IF THE EGYPTIANS DROWNED IN THE RED SEA WHERE ARE PHARAOH'S CHARIOTS?

Exploring the Historical Dimension of the Bible

Benjamin Edidin Scolnic

D1523914

Studies in Judaism

University Press of America,® Inc.
Lanham · Boulder · New York · Toronto · Oxford

Copyright © 2005 by
University Press of America,® Inc.
4501 Forbes Boulevard
Suite 200
Lanham, Maryland 20706
UPA Acquisitions Department (301) 459-3366

PO Box 317
Oxford
OX2 9RU, UK

Library of Congress Control Number: 2005921133
ISBN 0-7618-3147-9 (paperback : alk. ppr.)

Studies in Judaism

Dedication

This book is dedicated to my friend
Harvey Miller
For giving me an adventure I never even hoped to have.

Table Of Contents

Acknowledgements

I would like to thank:
Dr. James Hoffmeier for his inspiration and wisdom,
Dr. Jacob Neusner for his support and encouragement,
Dr. Leslie Wilson for his help and friendship,
And my students, congregants, and friends for their patience and openness.

Introduction

Presumed True

There is a very frightening moment in the novel *Presumed Innocent* by Scott Turow when the narrator realizes that he will soon be accused of murdering his former mistress. As an attorney, he knows he has a problem: he had motive and opportunity. He wonders, "How do I prove that I'm innocent? I know that I did not commit murder. I do not know who did but what can I say to convince others of what I know to be the truth?" [1]

Turow's title is, of course, a play on a well-known phrase. In the American system of law, the presumption is that the defendant is "Not Guilty." Guilt must be proved. A verdict of "Not Guilty" does not mean that the defendant has proved innocence but that the prosecution has not been able to prove guilt. Innocence is often impossible to prove. Even when a defendant has been declared "Not Guilty," the accusation of guilt often remains as a kind of stigma if others continue to dwell on the accusations.

Now think about the Bible as a defendant on trial for murdering the truth. In ages past, the Bible, as the Word of God, was considered to be factual and the repository of all truth. In our time, many are quite ready to disparage the Bible at every turn. There is a certain delight in taking the Bible apart, in finding its inconsistencies, its legendary aspects. The bias, when it is boiled down to basics, is that of moderns attempting to demonstrate superiority to ancients. With a sneer, we say, "We have science, they did not. The Bible has people living hundreds of years, a ship surviving a universal flood, lions sleeping with lambs, the good guys walking on dry land pursued by the bad guys who wind up sleeping with the fish. Why pursue a religious life if it is based on a book like that?"

Believers are on the run. If someone gets up and says, "Archaeologists state that the Exodus never happened!" the non-believers cheer and the believers feel defensive.

There is, however, a more reasoned approach, of evaluating the evidence in a calm, objective manner and with an open mind. It is difficult to prove the Bible's innocence. We can attempt to take the prosecution's case, point by point, weigh its evidence, and establish whether it makes its case that the Bible is "guilty" of killing the truth.

Does the Bible tell falsehoods? Is it guilty of this crime? Is the Bible innocent until proven guilty or guilty until proven innocent? Is the Bible right unless we know otherwise? Is it wrong only when we can prove that it is wrong?

---

1 James K. Hoffmeier *Israel in Egypt: The Evidence for the Authenticity of the Exodus* (New York: Oxford, 1997). My debts to the insights in that work will be evident throughout this book.

What would it take to execute someone? We would have to have incontrovertible evidence. Do we need such evidence in order to dismiss a Biblical text? I would say we do.

Can the Biblical data be taken as evidence? This is a key question. I believe that the Bible must be treated with respect. Others begin with the assumption that the Bible is so full of falsehood that it cannot be taken seriously. Any other text in the ancient world is considered evidence. Bombastic claims by tyrannical emperors are considered true. Every Biblical text, for these people, is worth less than nothing. I disagree and consider every Biblical text a set of data to be weighed and evaluated.

The present work is not a history book but a way of looking at the way the Bible thinks about historical events. I want to explain not only how we may look at Biblical history, but also our lives, in the same way.

Since this is a book about the Bible and history as opposed to a book of Biblical history, I will only present the history that is necessary to understand the issue at hand. Since this is not a scholarly book, I will keep references to a minimum and try to summarize scholarly debates as concisely as possible. Still, one of the things that you have to know about archaeology and the Bible is that you need to separate what is being said from who is saying it. If archaeology is a difficult art and science, be careful whom you trust. Try to understand the evidence yourself. In approaching the use of archaeology in trying to prove or disprove the Bible, you must proceed with caution. Whatever you read, whatever you hear, whether it is on television or in the newspapers or even in the pages of an archaeology magazine, remember to keep a yellow light at the top of your radar screen.

Let me, therefore, tell you about my personal prejudices. I am a rabbi and a person who believes in God. I believe that the Word of God can be found in the Bible. My sophisticated colleagues tell me that I'm in right field, that I am a throwback, almost a reactionary. I do not mind being to the right if it means that I may be right and I do want to react to what is going on in our intellectual world.

I presume that the Bible is innocent of killing the truth. I believe that the Bible is the Word of God that will lead us to a better understanding of history, of our lives, and of the future that God has in mind for us as individuals and as a world.

I also have a Ph.D. and a questioning mind. I would love to have proof that the walls of Jericho came tumbling down or, at least, that Joshua and the Israelites destroyed Jericho. I can only consider something to be proved by archaeology, however, if I have a preponderance of evidence. So how do I go about ascertaining what is fact that contains truth and what is fiction that contains truth? Very cautiously, case-by-case. My mind always remains open, waiting for new evidence.

Many believe that the Bible is guilty of falsehood. They are modern snobs. There is no falsehood here. At the very least, there is truth embodied in either stories or history. I could easily write a book focused on the question of whether the Bible is truth in a story or truth in a historical narrative or a mixture of the two.

However, that is too simple. Sophisticated readers would admit that there is at least some historical truth in every story of every culture.

That is not good enough. Most people who observe a religion are not satisfied with the idea that their core stories are simply stories, without historical reality.

I do not want to spend a lot of time on the definition of history. I mean it here in the simplest sense: History is something that actually was or actually happened.

When I talk to friends of mine who are ministers, and the subject turns to Christianity, they often discuss the distinction between the "historical Jesus" and the "Divine Christ." To reduce a very complicated matter to simple terms, my friends are quite open to the idea that Jesus the man may not have said and done what the Christian Scriptures says about him. They reflect the conclusion of many scholars that much of what is said in the Christian Scriptures is artificial and inauthentic.

If I were a Christian, however, I would care a great deal about who and what Jesus was. Is Christianity not based on the life of Jesus? If the historical conclusion is that Jesus was a minor revolutionary who wanted the Jews of his province to rise up against the Roman Empire, and who was crucified by the Romans for his rebellion, does this not change the foundation of Christianity? There are many who have reached this conclusion about the historical Jesus yet are unaffected in their Christian attitudes and beliefs.

The parallel to this kind of thinking in Jewish circles is the attitudes of those who just do not care whether the events of the Bible happened or not. They say that the Israelites were never slaves in Egypt and that the Exodus did not occur, but then celebrate Passover, the holiday on which we celebrate the redemption from Egyptian bondage.

We must be aware that all such statements have significant religious and political ramifications. If God is the God of history and His primary historical action is the rescue of the Israelites from Egypt (He identifies Himself by saying "I am the LORD thy God Who brought you out of the land of Egypt, the house of bondage" Exodus 20:1), whether there was an Exodus is a major religious issue. Politically, we live in a time when the origins of the Israelites and their relationship to the land of Israel have been questioned by those who would deny that ancient linkage. If the Israelites did not leave Egypt and come to the land of Canaan, that historical relationship is undermined, creating ammunition for the guns of the enemies of the modern Jewish state. All of this is part and parcel of the polemic and propaganda that ignite the dynamite on the international scene today.

Before we undermine belief in the truth of the Bible by accepting the conclusions of historical Minimalists and skeptics, let us see what cards these players are actually holding. They start with the assumption that there is no historical basis for most of the events discussed in the Bible and they finish where they start.

There are many people who believe in the truth of the Bible when they're young and lose that belief when they get older. While I have (almost) always believed in

God, my belief in the truth of the Bible has increased over the years. When I refer to those who can practice their religion while not believing in the truth of Biblical events, I am also referring to myself at an earlier stage. It is not because of increased faith that I have come to believe in the truth of the Bible. It is because of my experiences in the archaeological field and in learning to evaluate research about the Bible that I have come to be more open-minded about the possibility that the Bible is true, after all.

By reading this book, you place yourself on a jury. If I am acting, in a sense, as an attorney, I am asking you to rid yourself of any prejudices and preconceptions that you may have on the issues related to the case. Be a juror willing to change your mind if the facts indicate a different verdict than the one to which you had been leaning. Remember that skepticism can become its own orthodoxy, its own kind of fundamentalism, its own dogmatic stance.

Approach what you are about to read with an open mind. I promise to tell the truth, and nothing but, to the extent that I know it and to be humble before knowledge that I do not have. When we approach sacred truths and the wisdom of the world, humility is not a bad place to start.

Chapter I

The Source of Rivers and the Source of Texts

It must be that when God speaketh he should communicate, not one thing, but all things; should fill the world with his voice; should scatter forth light, nature, time, souls, from the center of the present thought; and new date and new create the whole.... Divine wisdom ... lives now, and absorbs past and future into the present hour. All things are made sacred by relation to it,—one as much as the other. All things are dissolved to their center by their cause.

Ralph Waldo Emerson *Self-Reliance*

Tracing the Rivers of Eden

The Garden of Eden story refers to four rivers that flowed from that special area. The passage that describes these rivers has been taken to be primitive geography; it is used as a proof that the Bible is wrong and full of the errors of ancient people who did not know any better. Many modern readers think that the story of the Garden of Eden is a fairy tale that does not have any historical reality and insist that it is naïve to even suggest the existence of a place that could be located on a map of real geography. It cannot, they say, be the work of God, Who would know simple geography. In this chapter, however, I am going to propose that the Garden of Eden story can be understood to have geographical and historical dimensions. I will discuss the rivers of Eden and demonstrate that the Bible is correct in its description.

More than that, I want to explore how these rivers start from perfection and flow into imperfection, how these rivers symbolize the movement of humans from an undifferentiated existence out into a differentiated one, how time itself moves forward, but like a river, cannot flow back upstream. We will see that once human beings differentiate themselves by eating of the "Tree of Knowledge," they will not be able to go back to a simpler existence, any more than time can go backwards. What we will learn from "The Rivers of Paradise" and the creation stories will tell us a great deal about the Bible's view of the development of human beings, the passage of time, and the nature of truth. The Rivers of Eden start from a single source, part and flow downstream. If we follow them theoretically upstream, we can find the location of the Garden of Eden. This means that we can find undifferentiated whole truth, a time before differentiation.

We will leave the geography, literally tracing the rivers back to their source, until the second part of this chapter. First, we will look at the texts of the two creation stories in Gen. 1-3. The fact that there are two presentations of creation means that God's truth is transmitted through a parting into different streams of tradition, by which it flows to us.

The Creation Stories of Genesis 1-3

Genesis 1, the narrative of the seven days of creation, like other stories of its type, is characterized by its markedly binary aspect,[1] setting up opposing categories: heaven and earth, light and darkness, evening and morning, the expanse above and the expanse below, land and sea, male and female, regular and holy time. Such binary oppositions are intrinsic to the process of human thought. Aspects of existence are defined through their opposites. When one describes the world, one needs to use categories. If something is a member of one category, it is not a part of another category. One could not even know the category "alive" if one did not know the category "dead." Religion is vitally concerned with the distinction and/or the link between life and death. One realm, the other world, is perfect; it is the world where the dead are perpetually alive. The other realm, of the living and reality, is imperfect. When religion considers the place of God in this setup, it must put Him into the perfect world. What then, is the relationship between God in one realm and human beings in the other? Religion's roles include building a bridge between God and humans and establishing and mediating basic binary discriminations such as superhuman/human, immortal/mortal, legitimate/illegitimate, and good/evil. In order to mediate the two categories, a third category is explored: a middle ground where one finds the holy, the legendary, the taboo, the anomalous, and the abnormal.

Religion communicates in many ways and one of them is narrative.[2] Since stories are a mode of communication, rules of communication can be applied to them. In any form of communication, repetition makes a point. If a story is repeated, it is emphasized; different versions of the same story might vary in their details but substantiate that emphasis. Redundancy on important matters is reassuring; we know that we are getting the right message if, even though the details vary, one story reinforces the other.

In modern times, different forms of criticism have been applied to the Biblical texts. Source criticism emphasizes the differences between stories and takes those

1 C.Levi-Strauss "The Structural Study of Myth" *Myth: A Symposium* ed. T. A. Sebeok (Bloomington, 1955); E. R. Leach "Levi-Strauss in the Garden of Eden" *Transactions of the New York Academy of Sciences* (New York, 1961) 386-96; idem "Genesis as Myth" in *Genesis as Myth and Other Essays* (London, 1969).
2 C.Shannon and W. Weaver *The Mathematical Theory of Communication* (Urbana, 1949); R. Jakobson and M. Halle *Fundamentals of Language* (The Hague, 1956).

variations as contradictions that point to different authors or schools. The notion is that one school would not produce two stories that contradict each other. This is all very interesting, as far as it goes, but the fact remains that understanding the message requires that we see not just the differences but the common elements in the supposedly contradictory accounts. The history of the texts may be found in the differences; the message is to be found in the common elements. Contradictions point to sources, but the commonalities point to the Source.

The Garden of Eden story in Genesis 2-3 follows the story of the creation of the world in seven days in Genesis 1. Critical scholarship is only too happy to show that these two stories are rival accounts of creation that contradict each other. If there are two contradictory stories, the line of reasoning continues, we should not accept either story as scientific or historical fact. This theory is based on the fact that Genesis 1, the story of the seven days of creation, presents an order that includes:

- Plants (on the third day)
- Animals (on the sixth day)
- Men and Women created together in the image of God (on the sixth day)

Genesis 2, the Garden of Eden story, states that creation happens in this very different order:

1. Man
2. Plants
3. Animals
4. Woman

One can avoid the contradictions in the order of the two chapters in various ways. One popular theory suggests that the entire story of the Garden of Eden happened on the sixth day. Another theory says that Genesis 1 is a general account of creation and that Genesis 2 focuses on a particular experiment that God conducted called the Garden of Eden where He created things in a different order.

These answers do not work on a simple level. In Gen. 1:11-12, plants and trees sprout and grow on the third day of creation:

And God said, "Let the earth sprout vegetation: seed-bearing plants, fruit trees of every kind on earth.

As clear as this is, the beginning of the Garden of Eden story in Gen. 2:4b –7 states something very different:

When the LORD God made earth and heaven—when no shrub of the field was yet on earth and no grasses of the field had yet sprouted, because the LORD God had not sent rain upon the earth and there was no man to till the soil, but a flow would well up from the ground and water the whole surface of the earth—the LORD God formed man from the dust of the earth. He blew into his nostrils the breath of life, and man became a living being.

The source critics are right to say that there is a logical problem here. Add to this problem the fact that the creation of Eve in Genesis 2 seems to bring woman into the world for the first time, which contradicts the fact that women were already created on the sixth day of creation in Genesis 1.

Again, many say that if there are two contradictory accounts, neither one of them should be taken seriously. Still, if there are two accounts of creation in these two chapters, we must ask the question of how to read these stories as they are presented to us, in sequential order. Moderns might say that one can do this, reading from a literary perspective, but that the fact remains that the existence of two stories should negate any attempt to think of the Garden of Eden as a place one can locate. They would agree, however, that both of the chapters are meaningful stories. The subject of Genesis 1 is God; the object is the world. Human beings are supposed to be fruitful and multiply and subdue the earth. Men and women are equal in that both are created in the image of God. Humans should rest on the Sabbath as God did on the seventh day of creation. The Garden of Eden story, they would say, is a beautiful and meaningful fable. The subject of Genesis 2 may initially be God but it quickly becomes the humans God puts in the Garden of Eden. The Garden of Eden is a dream of a place and/or a time when the human condition was different from the troubled and limited existence we experience now. Human beings have difficult lives, burdened with responsibilities, overwhelmed by the constant fear of war, sickness, and death. The Garden of Eden seems to be a place where human beings once lived in innocence, health, peace, and freedom from responsibility.

The popular idea of the Garden of Eden is that Adam and Eve:

- Are sexually innocent;
- Do not have to work;
- Are immortal.

When they eat of the "Tree of Knowledge" of Good and Evil, however, they

- Become sexually knowledgeable;
- Have to work;
- Are now mortal.

I disagree with all of these common notions. By refuting them, we may come to an understanding of this story that changes our understanding of the nature of the Garden of Eden; it will become a place in the development of human consciousness that is founded in a place that existed.

The Garden of Eden Story

When one reads about both ancient and later legends about perfect places, one tends to connect some of the aspects of these stories to the Garden of Eden story in Genesis 2-3. [1] I hear people make the mistake of saying that Adam and Eve lost their immortality when they were exiled from the Garden. I understand why people make this mistake. The Garden of Eden has become synonymous with Heaven, the eternal abode, in many traditions. For instance, the Jewish memorial prayer *'el male rachamim* asks God to let the Garden of Eden be the eternal resting place of the deceased. The Garden of Eden in Genesis 2-3, however, is not the abode of God. It is a park, a special paradise park, with many trees including two very special ones:

> The LORD God planted a garden in Eden, in the east, and placed there the man whom He had formed. And from the ground the LORD God caused to grow every tree that was pleasing to the sight and good for food, with the "Tree of Life" in the middle of the garden, and the "Tree of Knowledge" of good and bad.
>
> Gen. 2:8-9[2]

The relationship between the "Tree of Life" and the "Tree of Knowledge" is a mysterious one. The syntax is awkward at best; the "Tree of Knowledge" seems to be an afterthought. The verse does not say, "With the "Tree of Life" and the "Tree of Knowledge" of good and bad in the middle of the garden." This would be an easier way to say that both trees are in the middle of the garden. Yet it is the "Tree of Knowledge" that seems to be the focus in God's prohibition to Adam:

> And the LORD God commanded the man, saying, "Of every tree of the garden you are free to eat; but as for the "Tree of Knowledge" of good and bad, you must not eat of it; for as soon as you eat of it, you shall die."

The verse raises more questions than it answers. Why would God prohibit humans from the acquisition of knowledge? Is knowledge not a good thing? Why was the "Tree of Life" also not prohibited? The apparent simplicity of the story of the Garden of Eden is deceptive; there are many questions that beg for answers. Let us stick to the questions we've already raised about the implications of eating from the "Tree of Knowledge."

The man is supposed to leave his father and mother and cleave to his wife. Cleaving certainly does not sound asexual. The notion that Adam and Eve only know sexuality after they have eaten of the "Tree of Knowledge" seems undermined by the text. Indeed, Eve is created to be an `*ezer k^e negdo*, a "helpmeet" for Adam immediately after he named all the animals but could not find his sexual partner.

---

1 I am particularly influenced here by Martin Buber "The Tree of Knowledge" in *On the Bible* (New York, 1968) 14-21.
2 All translations are from *NJV*.

When Eve is punished, the husband's cleaving turns to her cleaving. The punishment does not change the relationship from childlike innocence to male dominance in a new sexual relationship; it changes the nature of an already sexual relationship. Pain in childbearing seems to be connected to this new male dominance in the relationship. It is not correct to say, then, that Adam and Eve were asexual or innocent like children before they ate of the "Tree of Knowledge."

As for the second popular impression, that Adam and Eve did not have to work, the fact is that Adam was placed in the Garden of Eden "to till it and tend it" (Gen. 2:15). The popular notion that Paradise means that one does not have to work is just a mistake. After their punishment, working will be incredibly harder, but work is not introduced at that time; it is already a part of life.

What about the third impression that humans would have lived forever if they had not eaten of the "Tree of Knowledge"? God tells Adam that if he eats of that tree, he will surely die on that day. However, when Adam and Eve eat of the tree, they do not die on that day, as God had threatened they would. While it may seem controversial to say this, perhaps God changed His mind out of mercy. Or perhaps He had only wanted to see how Adam and Eve would respond to the threat in the first place. Why are Adam and Eve not more affected by God's frightening threat? The serpent easily convinces them that they will not die. One explanation for Adam and Eve's lack of fear is that they do not understand the concept of death. As I said above, one only understands the idea of being alive if there is an opposing category "death." A short anecdote: A famous pediatrician, Dr. Morris Wessel, is an expert on children and grief. Once, tragically, a teacher of a second grade class died. Dr. Wessel was asked to come to speak to the class about what had happened and listen to their questions and reactions. The session went very well, and Dr. Wessel was ready to leave, feeling rather good about helping in this difficult situation. A child raised his hand and asked, "Doctor, can I ask one more question?" Dr. Wessel nodded. "When is she coming back?" I cite this anecdote in this context because it tells us something about Adam and Eve. They can be told that they will die if they eat from the "Tree of Knowledge," but they may not comprehend what this means. Animals may instinctively fear death but are not aware of their mortality. Adam and Eve lived in that state of mind. After eating of the "Tree of Knowledge," however, they understood their mortality. God did not seem to be thinking about the death penalty until He started to worry that they will eat of the "Tree of Life" as well:

> And the LORD God said, "Now that the man has become like one of us, knowing good and bad, what if he should stretch out his hand and take also from the Tree of Life and eat, and live forever!" So the LORD God banished him from the Garden of Eden, to till the soil from which he was taken. He drove the man out, and stationed

east of the Garden of Eden the cherubim and the fiery ever-turning sword, to guard
the way to the "Tree of Life."

Gen. 3:22-24

God is right to be concerned that Adam and Eve will eat of the "Tree of Life"; if
they had lived just a little longer in the Garden, they would have eaten and become
immortal. So why did this worry God so much?

God distinguished between night and day, light and darkness; He created and
ordered through binary oppositions and was above those oppositions. The
oppositions were His world order. Humans, on the other hand, were created *within*
these oppositions; it is only after they eat of the "Tree of Knowledge" of Good and
Evil, with good and evil representing all oppositions, that they know it. The
realization is shocking. Before they eat of the fruit of the "Tree of Knowledge,"
Adam and Eve live in an undifferentiated existence. Once they have eaten of it, they
know what God knows. Which is exactly what the serpent told them would happen.[3]
The artful use of the Hebrew word `arum illustrates this point. Before they eat of
the "Tree of Knowledge," Adam and Eve are one kind of `arum, "naked."
Nakedness is a metaphor for undifferentiated simplicity; they are so simple that they
do not know the opposition clothed/naked. In a fascinating turn of phrase, we see, in
the very next verse, that the serpent is the most `arum, the "shrewdest" of all of the
creatures. Once Adam and Eve eat of the "Tree of Knowledge," they now know
what nakedness is. They know both sides of the 'arum coin; they now know
complexity. Adam and Eve also learn that the serpent was wrong about the wages of
sin; that is why they hide, fearing punishment. They know that they will be punished
because they are guilty as opposed to innocent. They are no longer innocent in the
sense of no longer being simple; they now see the garden and not just the trees. God
cannot let them both know and transcend. This would wreck the opposition
Divine/human. That which is "Divine" knows oppositions but transcends them. To
know and live forever is transcendence, and this cannot be. Now humans cannot live
forever because to know differentiation but to transcend it is divine. God does not
want them to be immortal because He has set up the opposing categories of Divine
and human; immortality with transcendence of categories is not for humans. For
humans, there are two choices:

---

3 An interesting point here is that God does not destroy the Garden of Eden. The "Tree of
Life" is still there. It may be hidden and protected, but it still exists. Adam and Eve may
never have been immortal, but, it seems, they could have been. Remember that the "Tree
of Life" was not initially prohibited. Perhaps it was only forbidden after God saw that
humans were disobedient. The end of the story reminds us that God had given humans
the opportunity to live on this earth in an ideal state. Human life does not have to be lived
in misery. The world was given to humans to tend, a place in which to live in happiness.

1.   Undifferentiated simplicity with the possibility of immortality
2.   Mortal complexity
3.   God is One; humans are two.

The two, in Genesis 1, are both created in the Divine Image. The "we" of Gen. 1:26 is the "we" of oneness, of complexity that is One. That works for God but does not work for His new creation, the human. Adam is one, but one is the loneliest number, insufficient for human existence. There must be two and so the human one is divided into two.

The result of both accounts is the same: the commonality of the stories, rather than their differences, comes into view. In the first story, God, Who is One, differentiates the One Image and creates two. In the second story Adam, God's creation, is eventually literally divided into two. Both the Seven Days of Creation and the Garden of Eden stories tell us how the world became what it is and how God tried to lead us within our limitations. Genesis 1 expresses differentiation in a positive way, skipping some of the steps by which humans became differentiated; Genesis 2 sees differentiated existence as something we played a role in developing. Differentiation occurs through a necessary catastrophe.

The source critics see difference as contradiction. Religiously speaking, they do not live up to their name. They do not see that their results can lead us back not only to sources but ultimately to the Source, God, Who in His unique undifferentiated complexity, gives us two texts of Creation. Indeed, the critics have shown that in the Torah there will be no less than four streams of tradition. I agree, but I know that they are flowing from the Source. Seeing the different streams allows us to trace them back to whence they came, namely, from God, the one perfect being, flow the sources, each imperfectly bringing its gifts to the accumulation of truth. Four streams of texts: four rivers. Eden is the source of the four rivers; rivers of complexity flow in every direction, watering the world.

The Rivers of Eden
I can now turn to the rivers that flowed from Eden. In this section, I will study the geography of these rivers to show that they can be traced on a map. The reality of these rivers will lead us back to a historical dimension of the Garden of Eden story. More important, the paths of these rivers will reflect how time has flowed since the Era of Eden, and indicate why the Garden is no longer there.

Many modern readers are quick to point out that the concept of an idyllic place such as the Garden of Eden is one that existed long before the Hebrew Bible. People have probably always dreamed of a perfect place where human problems did not exist. For instance, in Sumerian myth,[4] Dilmun is a mysterious island in the Persian Gulf, a perfect place of great natural beauty where the lion does not kill and the wolf does not hurt the lamb.[5] No one is in mourning or grief because there is neither sickness nor death. In Greek mythology, one of the twelve labors imposed on Hercules was to obtain golden apples from the Garden of the Hesperides. This was a difficult task because the garden was situated at the end of the world and Hercules had to overcome a dragon that guarded it.[6] In Islam, paradise is to be found in the afterlife. The Koran states that those who fear Allah and follow the tenets of Islam will find eternal bliss.[7] All of this is in heaven; on earth, Islamic gardens from Morocco to India are designed to mirror this celestial paradise. The gardens are rectangular and are divided into four quarters by water channels that meet in the center. These four water channels are reflexes of the four rivers in the Garden in Eden that are the focus of this chapter. Western botanic gardens, such as the one at Oxford University, follow the same pattern.[8] These gardens are to give us the sense of being one with nature again, as Adam and Eve once were.[9]

If paradise is only to be found in heaven, however, there are limited possibilities for life on this earth. If paradise is only to be found at the end of the world, and regular humans cannot get there, it does not do us much good. A paradise that is of this world is indeed a significant fact. If such an idyllic place ever existed, if life once were different for human beings, it becomes an important place in human metaphorical and symbolic geography; the Garden represents the childhood of humankind. It is not so much a place in the world as a place in time, or it seems to be outside of time and space altogether. Since there seems to be a relationship between the Garden of Eden and the idyllic places of legends, the quick temptation is to say that the Eden story is also a legend and leave it at that.

For many, it is ridiculous to think in any other terms. It takes intellectual courage to say that the story may be a legend based on something that really existed.

---

4 The Sumerians were a non-Semitic people who were already settled in the lower Tigris-Euphrates as early as the 4th millennium BCE. The well-preserved Sumerian myth of Enki and Ninhursag tells of the mythical island of Dilmun (*ANET* 37-42; Kramer *History Begins at Sumer* 144ff.).

5 This passage reminds us not only of the Garden of Eden but also of later passages about the Messianic age (as in the Book of Isaiah).

6 The Garden of the Hesperides has some relationship to Elysium (or the Elysian fields), mentioned by the Classical poet Homer (8th century BCE?) that was also at the end of the world. Hesiod (probably from the same period) speaks of the Isles of the Blessed where heroes live a life without cares; all their desires are provided for by the earth.

7 They will be dressed in green silk robes and will be served their meals on silver dishes; their waitresses will be beautiful virgins.

8 After the discovery of the Americas, the four parts of the garden came to represent the four known continents, Europe, Asia, Africa and America.

9 J. Prest *The Garden of Eden: The Botanic Garden and the Re-Creation of Paradise* (New Haven, 1981).

What if this story is based on a real-life place that the millennia looked back on as a perfect place? I ask you to open your mind and consider the possibility that the Garden of Eden is at least a reflex of a real place. For there is another approach, one based on a fascinating passage in Genesis 2, which will send us not to a map of symbolic geography but to the map of the real world. If this is true, the story of the Garden of Eden will open up to us in a new way. If we know where the Garden of Eden is but also realize why we cannot get there, we will understand the process that all human beings go through on their way to a mature understanding of their lives.

I am not suggesting that we should all put on our explorers' coats and go looking for the Garden of Eden. I am saying that there is something quite profound about the idea that the Bible, as we shall see, presents us with a verbal map about the location of the Garden.

Some who do not take this map seriously might do so because they think ancient peoples did not have a sense of geography. We now know, however, that maps were basic to civilization. We have learned that the human activity of graphically translating one's perception of his world was a universally acquired skill that pre-dates other forms of written communication. It is fascinating to think about what this might mean about the human mind. In *The Nature of Maps*, Robinson and Petchenik explain that mapping is a way that one converts personal knowledge of spatial relationships to knowledge that one can transmit. Consider the philosophical premise that spatial elements are fundamental to all existence, even more than temporal elements. One needs to know where one is even more than one need to know when this moment of existence is in relation to other moments. Maps are about spatial relatedness, a quality "without which it is difficult or impossible for the human mind to apprehend anything."[10] One maps those spatial relationships that one requires for existence.

The Bible gives us a map relating to the Garden of Eden because it is a spatial relationship that we require for our existence. That there is a map is therefore in itself significant. Let us look at the map:

> A river issues from Eden to water the garden, and from there it divides and becomes four branches. The name of the first is Pishon, the one that winds through the whole land of Havilah, where the gold is. The gold of that land is good; bdellium is there, and lapis lazuli. The name of the second river is Gihon, the one that winds through the whole land of Cush. The name of the third river is Tigris, the one that flows east of Asshur; and the fourth river is the Euphrates.   Gen. 2:10-14

---

10 Arthur H. Robinson and Barbara Bartz Petchenik *The Nature of Maps: Essays Toward Understanding Maps and Mapping* (Chicago, 1976) 13.

This passage does not read like a fairy tale at all; it certainly seems to be historical geography. There is an earnest attempt to identify the two rivers that may be unfamiliar to the reader and to tell us where these rivers originated. If the Biblical writers did not want to tell us where the Garden of Eden was, if it were all just a legend, the passage would simply leave out 2:10-14. The Garden of Eden, for all its mystery, was, at least for the writer of this account, a geographical reality. The Biblical narrative states that the garden was planted in "the east" (v.8) and that the four rivers begin in a single body of water (v.10). Since we know where the Tigris and Euphrates are, we should not look for the two unknown rivers, the Pishon and the Gihon, in other areas of the world such as Africa.The Israelites might not have known the geography of the world but they knew the geography of their part of the world. The headwaters of the Tigris and the Euphrates were just north of familiar places like Harran, where Abraham lived, and Nineveh, to which Jonah traveled. The Israelites knew, for instance, that the Nile did not connect to the Persian Gulf. One should not suggest that the Bible could present these rivers in a purely mythical and non-geographical fashion. Yet this is exactly what has been suggested.

Since the Garden of Eden is so famous, and since it represents the kind of paradise we all long for, people throughout the centuries have been fascinated with establishing its location. The attempt to locate the Garden floundered, however, because of the inadequacy of ancient and medieval geographical knowledge. For instance, one of the earliest commentators on the Garden of Eden story is the general-turned-historian Josephus (37-100 CE) who says that the Garden "was watered by one river, which ran round about the whole earth, and was parted into four parts." [11] For Josephus, the Pishon is the Ganges that runs into India and the Gihon is the Nile in Egypt. A river that runs around the whole earth, that feeds the Ganges and the Nile as well as the Tigris and Euphrates, is either primitive geography or naïve legend. The more that we know about ancient geography, the more it seems that Josephus' explanation of the four rivers may point to the interpretation of the Garden of Eden story as a Biblical example of the way that the ancients thought about the world. We know enough about ancient geography to compare our Biblical account to other maps and views. The Babylonian concept of the shape of the earth is that of the sea encircling the land. The early period of cartography, from 4,000 BCE to 200 CE culminates with the contributions of the famous Greek scholar named Claudius Ptolemy[12] who created the first general atlas of the world.[13] His hypothetical map was excellent but his world of reality was faulty.[14]

---

11 Josephus *Antiquities* I: 3.
12 Ptolemy lived ca..90 to 168 CE in or near Alexandria Egypt.
13 In spite of the egregious errors on all of Ptolemy's maps, his atlas was considered an unsurpassed masterpiece for almost 1,500 years. Its wealth of detail still constitutes one

One way to think about the geography of the Bible involved in the Garden of Eden story is this: If the story were written anywhere in the period 1300-500 BCE, well before Ptolemy, its writers should not be expected to have known the real map of the world.[15] I reject this alibi and will maintain, as opposed to so many others, that the Garden of Eden was a place that the Bible thinks of in a very realistic geographical way. I am bold enough to argue for the Bible's accurate geographical sense because of some remarkable archaeological discoveries.

A. One of the earliest maps comes from the extensive Neolithic settlement of Çatal Hüyük in the Konya Plain in modern Turkey.[16] In 1963, James Mellaart found

---

of the most important sources of information for the historian and student of ancient geography.

14 His geographical errors arose from the fact that he lacked the fundamental data necessary to compile an accurate map.

15 Medieval world maps that locate the Garden of Eden constitute an interesting subject. A Byzantine map in Christian Topography, a book by Cosmas Indicopleustes ("Indian sea traveler") (c.sixth century CE), presents four rivers flowing out of a paradise in the east. The Psalter Map is a thirteenth-century English example of a *mappa mundi*, a world map that combines elements of geographical knowledge with religious symbolism and a variety of legendary features. At the top of this map, where the sun rises (which is to the extreme east in this presentation), Eden appears; it is the source of the Ganges, the Euphrates, the Tiger and other rivers. The Hereford *mappa mundi*, the largest surviving medieval world map, was the work of the cleric Richard of Haldingham in the 1280s. Nothing short of an encyclopedia of medieval belief, it is crammed with literally hundreds of pictures and captions. Near the top of the map, just inside time and space, is a roundel that represents the Garden of Eden. It is located somewhere beyond India and China in the Far East. Adam and Eve are shown being expelled from the garden by an angel. In the fourteenth century, a Benedictine monk, Ranulf Higden, from Chester, England, presented an Eden at the top of his world map. Three rivers branch out into one long river that flows horizontally across the map. After his third voyage, Christopher Columbus (1451-1506) came to conceive of the world as being in the shape of a rounded pear, or a ball with a nipple-shaped projection on it. Columbus suggested that on top of the ball's nipple was the Garden of Eden "whither no one can go but by God's permission." See J. E. Duncan Milton's *Earthly Paradise: A Historical Study of Eden* (University of Minnesota, 1972); A. B. Giamatti *The Earthly Paradise and the Renaissance Epic* (Princeton, 1966); R. Graves and R. Patai *Hebrew Myths: The Book of Genesis* (London, 1964).

16 J. Mellaart "Excavations of Çatal Hüyük, 1963, Anatolian Studies", *Journal of the British Institute at Ankara* vol. XIX, 1964. The archaeologist D. G. Hogarth had heard a local tradition that Konya had been the first city to emerge after the Flood. In about 16,000 BCE, the Konya Plain was a lake. The waters gradually retreated and left a fertile alluvial plain that supported a population that constituted what was in effect the first known city. The city seems to have dated from about 7000 BCE and covered 32 acres.

a cartographic artifact from Çatal Hüyük. This map-form is a wall painting that is approximately nine feet long and has a radiocarbon date of 6,200 BCE.[17] Mellaart believes that the map depicts a town plan, matching Çatal Hüyük itself, showing the congested "beehive" design of the settlement and displaying a total of some 80 buildings. In the foreground is a town arising in graded terraces closely packed with rectangular houses. Behind the town an erupting volcano is illustrated, its sides covered with incandescent volcanic bombs rolling down the slopes of the mountain.[18]

B. A Babylonian clay tablet that has been generally accepted as "the earliest known map" was unearthed in 1930 at the excavated ruined city of Ga-Sur at Nuzi, near the towns of Harran and Kirkuk, 200 miles north of the site of Babylon. Most authorities place the date of this tablet from the dynasty of Sargon of Akkad (2,500-2,300 BCE). The surface of the tablet is inscribed with a map of a district bounded by two ranges of hills and bisected by a watercourse.[19] Whether the map shows a stream running down a valley to join another, or running from that to divide into three, and whether they are rivers or canals, cannot be determined. The geographic content consists of the area of a river valley that may be that of the Euphrates flowing through a three-lobed delta and into a lake or sea in the northern part of Mesopotamia. Also shown on this tablet may be the tributary river the Wadi Harran, the Zagros Mountains in the east, the Lebanon (or Anti-Lebanon) in the west, and cities symbolized by circles. Inscribed circles indicate north, east and west,

---

One of the earliest settlements known to have made the transition from hunting/gathering to agrarian society developed here as early as 7400 BCE. The city was not only prosperous because of agriculture but also because of the great reserves of obsidian, a hard black stone that can be worked to a finish as smooth and sharp as glass but much harder. Before the discovery of metallurgy, obsidian was in great demand for the making of tools. Obsidian was one of the first objects traded among prehistoric human beings; this trade no doubt helped the prosperity of Çatal Hüyük. The archeological dig of Çatal Hüyük is located on the Anatolian plateau near modern Konya.

17 James Mellaart *The Archaeology of Ancient Turkey* (London, 1978) 13.

18 Other such bombs are thrown from the erupting cone; a cloud of smoke and ashes hovers above the cone. The twin cones of the volcano suggest an eruption of Hasan Dag 10,672 feet high (standing at the eastern end of the Konya Plain and visible from Çatal Hüyük). These local volcanic mountains were important to the inhabitants of Çatal Hüyük as a source of obsidian used in the making of tools, weapons, jewelry, mirrors and other objects. Further, from graphic embellishments around the mountain, Mellaart has speculated that the depiction of the volcano in an active state is accurate since volcanic activity in this area would continue for some 4,000 years after this.

19 Although the exact location is still unknown, the map is identified as of a region near present-day Yorghan Tepe.

implying that maps were aligned in the cardinal directions then as they are now. This tablet represents the earliest known example of a topographic map.[20]

These ancient maps, far older than the Biblical narrative, describe places and areas with a very fine and exacting geographical sense. I am willing to accept that the ancients may not have had a very developed sense of the geography of the world. This does not mean, however, that they did not know areas closer to their own.

I have emphasized these two examples for another reason: They portray areas close to where I will argue the Bible places the Garden of Eden. None of these places were outside the worldview of Biblical Israel. To reject a geographical

---

20 This particular tablet is drawn with cuneiform characters and stylized symbols impressed, or scratched, on the clay. Inscriptions identify some features and places. In the center the area of a plot of land is specified and its owner is named Azala. None of the names of other places can be understood except the one in the bottom left corner. This is Mashkan-dur-ibla, a place mentioned in the texts from Nuzi as Durubla.

Other ancient Babylonian maps are instructive. The Babylonian would look to the southeast and see the Persian Gulf and the Indian Ocean, to the southwest and see the Red Sea, to the West and see the Mediterranean. L. W. King Babylonian *Religion and Mythology* (London, 1889) 29-30. Jean-Claude Margueron *Mesopotamia* trans. by H. S. B. Harrison Archeologia mundi (New York, 1965) facing 93; Campbell Thompson Cuneiform Texts 22, pl. 48; E.Unger *Babylon: die heilige Stadt...* (repr. Berlin, 1970) 254-8; A. L. Oppenheim "Mesopotamia" in C.C.Gillispie, ed. *Dictionary of Scientific Biography* vol. 15 (New York, 1978) 637. The very famous "Babylonian map of the world" is a late Babylonian clay tablet, dated to about 600-500 BCE. Its identity as a map of the world seems to be demonstrated by the accompanying cuneiform text that refers to seven outer regions beyond the encircling ocean. The earth seemed to be a mountain; the center of this mountain consisted of the high mountain ranges of Kurdistan. The map provides a view of a round, flat world with Babylonia in the center. Babylon was a prosperous and mighty city and it would be natural for the people there to see it as the hub of the world. Babylonians had seen their city at the center for a millennium and a half. The seven distant regions are marked with triangles. The tablet states that these islands are at equal distances of seven miles (from either each other or from the Babylonian world), around the outer periphery of the Earthly Ocean, "the Bitter River", creating a gulf (what we often, controversially, call the Persian Gulf today). The circle of the Ocean encloses an oblong marked "Babylon", with two parallel lines running to it from mountains at the edge. There is a marsh that is identified by two parallel lines near the bottom of the circle; the marsh is the swamp of what we call southern Iraq. An arm of the ocean curves around the right end of the marsh; its neck touches the lines from Babylon and seems to be the Euphrates. Assyria is to the right of Babylon, with what may be Urartu (eastern Armenia) above Assyria. The map, then, is a diagram to show the relation of other places in the world to the area known to the Babylonians.

reality for the Garden of Eden ignores the growing evidence that the writers of Genesis 2 did not see the Garden as a fictional place but as a place in the real world.

The Biblical Location of the Garden of Eden

While Jon Levenson states, "It is naïve to read a description of the primordial paradise in terms of scientific cartography,"[21] Gerhard von Rad says that the passage connects the garden to the historical and geographical world, that the cosmological is related to the spatial. I find the latter remark to be very important.[22]

Let us take a serious look at what we know. The only evidence that we have about the location of the Garden of Eden is from the Biblical text. Gen. 2:10-14 is often called "The Rivers of Paradise":

> A river issues from Eden to water the garden, and from there it divides and becomes four branches. The name of the first is Pishon, the one that winds through the whole land of Havilah, where the gold is. The gold of that land is good; bdellium is there, and lapis lazuli. The name of the second river is Gihon, the one that winds through the whole land of Cush. The name of the third river is Tigris, the one that flows east of Asshur; and the fourth river is the Euphrates.

The rivers that are mentioned are the key set of clues for determining the area where the Garden of Eden was situated. There are four rivers mentioned here, two of which, the Tigris and Euphrates, are extremely well-known, as well-known as any rivers in the history of the world, and two rivers, Pishon and Gihon, which are completely unknown to us.

We will proceed on the basis that the writers of the Hebrew Bible knew their geography better than the ancient and medieval mapmakers. Let us assume that there were four rivers that originated near each other.

The Tigris and Euphrates river basin and its network form the greatest river system of Southwest Asia. The Tigris and Euphrates rivers have sources within 50 miles of each other in eastern Turkey. The two rivers rise in close proximity in the Armenian Highland of Turkey.[23] The two areas that are the sources of the Tigris are Lake Van and Lake Hazar. The rivers flow in a southeasterly direction through what is now called northern Syria and Iraq to the head of the Persian Gulf.[24] The ancient

---

21 Levenson *Sinai and Zion: An Entry into the Jewish Bible* 131.

22 Gerhard von Rad *Genesis* (Philadelphia, 1961) 77.

23 The Tigris and Euphrates diverge sharply, however, in their upper courses, to a distance of some 250 miles at their points of greatest separation, near what is now the Turkish-Syrian border. Their middle courses gradually move toward each other, creating a triangle of limestone desert known now known in Arabic as Al-Jazirah, "The Island". Along the northeastern edge of Al-Jazirah, the Tigris drains off the rain-fed land ancient Assyria, while along the southwestern limit the Euphrates crosses true desert.

24 The Euphrates is called "The River" (Gen. 31:21; Exodus 23:21; Numbers 22:5, etc.) or "The Great River" (Gen. 15:18; Deut. 1:7. Joshua 1:4). The Euphrates is about 1,740

Greek name for the lower portion of the region that these rivers define was Mesopotamia, "The Land between the Rivers." As every schoolchild knows, this area was one of the cradles of civilization.[25]

So we know everything we need to about two of the rivers in the passage. We know that these rivers rise in close proximity in the Armenian Highland of Turkey and we know that the Tigris and Euphrates flow in a southeasterly direction. These two points, as basic and simply factual as they are, will be extremely important in our search for the Biblical location of the Garden of Eden.

Now we come to the two unknown rivers, the Pishon and the Gihon:

> The name of the first is Pishon, the one that winds through the whole land of Havilah, where the gold is. The gold of that land is good; bdellium is there, and lapis lazuli. The name of the second river is Gihon, the one that winds through the whole land of Cush.

What do we know about these two rivers?

Is the Gihon in Israel

There is a Gihon that is a spring on the eastern side of the city of David; it served as the principal source of water for Jerusalem. This has led to one theory about the location of the Garden of Eden. Solomon is anointed at the Gihon in Jerusalem (I Kings 1:33, 38, 45) indicating that the spring had a sacramental capacity. If we are not speaking of a river but a spring, the reference to Gihon in the Garden of Eden story is related to the concept of Zion as the cosmic mountain and the primal paradise.[26] The idea would be that the Gihon goes from Eden (Jerusalem) out to the whole world, flowing across the Syrian desert and across the Tigris and Euphrates and up to the land of Cush (western Iran). The theory about the Gihon River as the Gihon spring in Jerusalem, and the construction that Jerusalem as Cosmic Mountain is related to this passage, is fascinating. Personally, I believed this for years; I was intrigued with the idea of the Bible connecting the origins of humankind to Jerusalem, which had become the center of the world in the Israelite consciousness. The Gihon/Jerusalem connection is, however, just a theory, and one that sends us off course. In order to believe it, you have to think that the Bible was dealing in a symbolic geography that defied all common knowledge. The Israelites

---

miles long, the length of the Tigris about 1,180 miles. For 7,000 years, irrigation farming has been conducted in the alluvium. The Euphrates was the main source of Mesopotamian irrigation.

25 This rich history is reflected in a complex landscape of abandoned canal systems and thousands of ancient settlement sites.

26 Levenson *Sinai and Zion* 129.

knew that the Gihon was just a spring and that it did not flow across the Syrian desert and the Tigris and Euphrates and up to Iran.[27]

It is possible that the Bible gives us a map of the world that is not more sophisticated and not less ethno-centric than the Babylonian world-map. However, I do not think so. If the Garden of Eden were in Israel, it would not be described as the source of the Tigris and the Euphrates. The Israelites of Biblical times knew that their country was not the source of life and not the geographical center of the world. Instead of thinking about a spring in Jerusalem that becomes an imaginary river that flows into Syria and Iran, let us look again at what the Bible says: "The name of the second river is Gihon, the one that winds through the whole land of Cush" (Gen. 2:13). There is a great deal of confusion about the identity of the land of Cush. While it is true that the Hebrew term Cush can refer to the region of the Upper Nile, the Bible also speaks of a Cush in or near Mesopotamia.[28] For the Gihon, we need a river that flows through the land of Cush, the land of the Kassites. This river would not originate in Jerusalem. Instead, it should originate near the source of the Tigris and the Euphrates, in Turkey.

Was the Pishon in Arabia?

The name Pishon[29] appears nowhere else in the Bible; we do not know anything about it. We do know the name Havilah which appears as southwest Arabia in one case in Gen 10:28 but as the eastern frontier of the Ishmaelite Arabs, which would be not southwest but northeast Arabia, in Gen. 25:18. How does this fit the description of precious stones in this place? Any theory about the location of the Garden of Eden needs to account for these terms and minerals. "Bdellium" seems to be a fragrant resin, found in abundance in Arabia, as are various types of precious and semiprecious stones. The only known Arabian source for "good gold" is the so-called "Cradle of Gold" (Mahd edh-Dhahab), located about 125 miles south of Medina, in the Hijaz Mountains, which currently produces more than five tons of gold a year. The problem is that there is no river flowing today from this area toward the confluence of the Tigris and Euphrates. However, that is based on today's geography. A Boston University scientist, Farouk El-Baz, took clues from

---

27 As Luis I. J. Stadelmann writes, "It is interesting to note that none of the rivers of Palestine is referred to as a *nhr*. Instead, there is mention of the rivers of Mesopotamia, Egypt and Syria." The Gihon was a spring, not a river. Luis I. J. Stadelmann *The Hebrew Conception of the World: A Philological and Literary Study* (Rome, 1970) 161.
28 Biblical evidence for the latter statement can be found in Gen. 10:8-12's reference to Nimrod, who may have been Tukulti-Ninurta. This king reigned ca.1246-1206, within the Kassite period of Babylonian history; he was victorious over a Kassite ruler. Since Kassite rule over Babylon ended by the 12th century, we might have an indication here of how early this narrative was written. Additional evidence for Cush in the north may be Zeph.2:12-13. Zeph.3:10 even has an intriguing reference to the rivers of Cush.
29 We can guess that it is an appellative from the root *puš/*"spring forth."

alluvial deposits in Kuwait and examined satellite photos of the Arabian Peninsula. He spotted the unmistakable signs of a river channel cutting across the desert. Originating in the Hijaz Mountains near Medina, the ancient waterway, currently concealed beneath sand dunes, runs northeast to Kuwait. The "Kuwait River" (as El-Baz calls it) once joined the Tigris and Euphrates at the head of the Persian Gulf. Climate changes caused it to dry up between 3500-2000 BCE. The agreement of all of these details of the Kuwait River with the Biblical description of the Pishon, has led some scholars to make the obvious connection. James A. Sauer, a self-described "former skeptic," connects the Kuwait River with the Pishon.[30] If this connection is correct, we have a reason to look for the Garden of Eden near the Persian Gulf.

The Theory That the Garden Was Near the Persian Gulf

Since the Tigris and the Euphrates are the rivers that created the famous "cradle of civilization" in Mesopotamia, a popular place to look for the Garden of Eden is in modern Iraq.[31] Since the Sumerian legend about Dilmun is at the head of the Persian Gulf in Iraq, most scholars place the Garden of Eden near that body of water. The most important scholarly theory about the location of the Garden of Eden is found in E. A. Speiser's classic article "The Rivers of Paradise"[32] Speiser

---

30 James A. Sauer "The River Runs Dry" *BAR* July/August, 1996.

31 The English explorer Sir Walter Raleigh (1552-1618), in his *History of the World*, placed the Garden of Eden in Mesopotamia.

32 Ephraim Avigdor Speiser "The Rivers of Paradise" in *Oriental and Biblical Studies* ed. by J.J.Finkelstein and M.Greenberg (Philadelphia, 1967) 23-34. In the decades since its publication, this article has remained the basis for most discussions on this topic and a principal reason that most believe that the Garden of Eden is to be found in modern Iraq. It is also a model of scholarly logic and brilliance. Speiser looks at the two rivers we are sure about, the Tigris and the Euphrates. The Tigris is to the east of the Euphrates. This is not what we would have expected from an Israelite point of view; we would think that the perspective would have been from west to east. The narrator is working with an order from east to west. The map now requires that the Gihon would be to the east of the Tigris, and the Pishon to the east of the Gihon. The central river of the Garden of Eden would be to the east of all of these. The river Gihon could be the Diyala, which meanders through the land of the Kassites. According to modern hydrographic studies, the mouth of the Diyala was much further to the east than it is now. In this case, the Pishon would be the Kerkha, a river that comes down from the Central Zagros in the Iranian plateau. If the Gihon is the Kerkha, then, working backwards in the list, the Pishon must be a river to the east of the Kerkha, the Karun or the Wadi er-Rumma. This is a brilliant and logical set of deductions. I am not at all sure, however, that it is based on a solid premise. It is true that the Tigris is to the east of the Euphrates. We might just as easily say, however, that the narrator begins with the rivers that he needs to say the most about and then refers to the ones that are more familiar. The amount of information required to make the identification of the various rivers becomes less as the

states that all four streams once converged near the head of the Persian Gulf to create a rich garden land.

Rivers, however, flow downstream, from the heights.[33] One way to determine the location of the Garden of Eden is to identify the origination points of the four rivers:

> A river issues from Eden to water the garden, and from there it divides and becomes four branches

There are two important Hebrew words that must be understood. The word translated by Speiser and his colleagues here as "branches" actually says "heads", the Hebrew *rašim*, as in the Hebrew term *Rosh Hashanah*, "the New Year, the Head of the Year." The issue is whether the "four heads" of the rivers are upstream or downstream. This is an important question for determining the location of the Garden of Eden. If the four heads are downstream, then the Garden of Eden will be found near the Persian Gulf; the Tigris and the Euphrates flow into that body of water. Speiser notes that all four rivers "would then have converged" in the shallow lake area near the Persian Gulf. [34]

The problem is that the "heads" are the headstreams or upper courses of the rivers. The Bible tells us that Eden is near the four heads of the rivers. Thus a theory about the Pishon as the Kuwait River that originates in Arabia ignores the simple

---

list moves on. It is also quite possible that the four rivers are not listed in any particular order at all. Still, Speiser has other evidence to substantiate the possibility that the Pishon is the Kerkha. Speiser cites the early Samaritan version of the *Torah* that renders the Gihon as the modern Kerkha, and so is thinking about the Gihon as a river in Iran, not Egypt or Ethiopia. Assyrian records mention gold in Media; the Bible refers to the Pishon flowing through Havilah where there is gold. The Bible states that there is *šoham*-stone in Pishon territory. *Šoham*-stone seems to be *lapis lazuli* (Exodus 25:7; 28:9, 20; 35:9, 37; 39:6). NJV is inconsistent in how it renders *šoham*. In Gen. 2:12 the translation is *lapis lazuli* with a footnote stating that other translations indicate onyx and that the "meaning of Heb. *shoham* uncertain." In Job: 28:16, *NJV* translates precious onyx; in Gen. 2:12, Ex. 28:9 and 20; 35:9 and 37; 39:6 it is translated as *lapis lazuli*. *Sapir* is sapphire stone that is blue but different from *lapis lazuli*. Job 28:16 mentions both *šoham* and *sapir* which, Speiser says correctly, "may suggest similarity but precludes identity." If *šoham* is *lapis lazuli*, then the Pishon might very well be the Kerkha, called in cuneiform the Uqnû, "the Blue River", "Lapis Lazuli River". The Kerkha comes from a land of *lapis lazuli* and so does the Pishon. It is also interesting that in Ezekiel 28:4-5, 13-14 there is a reference to precious stones in the Garden of Eden and the mountain of God. This passage about the rivers of Paradise also refers to precious stones associated with the Garden of Eden.

33 For instance, as we have just seen, the Kerkha comes down from the Iranian plateau; this would fit the idea that the four rivers flow from the north, but it is another problem for Speiser's notion (his most serious mistake) that the ancients thought that the rivers flowed to the north.

34 "Rivers of Paradise" 27.

meaning of the text. So does the Persian Gulf theory in that none of these rivers have their sources there.

Shalmaneser III of Assyria (858-824 BCE) claims that he "has visited the sources of both the Tigris and the Euphrates." [35] In his famous "Black Obelisk," Shalmaneser III states: "To the head of the river, the springs of the Tigris, the place where the waters rise, I went."[36] This text discusses how the Assyrian emperor has conquered kingdoms far to the north in what we call Turkey.

The second important Hebrew term is *yotze' me* that is explained as "issues from…with special emphasis on the idea of origin, source." [37]

Speiser creates a mess for himself: While he says that it was the ancient Mesopotamian misperception that the rivers went upstream, he also says, "numerous rivers descended" into the shallow lake area. The ancients knew which way the water flowed. Speiser knows that the rivers did not start in the south but in the north.[38]

---

35 *ANET* 277.
36 *Babylonian and Assyrian Literature* Translator: Rev. A. H. Sayce (New York, 1901). This inscription is engraved on an obelisk of black marble, five feet in height, found by A. H. Layard in the center of the Mound at Nimrod, and now in the British Museum.
37 So *BDB*. See two passages in Isaiah:

> You shall be like a watered garden
> Like a spring whose waters do not fail.
> > Isaiah 41:18

> I will open up streams on the bare hills
> And fountains amid the valleys
> I will turn the deserts into ponds
> The arid land into springs of water.
> > Isaiah 58:11

The Siloam Inscription, which I will be discussing for its archaeological value in a later chapter, speaks of *hamotza'* the source (of water)" see II Chronicles 33:29. The Syriac equivalent means "go forth" in the sense of germinating, growing. The verb *yotze'* means "to go forth from a place," especially Egypt. See also II Kings 2:21; Isaiah 58:11; Psalms 107:33, 35 = Isaiah 41:18. It means, "to depart from" in Gen. 35:18. Water comes out of the rock in Exodus 17:6. Children go forth from their parents (II Samuel 7:12, 16:11). Words go forth from the mouth of the speaker (Joshua 6:10).
38 The Biblical verse itself can help in determining if the rivers flow from Eden or into it. Speiser says that the rivers flow into the Garden of Eden. Before reaching Eden, he says, the river consists of four separate branches. Von Rad, on the other hand, says that the rivers flow from the Garden of Eden. Von Rad is right and, frankly, Speiser knows it. In *NJV*, the translation of the *Torah* that Speiser was heavily involved with, the verse is

If the Persian Gulf theory is correct, if the Garden of Eden was near Eridu, then this means that Ur, the birthplace of Abraham, not far from Eridu, may be somehow connected. It is fascinating to think that just as the rivers of Eden went out to water the world, it was Abraham, as God's agent, who left Ur to water the world with truth and morality. As neat as this theory would be, the Bible presents an anti-Babylonian bias and responds to Babylonian stories. The Tower of Babel story in Genesis 10 is an anti-Babylonian polemic. Perhaps, in complete opposition to Speiser and all those who think that the Garden of Eden is to be found in Mesopotamia, one of the points of Gen. 2:10-13 is that it is not in Mesopotamia. The legend of Dilmun tried to transfer the idyllic place to their region. Not so, says Genesis; Mesopotamia, "the land of two rivers," was itself created by two rivers that flowed down from a primeval paradise. [39] The irony about the theory of the Garden of Eden in Iraq is that it may run exactly contrary to the purpose of the Bible in its discussion of the location of the Garden. The Bible consciously contradicts Babylonian lore:

• "You say Dilmun, and we say Anatolia." You think that the original garden was near the Persian Gulf; it was not, and it is not historically correct.

• "You say Babylon and we say Babel." You say that the center of the world was Babylon but that is not how things are supposed to be. If everyone would live in one place, it would go against part of the idea of creation, which is

• "You say gather, and we say spread." If we do not spread throughout the world, if we do not follow God's commandment in Genesis 1, what a waste of space!

The Bible is saying to the Babylonians: You are not the center of life. Life started somewhere else. Our ancestors, and your ancestors for that matter, came from the same place. That place was in what we call Turkey.

The Theory That the Garden of Eden Was in Turkey

We know that the sources of the Tigris and Euphrates are found near each other in Armenia, in modern Turkey. This theory has the virtue of taking the Biblical verses seriously. In the Gilgamesh Epic, the epic hero, looking for immortality, arrives at a mountain range whose peaks rise into the sky. His route moves northward through from Mesopotamia into the headwaters of the Euphrates, to the perilous mountain peaks surrounding the region of Lake Van in Anatolia:

---

rendered: "A river issues from Eden to water the Garden, and it then divides and becomes four branches."

39 In the narrow sense, Mesopotamia is the area between the Euphrates and Tigris rivers, north or northwest of the bottleneck at Baghdad, in modern Iraq. However, in the broader sense, the name Mesopotamia has come to be used for the area bounded on the northeast by the Zagros Mountains and on the southwest by the edge of the Arabian Plateau and stretching from the Persian Gulf in the southeast to the spurs of the Anti-Taurus Mountains in the northwest.

"Utnapishtim shall reside far away, at the mouth of the rivers." Notice "the mouth of the rivers." Gilgamesh certainly seems to be in the same area as that of the Garden of Eden. In both the Bible and the epic, nature in this area is in an idyllic state.

If the Bible says that the Garden of Eden was near where the Tigris and Euphrates started, let us look in that area for other rivers that originate there.

One method is to look for rivers leading into different seas, the Tigris and Euphrates into the Persian Gulf and the Araks-Aras into the Caspian Sea. The Araks rises south of Erzurum in the Bingöl Daglar Mountains of Turkish Armenia; it flows eastward, forming for approximately 274 miles the international boundary between Armenia on the north and Turkey and Iran on the south. About 666 miles long, it joins the Aras River in Azerbaijan 75 miles from its mouth on the Caspian Sea. The swift-flowing unnavigable Aras deposits most of the sediment composing the Kura-Aras delta.[40] Perhaps the Gihon is the Aras-Araks that originates in the highlands and flows into the Caspian Sea.

While the Pishon has been identified with a certain river Phasis known to the ancient Greeks, which rose in the Caucasus and flowed into the Black Sea, an interesting possibility for the fourth river is the Murat, the major headstream of the Euphrates. The river rises north of Lake Van near Mount Ararat, in eastern Turkey, and flows westward for 449 miles through a mountainous region to unite with the Karasu Çayi and form the Upper Euphrates near Malatya. The Murat River runs through Samsun on the coast of the Black Sea. Havilah is perhaps that area known by this name between the Black Sea and the Caspian Sea, where gold and precious stones have been found. Jason, whose name is associated with the "Golden Fleece," went to Colchis, a district through which the river Phasis (or Pishon?) flowed.

I am suggesting that the Gihon and the Pishon are the Araks-Aras and the Murat. Even if we cannot establish what the other two rivers are, we see that there are rivers in the area that might fit the Biblical information. In order to confirm or reject all of this, we will have to reconstruct what the natural area looked like in ancient times. We have to understand that to look at the map of today's topography is to do an injustice to the study of the accuracy of Biblical geography. It is difficult, if not impossible, to reconstruct the courses of the rivers. It is a scientific fact that many of the rivers of the world have changed their courses, dried up, and changed in various ways over the course of time. As we saw in the case of the river in the desert, rivers could have existed where no river runs today. One of the points of this book is to state that we must not use modern geography to study ancient complexities. We know that this area in Turkey has gone through incredible change since ancient times. While some upland Armenian towns have an average temperature of as low

---

40 Principal tributaries of the Aras are the Razdan, draining Lake Sevan and the Qareh Su, flowing off the Kuhha-ye Sabalan in northeastern Iranian Azerbaijan.

as 12 degrees Fahrenheit, archaeology has found that the climate was much milder and the vegetation in upland zones much more abundant in ancient times than it is today. We also know that destructive earthquakes often shake this area.

In attempting to reconstruct the area as it was in Biblical times, a good starting-place might be the ancient Roman geographer Strabo (ca.64 BCE–25 CE) who speaks with great accuracy about the region of Anatolia/Armenia. He describes Lake Arsene:

> ...which contains soda, and it cleanses and restores clothes; but because of this ingredient the water is also unfit for drinking. The Tigris flows through this lake after issuing from the mountainous country near the Niphates; and because of its swiftness it keeps its current unmixed with the lake; whence the name Tigris, since the Median word for "arrow" is "tigris." ... Near the recess of the lake the river falls into a pit, and after flowing underground for a considerable distance rises near Chalonitis.[41]

Here we have a fascinating and detailed example of how different the topography of this area may have been in ancient times. Very specifically, we see the relationship between the sources of the Tigris and Lake Van (Arsene). Is it really so far-fetched to think that it was this region that was once the site of the Garden of Eden?

A New Theory: Lake Van

We have another line of inquiry based on the Biblical text. Gen. 2:8 states that "The LORD God planted a garden in Eden, in the east, and placed there the man whom he had formed." "In the east" may mean east from the perspective of the Biblical writers, that is, east of Israel, but it may mean east of where God had created human beings. It also may mean that God placed Adam in the east of the Garden of Eden. Gen. 3:24 states, "He drove the man out, and stationed east of the Garden of Eden the cherubim and the fiery ever-turning sword, to guard the way to the "Tree of Life.""[42] The question is, "Why did God not need to protect the "Tree of Life" from the other directions? Why only in the east?" It seems that there was only one entrance to the Garden and that there must have been natural barriers in the other directions. Is there any area we know of that fits this description? The Garden of Eden would be an area that had only one entrance, on the east. If it were a mountain (Ezekiel 28:14), perhaps the area around Lake Van is intriguing. We look in the area of Lake Van that can only approached on the east.

Lake Van, the largest lake in Turkey, is 5640 feet above sea level, has a maximum length of 75 miles, a maximum width of 50 miles, and an area of 1450

41 Strabo *Geography V* Books 10-12 trans. Howard Jones (Cambridge, 2000) 328-9.
42 There is probably some relationship to another verse as well: Genesis 4:16 states that "Cain left the presence of the LORD and settled in the land of Nod, east of Eden."

square miles. With its deep blue waters, the lake is surrounded by volcanic formations on the northern and western parts. Mount Suphan, the third highest mountain in Turkey (13,188ft.) is situated in the north; it towers over the neighboring hills and provides a landmark for the entire region. Once an active volcano, it has black basalt slopes. The second peak, Mount Nemrut, which lies to the west of the lake, boasts a lake at its summit. The explosion of the Nemrut volcano led to the formation of Lake Van. Lake Van has been described as "superbly queer ... unique and fascinating... Lake Van is old, even as geological time is measured; since the volcanic upthrusts that isolated this basin, water can flow in, down from the mountains, but not out. With no circulation, the lake is left to stew in its own juices."[43] It is now a saline (salty) lake.[44] There are many bays and capes around the lake and four islands in the northern section. Surrounding the lake are agricultural areas where fruit and grain are grown.

The area around Lake Van has been inhabited as early as the Stone Age.[45] The mountains circling Lake Van are full of cave paintings, some dated as far back as 15,000 years. The Tirsin pasture in Van is a unique area. The rocky area of this 2,400 meter-high pasture is an outdoor archeological museum.[46] There are thousands of pictures on as many rocks: schematic pictures of "taurus," bison dating

---

43 Dana Facaros and Michael Pauls *Turkey* (Chester, Connecticut, 1988) 350.

44 Because the water enclosed here has no outflow, Lake Van has bitter, salty and carbonated (soda) waters. Sodium carbonate sedimentations form along the shores of the lake into which many of the rivers coming from the mountains empty. It is said to be an interesting experience to swim in these "soda" waters.

45 We have evidence of human habitation in Prehistoric Anatolia going back to the Paleolithic period (500,000-12,000 BCE), including flint hand-axes, scrapers and other tools, as well as paintings on cave walls, becoming more prominent during the Upper Paleolithic (40,000-12,000 BCE) and the Mesolithic period (12,000-6500 BCE). These periods are divided by the gradual warming of the climate and the retreat of ice to the higher regions of the mountains. It is true that a great deal of visible evidence of the earliest cultures of Anatolia may have been lost due to the large rise in sea levels that followed the end of the last Ice Age. Still, there are widespread—though little studied—signs of human occupation in cave sites from at least the Upper Paleolithic Period, and earlier Lower Paleolithic remains are evident in Yarmburgaz Cave near Istanbul.

46 The beginnings of archaeology in Van began with the first treasure hunters. The materials found gave stimulus for the first scientific archaeological work at Van. In 1877, Henry Layard sent his assistant Hormuzd Rassam to Van. At the almost three thousand year old site, he unearthed the magnificent bronze palace doors, decorated with scenes from Shalmanesers's campaigns, in particular his campaigns against Urartu. The door had representations of Urartian fortresses, warlike operations, and sacrifices on the shore of Lake Van.

back to Mesolithic times. These pictures created by the hunters support the thesis that the area was thickly forested in prehistoric times. [47]

Lake Van was the sacred center and capital of the once powerful kingdom and civilization of Urartu.[48] The eastern part of Lake Van, where the city was located, used to be called "Waini" in the Urartu language. The lake was ringed with beautiful trees and mountains; now one can see fortresses, mosques, and ruins.[49] The Urartians had outstanding success in architecture having constructed unique temples, palaces, castles, waterways and artificial lakes despite the tough climate and geographical difficulties of the region. Urartu art contains depictions referring to the "Cult of the Tree." There are images of sacred trees guarded by *seraphim* and genies and sometimes attended by a king or kings. For generations, personal seals imprinted the sacred tree on correspondence carried throughout the empire. Rulers and administrators sipped wine from bronze cups stamped with the emblem of the tree. Urartian warriors carried the symbol of the sacred tree to battle on bronze belts and pointed helmets. Colorful wall paintings, carved columns in palaces and other buildings repeated the recurring theme. Examples of this can be found on a bronze helmet of King Sarduri II (760-743 BCE).[50]

I am not limited to, nor sold on, the suggestion that I am making about the exact area of the Garden of Eden.[51] I am fascinated by Lake Van, and I will hold this

---

47 The Hurrians, the shadowy late Neolithic people who may have provided the indigenous stock of so much of Anatolia, arrived around the 3rd millennium BCE, and the population increased markedly in the 2nd millennium when a prolonged drought in the plains to the south-west caused many of the semi-nomadic tribes of that area to migrate into the mountains. Today that migration is echoed in the annual spring wanderings of the shepherds, sometimes covering great distances, to their yayla, or summer pasture, in these highlands.
48 Troy R. Bishop Urartu: *Lost Kingdom of Van*; Boris B. Piotrovsky *The Ancient Civilization of Urartu* 18-21, 38-39, 50 and 81.
49 Urartian culture is believed to arise from the Hurrians. These mountaineers built great fortresses on overlooks throughout the highlands of Urartu. Their kingdom supported huge building programs. Palace remains show economic might. Much of their art has been recovered, particularly works in bronze.
50 Now found at the Hermitage Museum in Leningrad.
51 We can briefly hint at another theory about the location of the Garden of Eden. If the two sources of the Tigris are Lake Van and Hazar Lake, it becomes important to take a look at the latter area as well. Elazi is a city and a province in eastern Anatolia. The Hazar Lake is located in the tectonic depression between the Mastar and Hazar Mountains that occupy the center of the province. Elazi has rich surface water resources. The Tigris and Euphrates Rivers collect all the waters of the rivers of the province. Hazar Lake is the most important natural lake in this region. This crater lake, 4000 feet above sea level, used to discharge its water into the Tigris River Basin. Hazar Lake now discharges its water into the Euphrates Basin through a tunnel constructed to operate hydropower plant in 1957. Keban Dam Lake is the second largest artificial lake of the Turkey (675 square kilometers). The Keban Dam Lake now inundates the point where the Murat and Karasu Rivers join and where the Murat and its tributary Peru intersect. The major tributaries of the Murat River that are located

theory unless or until a better one comes along. I will maintain this position because the area around Lake Van:

1.   Is near the sources of the Tigris and Euphrates and other rivers as well;
2.   Is an area where there was an astounding amount of provable prehistoric activity;
3.   Is an area that is associated with a sacred tree;
4.   Is an area that can only be entered from the east, corresponding to the Biblical text.
5.   Is an area known for its famous volcanoes, which may correspond to the flaming sword guarding the way to the "Tree of Life."

The Garden of Eden is a reflection of a memory of a very special place, a region near a freshwater lake in what we now call Turkey.

Conclusion

The Bible tells us that the origins of humankind were in Turkey. By doing so, it refutes Babylonian theories that Mesopotamia was that place of origin, which would make that land the center of the world. Ironically, the prevalent modern theory on the location of Eden agrees with the Babylonians and misses part of the Bible's point. The Bible uses its verbal map of the rivers that flowed from the real point of origin, Turkey, in order to show that these rivers flowed downstream into Mesopotamia, thus creating the fertile area. Another theory suggests that the Garden of Eden is in Jerusalem. The Biblical evidence is clear that the Gihon in Jerusalem is just a spring and a spring is not a river. The Gihon River is in Turkey; the Gihon spring is just a spring. Unlike Mesopotamian stories that portray life beginning with their culture, the Book of Genesis does not start with the progenitors of the Hebrews, Abraham; it starts with the common ancestors of all humans, Adam and Eve. Israelites did not pretend that theirs was the original culture of the ancient Near East. Israelites were not self-conscious about the fact that civilization did not begin with them. In their minds, God selected a relatively undeveloped area, Canaan, between the great civilizations of Mesopotamia and Egypt, so that the religion of monotheism could radiate out in all directions and transform the world.

---

within this area are the Haringet and Cip streams. The Peri stream and other narrow plains located in the valleys of Euphrates and Mura Rivers are the other low-lying areas in the province. Plains which occupy high zone of Karaboa and Ak Mountains are very important for stock-breeding.

Still another possibility might be the enormous alpine Lake Sevan, surrounded by a ring of mountains (which reminds me of both passages in the Bible and the Gilgamesh Epic). It is some 6000 feet above sea level. It is smaller than it used to be because of hydroelectric work in the area.

The fact that Eden was not in Iraq or Israel does not make Turkey the center of the world. The center of the world is its spiritual center, not its historical point-of-origin. The Bible gives an accurate assessment of where civilization as we know it began. The fascinating thing is that, as I shall explain in the next chapter, modern scientific study corroborates this assessment.

We humans had a place in the world before we knew our place in the world. The four rivers can tell us where it was. If one were to go back there, one would not find paradise; any more than one could find undifferentiated existence again. It was a place that represents human existence as it was and now is not. Lake Van is now salt. Volcanoes erupted like *cherubim* with flaming swords and it all changed. Like the Valley of Siddim that is now the Dead Sea,[52] it is not the same kind of area anymore.

Some will insist that the four rivers are just symbolic geography, mere details in a fairy tale, examples of the primitive state of knowledge about the real world. However, we have seen that this description is more focused than that; there was a place that fits this location. It is transformed now, just as our perception of life itself has been transformed. There's a famous popular song that states, "We've got to get ourselves back to the Garden." That is very pretty, but we cannot get there from here. Genesis was, indeed, just the beginning. We no longer live in a perfect world (or even in a very good one). What happened to the world of the Garden of Eden? Just as the topography has changed over the centuries, Paradise (simple human interaction before the will to power changed such interaction into power games) is gone forever.

The Garden of Eden is not a locus of hope for the future of humankind but it is a locus of understanding. In understanding the beginning of the human condition, we reflect deeply on our lives. We are not immortal; we cannot eat of the "Tree of Life" and live forever. We must work for what we have, and even when we have what we want, we must prune and tend. As individuals who live apart from each other, separate in our differentiated existences, we must cleave to others.

At the beginning of this chapter, I cited Emerson who says that when God spoke He communicated all things, filling the world with His voice, spreading and scattering "light, nature, time, souls," paradoxically creating a whole through those diverse emanations. God, in His "present thought," paradoxically absorbs past and future into that present. The Biblical texts have come down to us from that present, those moments of revelation, and all of the texts are equally sacred in that they emanate from God. If we look at the texts as manifestations of those revelations, we can find our way back to God.

---

52 See Genesis 13 and 19.

Truth emanates from Eden; rivers flow downstream from the source on high. The Bible, with its different rivers of truth, is filled with what some call contradictions and discrepancies. Instead, those so-called problems should be seen as functions of the heterogeneous nature of the truth, indications of the richness of God's complex message for the changing nature of life.

CHAPTER II

Missing the Boat

Why Noah's Ark Sailed Without Us

"The Incredible Discovery of Noah's Ark" was a two-hour prime-time special on CBS-TV in February 1993. It featured a man named George Jammal who had some interesting things to show and tell the world. In 1984, he said, he and his companion Vladimir had searched for Noah's Ark on Mount Ararat in Turkey. He and Vladimir had crawled through a hole in the ice into a wooden structure. "We got very excited when we saw part of this room was made into pens, like places where you keep animals," he remembered, "We knew then that we had found the ark!" To prove he had been in the famous ship, Jammal cut out a chunk of wood.

Then, Jammal said, the worst possible thing happened. As Vladimir backed up, taking pictures of Jammal and the whole scene, he fell, "and that made some noise, and there was an avalanche ... and that is where he died." The photos were lost. Jammal was so upset by the tragedy that he had to wait nine years before he had the emotional strength to tell his story.

Jammal held up a piece of wood and said: "This piece of wood is so precious - and a gift from God."

The host of the show, the renowned archaeologist and Biblical scholar Darren McGavin (whose credentials include playing a murderer on the classic television series "Columbo" and a weary detective on the less-famous "Night Stalker") was very impressed: "These demonstrations support the biblical story of the Deluge in every detail," he pronounced somberly. He stated at the beginning of the show that it was a "scientific investigation." On this two-hour special, other so-called experts brought other testimony:

• People in Biblical times made batteries and had air-conditioning;

• The flood occurred when water from beneath the earth chambers burst through the surface with an energy exceeding "the explosion of 10 billion hydrogen bombs";

• Fossils of animals have been discovered which were "buried in swimming positions" and fish have been "found in positions of terror, fins extended and eyes bulging."

All these notions and more were brought forth, on CBS-TV, in prime time, in 1993, to reflect the literal truth of the Bible. Why did CBS buy all of this nonsense? The CBS executives should not only be accused of gullibility but of perpetrating a dangerous misunderstanding of the Bible and the nature of its truth. In all fairness, it is not only one television network that gets the Bible wrong; it is most people in this country. The mistake about Noah's Ark is a perfect example of how we can have the best intentions in the world and hurt the authority of the Bible and of religion in general.

A hoax has been foisted on people but not by just one con man or one television program. People who fervently believe in the Bible have perpetrated the hoax. In so doing, they not only fail to understand what the Bible is about but also set up a straw man that objective thinking will knock over with a feather.

George Jammal, according to *Time* (July 5, 1993), has never even been to Mt. Ararat. Vladimir never existed. The piece of wood is a piece of pine that Jammal soaked in juices (one report said teriyaki sauce!) and baked in the oven in his home in Long Beach, California.

George Jammal's fictitious tale is not a new phenomenon. The world has heard such stories before. At the beginning of the nineteenth century, the British diplomat and traveler James Morier visited the region of Mt. Ararat and heard stories that presented the mountain as possessing an almost mystical aura.[1] In September 1829, Johann Jacob von Parrot, a German, made the first recorded successful ascent.[2] When Parrot, a German professor, scaled the mountain for what may have been the first time (after two failed attempts of his own), he raised a wooden cross and had a drink of wine to toast Noah, the father of winemaking. J. Bryce, a British historian and statesman, led an expedition in 1876 and later wrote:

> If it was indeed here that man first set foot again on the unpeopled earth, one could imagine how the great dispersion went as the races spread themselves from these sacred heights along the courses of the great rivers down to the Black and Caspian Seas.... No more imposing center of the world could be imagined.

Bryce found a piece of wood cut by a tool; he found it well above the tree line.[3] Since then several explorers have scaled Ararat; some of them claimed to have sighted the remains of the Ark. Russian aviators in World War I claimed that they had seen the Ark resting on a shoulder of Mt. Ararat. The Czar sent out an expedition but the leaders of the Russian Revolution destroyed the records. Actually, there was nothing to the story in the first place, but that did not stop its wide circulation in America.Some explorers have even brought back, as Jammal allegedly did, interesting pieces of wood. Radiocarbon testing of these pieces of wood certainly has not

---

1 James Morier *A Second Journey Through Persia, Armenia, and Asia Minor, to Constantinople, Between the Years 1810 and 1816* (London, 1818).
2 Johann Jacob von Parrot *Journey to Ararat* trans. by W. D. Cooley (London, 1845).
3 J. Bryce *Transcaucasia and Ararat* (London, 1877).

substantiated the antiquity of this evidence. At best, medieval monks who had made the mountain a site for pilgrimages may have left some of the pieces.

What is going on here, and frankly who cares? What is at stake in the study of the Noah story?[4] For many, the scientific evidence for a flood and the archaeological evidence of an Ark constitute nothing short of a representative case of Biblical veracity.

Both those who think the story is historical and those who think it is purely mythical have some interesting questions to puzzle over: Is "Mt. Ararat" a knowledgeable reference to a particular mountain? Where was this mountain? If so, how do we know this from the Biblical evidence? What is the evidence that the mountain that is called "Mt. Ararat" is the resting-place of the Ark referred to in the Bible? Most intriguingly, is there a connection between the mountain known from the Noah story and the location of the Garden of Eden?

I will come to some conclusions that are very different from both the usual common perceptions and the usual scholarly position that these stories are purely mythical. Over the next three chapters, I will show:

• That the Flood story is not just a "myth" but instead is a narrative expression of a catastrophic flood that has been proved scientifically and that changed the course of history;

• That those who think that they know where Noah's Ark landed, on "Mt. Ararat," have never really read the Bible, which does not even mention a "Mt. Ararat";

• That the Bible places the resting-place of the Ark in Turkey in the same general area as that of the Garden of Eden.

---

4 In Genesis 5:29, Noah, the son of Lamech, is listed as the direct descendant of Adam. In the Flood story (Genesis 6:11-9:19), Noah, a righteous man, is chosen by God to perpetuate the human race while his wicked contemporaries perish in the catastrophe. When God sees the moral corruption of humanity and decides to destroy it, He gives Noah a warning of the impending disaster and makes a covenant with him, promising to save him and his family. Noah is instructed to build an Ark, and, in accordance with God's instructions, takes into the Ark male and female specimens of all of the world's species of animals, from which those species might be replenished. After Noah's heroic survival, he builds an altar on which he offers sacrifices to God. God promises that He will never again bring such a catastrophe on the world; never again will He curse the earth because of human evil. God then sets a rainbow in the sky as a visible guarantee of this promise. He hangs up his bow, as it were. God also renews His commands given at creation but with two changes: humans can now kill animals for food and murder will be punished. Consequently the entire surviving human race descends from Noah's three sons.

A Quick Review

I am going to discuss the stories out of order, so let me just quickly review the first part of the Book of Genesis:

• Chapter 1–God creates the world, including men and women, who He commands to be fruitful and multiply and spread over the world;

• Chapters 2 and 3–God puts one human being, Adam, in a garden in Eden. Adam and then Eve live in the garden and can eat of the fruit of any of the trees in this paradise save one, the "Tree of Knowledge." When, with guidance from the snake, they break God's command, God exiles them from the garden. He doe not want the human beings to eat of the "Tree of Life" and gain immortality.

• Chapter 4–Adam and Eve have two sons, Cain and Abel. In a jealous rage, Cain kills Abel and is condemned to wander. Cain builds the first city.

• Chapter 5–Adam and Eve have another son, Seth. There are now two lines, those of Cain and Seth.

• Chapter 6-9–People are so evil that God sends a Flood. He warns one righteous man, Noah, to build an Ark and save himself and his family. The Ark lands on a mountain and the family is the new beginning of humankind. Noah plants a vineyard.

• Chapter 10–Noah's sons are the progenitors of the many nations of the world. These nations spread and have different languages.

• Chapter 11–The whole world has one language; everyone lives in one place, Babel. The people build a tower and are condemned to scatter throughout the world and have different languages.

This simple outline raises more questions than it answers. I will point out just two that jump out of the sequence presented. If human beings have multiplied and spread through the world in Chapter 1, why does Chapter 2 have a story about the (apparently) first human beings? If Chapter 10 states that there are a multitude of nations and languages, why does Chapter 11 say that everyone lived in one place with one language?

A book that can present truth in different modes, and place those modes next to each other, is an incredibly sophisticated and complicated work. Whatever the case, do not sell the Bible short. The Bible is a lot more complex than its detractors, and a great many of its supporters, will ever understand.

Mt. Ararat

Our entry-point will be the story of the Flood (Gen. 6-9). What I've said so far is that there are people who look for evidence of the Ark on Mt. Ararat.

Local traditions agree that the explorers who climb "Mt. Ararat" are looking in the right place. "Mt. Ararat" is sacred to the Armenians, who believe that they were the first race of humans to appear in the world after the Deluge. A people who spoke a language unlike any other now known inhabited this part of Armenia. A Persian legend refers to the Ararat as the cradle of the human race. The Persians call Ararat *kuh-i-nuḥ*, i.e., "Noah's mountain." There used to be a village on the slopes of the Ararat high above the Aras plain, at the spot where, according to local tradition, Noah built an altar and planted the first vineyard. Above the village, Armenians built a monastery to commemorate St. Jacob, who is said to have tried repeatedly but failed to reach the summit of Great Ararat in search of the Ark. Local tradition says that the Ark still lays on the summit but that God had declared that no one should be able to see it.

Despite all of these traditions, after all of the accounts, "sightings" and claims of discovery, after the extensive research which has taken place on Mount Ararat, after all the ground and aerial expeditions (some with sophisticated mapping capabilities), we do not have any scientific evidence or photo that shows that Noah's Ark exists today. Some think that it must be buried in the ice, so they have sent expeditions using Ground Penetrating Radar; they have not found any evidence of the Ark under the ice. If Noah's Ark survived into modern times and is somewhere on Ararat, there are very few places left on the mountain to search. Some cling to the possibility that Noah's Ark landed on Mount Ararat and was subsequently destroyed. They insist that even if Noah's Ark is not proven, Noah's Ark still could have landed on Mount Ararat.

All of this assumes that we know what "Mount Ararat" is. Most readers do not seem to have any idea that the very term "Mt. Ararat" is based on a simple mistake.

Why the Term "Mt. Ararat" is a Mistake

> At the end of one hundred and fifty days the waters diminished, so that in the seventh month, on the seventeenth day of the month, the ark came to rest on the mountains of Ararat.
>
> (Gen. 8:3-4)

Notice carefully here that Ararat is the name of a country or region; the Ark rests on one of its mountains after the Flood subsides (Gen. 8:4). The text does not say, "Mt. Ararat" but "on the mountains of Ararat."

Many ancient versions of and commentaries on the Bible are clear in saying that the Bible is referring to the "mountains" of the area and not to one particular mountain.[5] The famous modern commentator Umberto Cassuto sums it up well:

---

5 Josephus states that the ship landed "on the mountain of the Kordyaeans." This reference to the Kurds is echoed by the Aramaic translations and versions of the Biblical text. *Targum Onkelos*: "on the mountains of Qardu"; *Targum Pseudo-Jonathan* A: "on the mountains of Qardun"; the *Peshitta* (Syriac version): "on the mountains of Qardu". The rabbis of the Talmudic period, in the Midrashic work *Bereshit Rabbah* (xxxiii 4)

"...none of the identifications of the Biblical Ararat with a specific mountain has any basis in the Scriptural text, for the expression on the mountains of Ararat, correctly interpreted, only connotes a mountain –unspecified-in the land of Ararat."[6]

History and tradition misinterpret Genesis by limiting the Ark's landfall to the smaller Araxes valley area including Mount Ararat rather than the Urartian region or "mountains of Urartu" as described in Genesis. The Hebrew term Ararat, as it is found in the Bible,[7] is the equivalent of Urartu, the Assyrian-Babylonian name of a kingdom that flourished between the Aras and the Upper Tigris rivers.

In the year 860 BCE, the Urartian kingdom was formed under its first king, Aramu.[8] In the 13th century BCE, Assyrian documents gave the first definite reference about the peoples of the Armenian highlands. In inscriptions of the Assyrian King Shalmaneser (1280-1261 BCE), the term Ururti (Urartu) first occurs. The name Urartu was given to the alliance of the tribes of the Armenian highlands. The state of Urartu came into being in the early 9th century BCE as tribes coalesced to fight off the Assyrians. In 590 BCE, Urartu was sacked and burned by the Medes. The civilization of Urartu was completely forgotten. The name was lost and references in Assyrian inscriptions constituted a puzzle to later historians. Until, that is, Urartu was rediscovered by the archaeology of the late 1800s and early 1900s.

The area that was called Urartu is now called Armenia, part of Turkey. Armenia is Urartu and Urartu is Ararat. Turkey is predominantly mountainous; the only lowland is found on the coastal fringes. About one-fourth of the surface has an elevation above 4,000 feet. Mountain crests exceed 7,500 feet in many places, particularly in the eastern part of the country, in what was Urartu.

Again, Genesis simply says that the boat landed in the Urartian mountains. Since Mt. Ararat is the highest location in Urartu, it is understandable why it has been called the landing place of the Ark; this concept has been promoted in local traditions. If anyone were to arbitrarily select one mountain in the area of

---

state: "on the mountains of Qardunia". Nicolaus of Damascus, mentioned in Josephus' *Antiquities,* says that the people fled from the waters of the Flood to Mount Baris in Armenia. The Book of Jubilees, which often gives names to places and people who are not named by the Bible itself, states that the Ark rested on the summit of Mount Lubar, one of the mountains of Ararat (v: 28; vi: 1 and see vii: 17; x: 15).

6 Umberto Cassuto *A Commentary on the Book of Genesis: Part Two From Noah to Abraham* translated by Israel Abrahams (Jerusalem, 1974).

7 In II Kings 19:35-37 and Isaiah 37:37-38, the sons/assassins of Sennacherib, the king of Assyria who had recently unsuccessfully besieged Jerusalem, flee to "the land of Ararat" after they assassinate their father. In Jeremiah 51:27, the prophet summons God against several nations including "the kingdom of Ararat."

8 The Urartians referred to their country as the Land of Biaini.

Urartu/Ararat, Agri Dagi would be a terrific candidate. It is one of the largest single-mass mountains in the world. The mountain actually has two conical peaks, about 7 miles apart: Great Ararat (Büyük Agr Dag) reaches an elevation of 16,854 ft. above sea level and is the highest peak in Turkey; Little Ararat (Küçük Agr Dag) an almost perfect cone, reaches 12,782 ft. Both Great and Little Ararat are the products of volcanic activity. The snowcapped conical peak of Great Ararat is a majestic sight. There is a glacier near the summit on its northern side. The middle zone of Ararat, from 5,000 to 11,500 feet, is covered with pasture grass and some juniper trees. There are very few trees on Great Ararat. Despite the abundant cover of snow, the Ararat area suffers from scarcity of water. After the Flood, I like to think, this would be quite welcome.

So we can easily understand why people have thought that the Ark landed on this great mountain. If, however, the Bible wanted to say that the Ark landed on a particular mountain, or on the highest mountain in the area, it would have said it. The fact that the Bible simply says "the mountains of Ararat" is interesting in itself.

Where Did the Mesopotamian Noah Land?

Another line of evidence in studying the Biblical story of the Flood is to look outside of the Bible in other ancient texts. As most schoolchildren know, the story of the Flood has a close relationship to Mesopotamian traditions of apocalyptic floods in which Utnapishtim plays the part corresponding to that of Noah. These mythologies share many features of the Biblical story such as the building and provisioning of the Ark, its flotation, and the subsidence of the waters, as well as the part played by the hero. While there are clear and concrete parallels between the Mesopotamian and Biblical stories of the Flood, the Biblical story has a unique Israelite perspective. In the Babylonian versions, the destruction of the Flood was the result of a disagreement among the gods. In Genesis, however, it resulted from human evil. The polytheism of the Mesopotamian versions is transformed in the Bible into an affirmation of the justice and mercy of God. After the Flood, Utnapishtim and his wife become immortal gods; Noah and his family, however, are commanded to begin human history all over again.

Tablet XI of the *Gilgamesh Epic* speaks of Utnapishtim, who survives by following Divine instruction to build a ship. Since the Biblical story of the Flood is so close to that of Utnapishtim in the *Gilgamesh Epic*, any details about where Utnapishtim's boat landed and where he lived his life after the Flood, is of interest to our considerations. Searching for immortality, Gilgamesh reaches a mountain range whose peaks surge into the sky. His route moves north from Mesopotamia into the headwaters of the Euphrates, perhaps into the perilous mountain peaks surrounding the region of Lake Van in Anatolia (the region I have discussed above in relation to the Garden of Eden). Gilgamesh meets Utnapishtim, the son of Ubar-tutu (Ubar-tutu does seem to sound like Urartu). The sea of Utnapishtim is the Black Sea. Utnapishtim tells the story of how he built a boat and lived through the great catastrophe. He states that Mount Nisir is the mount on which the boat grounds in the *Gilgamesh Epic*:[9]

> I looked about for coast lines in the expanse of the sea;
> In each of fourteen regions there emerged a region (mountain)
> On Mount Nisir the ship came to a halt
> Mount Nisir held the ship fast, allowing no motion.

Where is Mount Nisir? Nisir seems to be a Semitic word meaning "Mount of Salvation."[10] It has been identified with the mountain now called Pir Omar Gudrun (about 9,000 feet high).[11] This mountain or mountain range is mentioned in the annals of King Ashurnasirpal II of Assyria (883-859 BCE) according to which it seems to be found in one of the ranges between the Lower Zab and the Adhem/Radanu. Still others say that the mountain is Elburz, the sacred mountain of the Iranians south of the Caspian Sea.

In his later version of the Babylonian story, Berossus[12] says that in his time the remains of the ship could still be seen on a mountain in Kurdistan, at what we call Mt. Cudi, a striking mountain southwest of Lake Van, commanding a panoramic view over the Mesopotamian plain, rising to a height of 7700 feet.[13] Cudi Dagh is located approximately 200 miles south of Mt. Ararat in southern Turkey, almost within eyesight of the Syrian and Iraqi borders, just east of the present Turkish city of Gizre. It is located about 25 miles from the Tigris River and still within the bounds of the Biblical region of Ararat. This would place the mountain in the southwestern part of Urartu/Armenia, far from "Mt. Ararat" which is northeast of Lake Van. The Koran states that it is this mountain that should be called "Mt. Ararat."

Cudi Dagh is notable for its many archaeological ruins in and around the mountain.[14] Mount Judi, called Cudi-Dagh in Turkish, means "highest" or "the heights" in Arabic and for this reason a number of people in Eastern Turkey, including many Islamic scholars, think Al Judi refers to Ararat. The local tribesmen

---

9 *ANET* 94.

10 A. Heidel *The Gilgamesh Epic and Old Testament Parallels* (Chicago, 1949) 250.

11 See E. A. Speiser *AASOR* VIII (1928) 17-18 and 31.

12 Berossus, a priest of Marduk in Babylon in 275 BCE, wrote a three-volume history in Greek. It is unfortunate that we only have excerpts of this work, because it would surely give us insights into all sorts of issues in the study of ancient texts. Berossus presents the Babylonian story in basic agreement with the *Gilgamesh Epic*.

13 Heidel *The Gilgamesh Epic* 118.

14 There are also many references to it in ancient history. The Assyrian king Sennacherib (700 BCE) carved rock reliefs of himself on the side of the mountain.

there maintain that the Ark drifted to a high point in the Cudi mountain chain and that the remains of it are still on the top of Cudi-Dagh, the highest mountain in the area. The Nestorians, a Christian sect, built several monasteries around the mountains including one on the summit called "The Cloister of the Ark."[15] In 1910, Gertrude Bell explored the area and found a stone structure still at the summit with the shape of a ship that the locals call *sefinet nebi nuh* "The Ship of the Prophet Noah." Bell also reported that every September 14, Christians, Jews, Muslims gathered on the mountain to commemorate Noah's sacrifice. As late as 1949, two Turkish journalists claimed to have seen the Ark on this mountain, a ship 500 feet in length!

Please notice that there are different texts and theories about the location of the resting-place of the Ark. If we recognize the ambiguity of the Bible at its word, the mountain is by no means the now-named Mt. Ararat. It is a simply unacceptable methodology to test the veracity of the Bible based on the search for the Ark on one arbitrarily-chosen mountain.

It is fine to say that the ancient texts say that the survivors of the Flood landed in the region of Ararat and not on one particular mountain. However, what is the point if there is no evidence of the Flood?

Those who have wanted to prove the literal truth of the Noah story have written of flood levels in certain archaeological sites and have pointed to the fact that there are ancient flood stories from all over the world. The most famous of the archaeologists who have dug down through strata of a city looking for levels of the flood was Leonard Woolley, who led twelve expeditions to the very ancient city of Ur in southern Mesopotamia (the same Ur that is called the birthplace of Abraham in Genesis 12). When Woolley got down to a level from the period 4000-3500 BCE, he found a stratum of mud ten feet thick. He concluded that this was evidence of Noah's flood. Woolley's conclusion is trumpeted by the kind of popular discussions of which the CBS-TV program is an example. What only scholars know is that Woolley dug *five* pits down through all the strata at Ur and only found water, or evidence of the flood, in *two* of them! The so-called universal flood did not even cover the whole site at Ur. When Woolley dug at a site only four miles from Ur, there was no flood level at all.

So where does this seem to leave us? While fundamentalist/Orthodox readers still want to find remnants of the Ark, many scientists and historians have assumed that the Flood story derives from local events in Mesopotamia.

Things have been at this impasse for a long time. Now science, of all things, has come to the rescue.

---

15 Lightning in 766 C.E destroyed it. The Muslims later built a mosque on the site.

A Breakthrough (in Two Different Ways)

In recent years, scientists have proposed the first exciting interpretation of the flood in over 150 years of study and speculation. Combining modern geophysics and archaeology with Biblical texts and ancient traditions, these scientists have presented astonishing evidence relating to the reality of the Biblical Flood. [16]

In the summer of 1967, geologists and chemists from the Wood Hole Oceanographic Institution were on board the research vessel Atlantis II, on their way to the Red Sea.[17] As luck (or destiny or God) would have it, the Six Day War between Israel and several Arab states began. The leaders of the expedition, David Ross and Egon Degen, decided to divert the ship to the Black Sea.

The Black Sea has unique hydrology; it is an environment unlike any other on the earth. It is almost completely landlocked, with only one narrow outlet in its southwest corner, the Bosporus. Water from the Aegean Sea flows through the Dardanelles and the Bosporus into the Black Sea and sinks under the layer of fresh water on the surface. The fresh water comes from the drainage of some of the major rivers of Eastern and Central Europe, the Danube, the Dniester, the Dnieper and the Don. All of this fresh water, which is less dense than the thick salty water from the Aegean, overflows through the Bosporus. The heavier Aegean salt water is trapped below, unable to circulate, completely depleted of dissolved oxygen. Normal life is impossible.

The Ross-Degen team wanted to study the hydrology by taking bottom core samples. Examination of the deep-sea sediments showed that a layer of black mud sediment was flecked with tiny white filaments above light gray clay. The strands turned out to be the skeletal remains of marine plankton that had descended like snow from the surface. When the clay was processed, it provided fresh water suitable for drinking.

Why was there evidence of marine life and fresh water at the bottom of this salt sea? The scientists theorized that the Black Sea had once been a freshwater lake, formed during the Ice Age. The world's oceans, and what we call the Mediterranean Sea, dropped drastically. When the glaciers melted, the rivers from Eastern and Central Europe carried their clays into the lake, which is what created the gray layer now at the bottom of the Black Sea. Eventually, the level of the Mediterranean rose to the point where it began to flow into the Black Sea through the Bosporus Strait.

---

16 William Ryan and Walter Pitman *Noah's Flood: The New Scientific Discoveries about the Event That Changed History* (New York, 1998).

17 Robert D. Ballard with Malcolm McConnell *Adventures in Ocean Exploration: From the Discovery of the Titanic to the Search for Noah's Flood* (Washington, D.C., 2001) 30ff.

This theory would explain why we have the evidence of marine life and fresh water at the bottom of what is now the Black Sea.

This evidence converged neatly with an earlier expedition from Woods Hole Institution, which, in 1961, had discovered that the northern mouth of the Bosporus had slashed a deep undersea gorge through the bedrock and sediment. The lack of sedimentation indicated that this gorge had been created with astounding pressure and speed. A student on that expedition, William B. F. Ryan, became fascinated with understanding the development and geological history of the Black Sea. On another expedition to do core-drilling of the Mediterranean in 1970, Ryan concluded that that sea had become separated from the ocean that went around the planet around five million years ago and as a result dried up into a desert. The core samplings showed a very thin edge between the desert layer below and the layer of marine ooze above it. Ryan concluded that the Mediterranean desert had been flooded in a single, catastrophic event.

How and why would this cataclysm have happened? Five million years ago, the Strait of Gibraltar had been dry land that separated the Atlantic Ocean from the Mediterranean basin. When a violent seismic event destroyed this natural dam, water filled that basin to the depth of 5,000 feet.

The parallel to the creation of the Black Sea became clear to Ryan, his colleague Walter Pitman and the British geologist John Dewey. Ryan and Pitman, now senior scientists at Columbia University's Lamont-Doherty Earth Observatory, realized that just as a violent event created the Mediterranean Sea, so the Black Sea became a salt sea due to a violent event. As opposed to the event that created the Mediterranean, the Black Sea event happened in a relatively recent age. The bottom of the freshwater lake that would become the Black Sea had dropped and was now lying hundreds of feet below the level of the world's rising oceans.

About 12,000 years ago, toward the end of the Ice Age, the earth began growing warmer. Vast sheets of ice that sprawled over the Northern Hemisphere began to melt. Oceans and seas grew deeper as a result. Over the next seven thousand years, to about 5600 BCE, the area of the Black Sea was isolated from the Mediterranean. In the meantime, the global sea levels were rising. Around 5,600 BCE, the mounting seas burst through. The salt water of the Mediterranean rose in Marmara, crashed through the natural dam of the Bosporus, poured into the lake with great force, and raised the level of the body of water 280 feet in twelve months. The gorge that Ryan had observed was first a tiny channel running down a grassy slope. Within 60 days, "the trickle had become a torrent, then an unimaginable cascade." The water cascaded over beaches and up rivers, destroying everything in its path. When the rising waters of the Mediterranean broke through the Bosporus, "ten cubic miles of water poured through each day, two hundred times what flows over

Niagara Falls...The Bosporus flume roared and surged at full spate for at least three hundred days."[18]

Again, the conclusion is that the Flood might have been a prolonged, huge flume of water from the Mediterranean that broke through a natural dam in the Bosporus Strait and plunged into the freshwater lake that then became the Black Sea. The rim of the lake had served as an oasis, a kind of Garden of Eden for farms and villages in a region of semi-desert. Pastoral people, Neolithic farmers, died as the level of the lake rose some 550 feet; it became a sea of death. The cascade inundated 60,000 square miles of land. Those who survived were those who successfully fled. Many may have fled by boat.

In 1993, a Bulgarian oceanographer, Petko Dimitrov tested the theory by diving off the Danube delta, on the western side of the Black Sea, in a manned submersible. 404 feet down, he found signs of an ancient beach. The shells from this beach were dated by radiocarbon tests to 7,000 BCE Russian scientists found submerged outlet channels of the old Don River (which flows from the north into the sea) as well as other streams and waterways that had once flowed out of the northern steppes across the grasslands of the shore into the freshwater lake. They found new evidence of a marine environment that had quickly destroyed a long-established freshwater system. In 1994, samples of Ryan and Pitman's shells from widely dispersed sites from the Black Sea were subjected to radiocarbon dating using a highly advanced accelerator mass spectrometry technique; all of them were dated 5,580-5,470 BCE. There was not some gradual influx but one great wave. These dates place the Flood within human memory.

The famous oceanographer Bob Ballard was compelled by all of these discoveries. He was especially interested in the submerged beach formations 400-600 feet below the present level of the Black Sea. Since the beach formations that had been discovered were on the northern coast, Ballard decided to test the findings scientifically: If this were true in the north, it should also be true on the southern coast as well. Hundreds of miles south of Ryan and Pitman's 1993 survey lines, Ballard did indeed find the distinct features of an ancient freshwater lake, 550 feet below present sea level. He also found the shells of two extinct freshwater species of saltwater shellfish; they became extinct c.5400 BCE. Ballard's conclusion: "We had closed the circle. No one could dispute that a Great Flood had occurred approximately 7,500 years ago."[19]

A skeptic might insist that all of this constitutes a fascinating gathering of geophysical and archaeological evidence to reconstruct the truth behind the Bible. However, we are not speaking of hoaxers, or amateurs with a camera crew and

18 Ballard *Ocean Exploration* 32.
19 Ballard *Ocean Exploration* 43.

some local guides. The evidence for the Flood is streaming in from prominent, working scientists.

The Flood and History

It is thus more than plausible that the Flood story of the Bible records a real and historic event. People lived around a freshwater lake. There was a Flood. They fled and many wound up in the mountainous area later called Urartu. Many of them might have fled by boat. Eventually, people moved south, maybe along the rivers. They dispersed; they spread their language(s), their genes and their historical memories. The story of the Flood was passed down orally from generation to generation. This would explain why the flood stories of various cultures, from Sumer to India, are remarkably similar. These tales not only tell of the destruction of the world, as it was then known, but also offer hope. Subsets of these people became, among others, proto-Indo-Europeans and Sumerians—the founders of two prominent early cultures of Europe and western Asia, respectively.[20]

People running for mountains may be the historical truth. It would make perfect sense: In a time of a flood, run for the high ground. Whether or not anyone built a big boat and put animals on it is of less importance to me (then again, if they could, they would have put animals on board so that they could start again). In this sense, the Flood story may be better history than a lot of us would have thought.

For Those Who Are Not Convinced:
The Flood Story as a Memory of the Ice Age

I find the Black Sea theory absolutely fascinating and, frankly, quite persuasive. It still does not explain the fact that there are traditions of a flood from the Arctic Circle to the southern tip of South America. Why are there are a hundred ancient stories from Greece to Polynesia to the Western Hemisphere? As different as all the stories are, they all tell of a very few people surviving a great deluge. They all seem to be memories of a great event. The easy answer is that the stories of the Flood that created the Black Sea spread throughout the world and became viewed as a universal event.

Perhaps a more complicated but more satisfying way to look at this question is to see the Black Sea flood as one example of Ice Age thawing. Flood stories constitute very ancient collective memories of the Ice Age. Noah represents the human beings who survived that horrible and frightening period. The flood came, froze, and took a long time to leave. There would be flood stories all over the world

---

20 The archaeological record is supported by DNA studies that reveal genetic connections between modern peoples of these regions and remains found around the region.

because there was an Ice Age; no other event, one could suggest, would have the same traumatic worldwide impact.[21]

From the Flood Story Back to the Garden of Eden

I have pointed out that the Bible says that Noah's Ark landed in the mountains of Ararat. Then I start to wonder: What was the Ark's starting-point? That is, where did Noah live before the Flood? Could he have been one of, or at least a legendary reflection of, the people who lived in Turkey and fled before the Flood that created the Black Sea? If so, pushing further back, does the Bible have stories that reflect the time before the Flood that relate to our new understanding of the origins of people in the Near East? What is quite intriguing to me is that all of this may have a relationship to the Biblical story of the Garden of Eden that may also be found in Urartu-Armenia. If so, we have an interesting connection between the Flood story and the Garden of Eden. Eden is in Ararat or at least close to it. So by starting again in Urartu, in the same region as the Garden of Eden, Noah became a second Adam.

Concluding Unhistorical Postscript:
The Religious Dimension of the Flood Story

Humankind survived. Noah and his ark represent the ingenuity of human beings and the mercy of God in the face of catastrophe. A Flood story is not so much about catastrophe as about surviving a catastrophe. We know that Noah will survive. The question is how. Such a story does not create anxiety; it gives us hope that God will be with us when our lives are threatened. The Ark becomes a symbol, a powerful symbol, and I do not need pieces of wood to lend truth to my beliefs.

Archaeology is interesting, as far as it goes. However, the Bible is a record of God's relationship with human beings, and archaeology cannot prove God's part in any historical event. Even if you had a piece of a real-life historical Ark, that

---

21 If this Ice Age theory does not attract you, maybe you will prefer the late Thorkild Jacobsen's theory of flood as metaphor for invasion. Jacobsen was the greatest scholar of Sumerian, the first written language, and he studied all of the ancient Mesopotamian parallels to the Flood story. Modern scholarship recognizes as a fact the idea that the Biblical Flood story has parallels in other, earlier ancient Near Eastern Flood stories. Jacobsen discovered an interesting expression in many of the ancient texts, "after the flood has swept over," and showed that this expression refers to "barbaric invaders from the eastern mountains, butchering the inhabitants and destroying and looting" the Mesopotamian cities. "After the flood had swept over" refers to near-fatal catastrophes, and not necessarily to floods. Could it be that a metaphorical expression became frozen into a story? Whatever you think of such theories, that the Ice Age thawed into a flood or that a metaphor froze into a story, they are attempts to understand the meaning of the flood in ancient terms.

wouldn't prove that God had commanded Noah to build it. If you found indisputable evidence not just of wood from that time period but Noah's autograph and his shipbuilder's license with his picture on it, you would not be forced to say that there was a Flood or that it was a punishment from God.

So what is the story of Noah's Ark really about? It is not about a ship of wood. It is about the evil of humankind, the justice of God, the mercy of God, the unity of all humanity, and the Divine promise that the world will never be destroyed again.

A *maggid*, a Jewish teacher and preacher, once told a community in Hungary this story about Noah: When God told him of the impending Flood, Noah went for help to the fathers of his three sons' wives, offering them all passage on the Ark. Shem's father-in-law, a pious man, said that we must accept God's will and refused to go onto the Ark. Japheth's father-in-law was a banker who would not spend his money on what he saw was a bad investment; he also refused to go onto the Ark. Ham's father-in-law, a carpenter (whose services would have been immediately useful), said that he was too busy to help out or come aboard.

You can guess the rest of the story. All three fathers-in-law came running to the Ark at the last minute, but it was too late, and they all drowned in the raging waters of the Flood. They all missed the boat. Those who do not see the profit potential of studying the Bible, and those who have no time for study, miss a dimension of their spiritual lives.

The materials that make up the only Ark that we will ever be able to get our hands on are literary materials. We can come up with theories about how the Ark was built by studying these materials. Why bother? Because this little story about a man and a boat and a Flood has captivated the world for thousands of years. It has held all sorts of meanings for all sorts of people. It is probably one of the first stories that we can remember hearing as children. This demonstrates the power of this story, and holds up the promise that its truths will speak to us now as well.

The Bible is an Ark that has sustained us through the worst possible nightmares, through the times of butchering tyrants, through the stages of history when the world was like a frozen wilderness. We survived by entering the Ark of study of the Bible; we did it as individuals or in pairs or as groups, but it preserved us until the deluges had ceased. The Flood is raging; meaninglessness and despair rage over the earth, chaos prevails; only one ship rises above the waves. The invitation presented by the way people such as I read the Bible is to ignore both the hoaxers and those who think it is all falsehood and get on board.

Chapter III

Follow the Dreams:
Joseph and the Meaning of Dual Causality

The story of Joseph is a familiar one. In recent years, it has been the subject of the Broadway play, *Joseph and His Amazing Technicolor Dreamcoat*, the rock opera by Tim Rice and Alan J. Weber, the animated movie *Joseph the Prince of Dreams* and the television movie *Joseph*. It is a great story, a kind of novel with all of the dramatic tension anyone could want: Parental favoritism, sibling rivalry, betrayal, grief, ambition, power, rises and falls. Joseph starts out on top; as the favorite son of his father, he is #2, second only to his father. His brothers throw him into a pit and sell him into slavery in Egypt. He rises to be the *major domo* (top slave) in Potiphar's house; he's #2 again. He is thrown into prison but wins the favor of the keeper of the prison; he rises to become the #2 man in all of Egypt, second only to Pharaoh.

The literary symmetry is flawless:

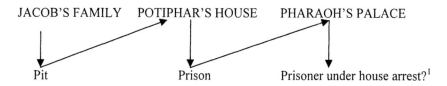

JACOB'S FAMILY   POTIPHAR'S HOUSE   PHARAOH'S PALACE

Pit   Prison   Prisoner under house arrest?[1]

Here's the story. Joseph is the eleventh son of Jacob; Jacob is the heir and grandson of Abraham, the one chosen by God to be a blessing to the nations. Several of Joseph's older brothers have demonstrated that they are not fit to succeed their father as chief. Reuben slept with his father's concubine (Gen. 35:22) and

---

1 One of the impressive things about the Joseph story is how it ends. Joseph cannot return to the land of Canaan. While he was able to bury his father, he cannot be buried himself in his homeland. Why not? Something has happened. His deathbed wish is that his bones will be brought home again. Joseph says that someday, God will remember His people and save them from Egypt. A powerful Joseph wouldn't say this. I am reminded of the Christian apologetic movie *Ben Hur*, where the title character starts as a prince, is thrown into prison and the galleys, rises to become the greatest charioteer in Rome by saving the life of a Roman general, goes home to Israel and gives up all worldly power to follow Jesus. Without the suffering and the prison and the galleys, the story wouldn't have its appeal. It is only the overcoming of adversity that gives any story dramatic tension.

Simeon and Levi conducted a violent massacre after their sister Dinah was raped (Genesis 34). Joseph, while young, is the oldest son of Jacob's beloved wife Rachel (Gen. 30:22-24). He is loyal to his father and points out his brothers' faults. Jacob gives his son the famous "Technicolor Dreamcoat" (really an ornamented tunic) and not because he wants to make Joseph a trend-setting fashion plate. The wearer of such a coat is the chief-to-be, and everyone knows it. The brothers are angry that he had reported their failings and envious about the coat but really become incensed when Joseph reports two dreams to them, dreams that have all of them bowing to Joseph. When Jacob gives them the opportunity by sending Joseph to see them when they are away from home, the brothers throw Joseph into the pit and sell him into slavery in Egypt for twenty shekels of silver.

In Egypt, Joseph becomes a slave to an officer of Pharaoh named Potiphar (Gen. 39:1). Joseph rises to become the overseer of Potiphar's house. Everything is going well until Potiphar's wife tries to seduce the young handsome Joseph, who resists her advances only to be accused of trying to rape her. Joseph is thrown into a new pit, the prison. There he becomes the #2 man again, the assistant to the prison warden. Joseph interprets the dreams of two of Pharaoh's cabinet officers, one of whom is lifted up out of jail and brought back into the Pharaoh's service (Genesis 40). Eventually, when Pharaoh has dreams that his magicians cannot interpret, the Cupbearer remembers the young Semite who interpreted his dream when he was in prison.

Joseph is brought before Pharaoh and interprets the king's mysterious dreams, which involve seven years of plenty followed by seven years of famine (Genesis 41). Joseph is made Vizier so that he can plan for the years of famine by creating reserves of grain for Egypt and the surrounding nations. Joseph does what he has planned and stores up huge amounts of grain for the bad times to come. When the years of famine overcome the region, Joseph is ready. Over the next few years, he proceeds to trade the grain for the land of the people of Egypt. They become serfs to Pharaoh. As another result of the famine, Joseph's brothers come down to Egypt for food. Joseph does not reveal himself to his brothers, who think that he is dead and certainly do not think that the Egyptian Vizier is the brother they sold into slavery. After a complicated game by which he can determine the brothers' repentance for what they had done to him, he reconciles with them. They bring Jacob down to Egypt, and the whole family lives in the area of Goshen. Joseph and his brothers take Jacob's body to Canaan where they bury him in the Cave of Machpelah in Canaan (Genesis 50) as Joseph swore to Jacob he would do (Gen. 47:29-31). When Joseph dies, however, his body cannot be brought back to Canaan. The Book of Genesis ends with Joseph's plea that his bones will be brought back to Canaan someday in the future when God remembers His people:

Joseph lived one hundred and ten years.... Joseph said to his brothers, "I am about to die. God will surely take notice of you and bring you up from this land to the land which He promised an oath to Abraham, to Isaac, and to Jacob." So Joseph made the sons of Israel swear, saying, "When God has taken notice of you, you shall carry up my bones from here."

Gen. 50:24-25

This prediction of the Exodus is striking because Joseph does not seem to have the power to arrange for his burial in the land of Israel. Egyptians were adamant about being buried in Egypt; Joseph is just as insistent on being buried in his native land. The fact that he cannot be buried where he wants to be would seem to indicate he had fallen in power for one last time. He knows that it will take Divine intervention to rescue the Israelites from Egypt.

The Debate: The Historicity of the Narrative, Pro and Con

Those who argue against the historicity of the Joseph narrative say that the fact that there is no extra-Biblical or archaeological evidence for Joseph is insurmountable. Many of their arguments point to the conclusion that the Joseph story is a product of the 1st and not the 2nd millennium BCE and does not reflect knowledge of the time and place in which the story takes place. The lead debater for the Cons is Donald Redford, distinguished Egyptologist and archaeologist. Sitting at his table are John van Seters and a group of scholars who think that the Joseph narrative is just a fictional story.[2]

The defense, led by Kenneth Kitchen and James K. Hoffmeier,[3] are quite eager to respond. As objectively as I can, I will draw a conclusion. You will have enough information to make a different conclusion if you see fit.

Exhibit I: Names

The subject is the Egyptian personal names mentioned in the Joseph narrative. Do the Egyptian names in the story reflect the 2nd millennium BCE, the period in which these events were supposed to have happened? Are Potiphar (Joseph's master), Asenath (Joseph's wife) and Zaphenath-Paneah (Joseph's Egyptian name) names that would fit in that time?

Think of the use of names to determine historical authenticity in this very simple way. If I said the name "Increase," you would not think about a person living in our age but might be quick to look back to Puritan Massachusetts in the 1600s. Scholars

---

2 Redford *A Study of the Biblical Story of Joseph VTS* vol.20 (Leiden,1970); J.Van Seters *Prologue to History: The Yahwist as Historian in Genesis* (Louisville, 1992) 20-42;
3 Kenneth Kitchen "Review of Redford's A Study of the Biblical Story of Joseph" *Oriens Antiquus* 12 (1973) 223-242. *idem* "Joseph" *ISBE* vol. 2 1127; Also for the defense see Hoffmeier *Israel in Egypt* 77-106; Alan R. Schulman "On the Egyptian Name of Joseph: A New Approach" *SAK* 2 (1975) 236.

can study names for their patterns and formulas and usage and determine when the name was used.

A.   Potiphar

Con - Redford states that Potiphar/Potiphera is the type of name that was used in the 1st millennium BCE (specifically in the seventh-third centuries). If the name Potiphar is a 1st millennium BCE name, the idea is, the narrative is late and fictional.

Pro- Kitchen finds this name on a stela ca.1070-945 BCE and shows that similar name formulas are found as early as the New Kingdom.

Conclusion: Where does leave us, the jury? If one expert says that the name and its formula do not exist in the early time under discussion, but other experts show that they do exist in that period, the cons lose.[4]

B.   Asenath (the name of Joseph's wife, Asenath, may mean "she who belongs to the goddess Neith")

Con: The problem is that this name does not exist anywhere in ancient Egypt. Also, if Asenath were the daughter of the priest of On, she would not bear a name with the component of the goddess Neith. So the name Asenath is seen as evidence that the narrative is false.

Pro: Kitchen solves the problem by showing that Asenath means "she who belongs to you" and is similar to a name formula from Middle Kingdom inscriptions such as "she belongs to her father/mother."

Conclusion: Now the name Asenath does not have anything to do the goddess Neith. While the name has only been found in the masculine so far, it does exist in early times, and the cons lose again.

C.   Zaphenath-Paneah (the name given to Joseph in Gen. 41:45. The name is mentioned as the Egyptian name given by Pharaoh to his Semitic Vizier.)

Con: The proposal for the name formula would make the name mean "The God has said: He will live".[5] Redford finds the name formula in texts between 664 and 331 BCE, which is very late for our purposes and is another sign of the inauthenticness of the Joseph narrative.

Pro: The name pattern here is still in dispute. Kitchen suggests a pattern that would mean "(Joseph) who is called 'Ip-Ankh'" ("Joseph who recognizes life"). This pattern is found in Middle Kingdom texts from 2000 BCE to 1300 BCE. Early attestations of the formula, "A who is called B," interestingly enough, are found

---

4 The name Potiphar appears in "The Tale of Two Brothers." Potiphar's wife calls him a Hebrew, a term that may be connected to the term Habiru found in the Amarna Letters.
5 Following the most popular suggestion made by George Steindorff in the 1890s, cf. *ZÄS* 27 (1889) 41-42 and ZÄS 30 (1892) 50-52.

referring to Semitic slaves at Egyptian estates.[6] The original Semitic name is retained and the given Egyptian name is added. Egyptians gave Egyptian names not only to slaves but also to foreign royalty who married into the Pharaoh's family.

Conclusion: While we can't be positive who is correct about the formula of the name Zaphenath-Paneah, it is very possible that it fits into the 2nd millennium BCE. At the very least, the name cannot be used as proof that the narrative is based on 1st millennium BCE background.

D.   Joseph (in Hebrew, Yoseph).
   Con: The name Joseph is never found in 2nd millennium BCE texts.
   Pro: The names Yitzchak (Isaac), Ya`akov (Jacob), Yoseph (Joseph), and Yishma'el (Ishmael) all begin with something linguists call the "Amorite imperfective." From studying lists of thousands of names found from the 3rd millennium BCE and later, Kitchen shows that 55 percent of the names during the time of the Patriarchs begin with an *i/y* sound, but already "by 1500 BCE the whole thing drops to a tiny percentage and never ceases dropping after that." Where, Kitchen asks, did the so-called fiction writers of the middle 1st millennium BCE get these names if they were composing their biblical novella a thousand or more years after the names had fallen from popular use?
   Conclusion: While the Cons do have the advantage that we have not found evidence of this particular name, the name itself would fit into the early period and is not evidence against an early date for the narrative.
   In general, the Cons have not made their case based on the names found in the Biblical story. They do, however, have the strong point that there is no evidence of Joseph himself. If he was such a major figure, where is the Egyptian evidence of his existence? We turn now to the subject of whether Joseph as Vizier was even possible in the New Kingdom.

Exhibit II: Is There Evidence of Semites Became Vizier of Egypt?
   Con: The narrative is inauthentic because no foreigner could hold the position of Vizier. Are the titles and roles given to Joseph by Pharaoh appropriate for a courtier of that time? Scholars such as William Ward state that Joseph's responsibilities and titles do not match those of a Vizier in Egypt in the time period under question.[7] Ward thinks other titles, such as "Overseer of the Granaries" or "Chief of the Entire Land," may have been those actually accorded to Joseph. For many scholars, the whole Joseph story is just a rags-to-riches fairy tale.
   Pro: The narrative is authentic because we have found evidence of Semitic Viziers. First, let us review a bit of background. For several periods in its history, Egypt's empire expanded into surrounding regions, including Canaan. During these

---

6 Kenneth Kitchen "Genesis 12-50 in the Near Eastern World" in *He Swore an Oath: Biblical Themes from Genesis 12-50* ed. by R. S. Hess et al (Cambridge, 1993) 82-83.
7 William Ward "The Egyptian Office of Joseph" *JSS* 5 (1960) 144-50.

times, young men and boys from those provinces were brought to Egypt to be trained in the pharaoh's ways and later sent back home as regional rulers who were loyal to the pharaoh. Also, a study on foreign children reared in the pharaoh's nurseries during the eighteenth dynasty shows that some of these children became court officials, and that a few eventually attained high government posts. The similarities to the stories of Joseph and Moses are obvious.

A. Bay - A courtier, Bay, was the "Great Chancellor of the Entire Land" after the death of Seti II in 1194 BCE. He helped to place Siptah on the throne. Bay was Semitic; he was born in Syria. Bay is a Semitic name; like Joseph, he was also given an Egyptian name as well, "Ramesse-Khamenteru."

The critics lose this general point about Semitic officials in the Egyptian court because this was a common occurrence. Think of it this way: In Egyptian affairs, the Semitic world and Asia were very much on the front burner. It must have been useful to have persons on hand that understood that world and could speak the languages of those countries.

B. Aper-el - One of these figures, Aper-el, with a name that includes the name of a Semitic, and Hebrew, god (El), was the Vizier during the end of the reign of one Pharaoh, Amenhotep III, and seems to have been a transitional figure who also served under the next Pharaoh, the famous Akhenaten. Is it realistic to think that a Semitic-speaking foreigner like Joseph, and later Moses, could have rose to the highest levels of Egyptian government? Hoffmeier answers by pointing to an Egyptian tomb discovered in Saqqara, Egypt, in the late 1980s. It contains the coffin of a Semite named Aper-el along with the coffins of his wife and children. His titles include "Vizier," "Mayor of the City," "Judge," "Father of God" and "Child of the Nursery." Hoffmeier points out that Aper-el's name was the first of a high-ranking, Semite official to be found there, even though Sacker has been excavated and explored for more than a century. "If such a high-ranking official as Vizier Aper-el was completely unknown to modern scholarship until the late 1980s, despite the fact that he lived in one of the better documented periods of Egyptian history [fourteenth century], and was buried in arguably the most excavated site in Egypt, it is wrong to demand, as some have, that direct archaeological evidence for Joseph should be available if he were in fact a historical figure." This is even more the case, he says, because Joseph lived during a period when surviving Egyptian documents of any kind are sparse and because Joseph operated in the Nile Delta, an area that remains "under-excavated" to this day.

Conclusion

It is intriguing to think that Aper-el was Joseph; the dates, under current theory, do not work. However, we should reserve judgment on this because our dates may be faulty. In the meantime, it is sufficient to say here that Aper-el is as close a parallel to the Biblical Joseph as could exist. He was a Semitic Vizier of Egypt in New Kingdom times.

Until the late 1980s, when the French Egyptologist Alain Zivie discovered a previously unknown tomb, no one had ever heard of Aper-el. If the Bible had mentioned someone by this name, scholars would have stated, with definitive aplomb, that Aper-el never existed because there was no extra-Biblical evidence of his existence. Now we know from extra-Biblical evidence that he did exist. If Aper-el is not Joseph, there may be evidence of Joseph that has not yet seen the light of day.

These viziers are still being discovered. They are at least background for Joseph. We have established the possibility of a Semitic vizier in the Egypt of that time. Since the Bible does not call Joseph a Vizier to begin with, I do not see whether he was Vizier or not as much of an issue. Even so, it is possible that Joseph was a Vizier and we have not yet found evidence of him.

Exhibit III: The Pharaoh of the Joseph Story
A.   The Title Pharaoh without a Personal Name.

Why doesn't the narrative tell us the name of the Pharaoh involved? The title Pharaoh, which means "palace" or "Great House," is a title that goes back to the Old Kingdom but only occurs as a title for the king in the 1400s BCE. The title becomes popular during the Ramesside period (1300-1100 BCE). Very often, the name Pharaoh occurs alone without the name of the individual. It was in the later periods such as those in which the cons want to place the narrative, that the personal name was indeed used alongside the title (Pharaoh Necho, etc.). The use of the title fits the time period of an authentic narrative.

B.   Pharaoh's Birthday

In the Biblical narrative, Joseph interprets the dreams of two highly placed officials from Pharaoh's court, the Chief Baker and Cupbearer, who had displeased Pharaoh and are sent to the same prison as Joseph has been condemned to. The Cupbearer is raised up out of prison on the occasion of Pharaoh's birthday (Gen. 40:20).

Let us consider this item as an historical question: Do we have evidence that the Pharaoh's birthday was the cause for celebration; was the Pharaoh's birthday a festival during the 2nd millennium BCE?

Con: Redford states that there is not any evidence for the celebration of the Pharaoh's birthday before the 1st millennium BCE. His point is that while the birthday-as-festival is authentic, it fits the wrong period and is thus evidence of anachronism and artificiality. Redford goes so far as to say that the king's birthday became a major event because of the influence of the Persians who brought the practice to Egypt in the seventh-sixth centuries BCE.

Pro: While scholars have argued about a Pharaoh's birthday-festival as early as the Second Dynasty (2890-2686 BCE), the evidence is unclear.

Let us take a step back and think about the idea of kingship in Egypt. When a prince became a king at his coronation, he was born as a god. That is, his birthday was no longer significant; what was very important was the day he became king and god. Redford himself has shown that the texts that speak of the "appearance of the king" concern the accession/coronation of the pharaoh. The festival is known from the Sixth Dynasty on (2345-2181 BCE); there is evidence of the feast during the 18th Dynasty (1570-1293 BCE) reigns of Thutmose I and II and Amenhotep II, a period in which we might look for Joseph.

Hoffmeier's brilliant and plausible suggestion is that the celebration of Pharaoh's birthday recorded in Gen. 40:20 is a celebration of his coronation. We would thus have plenty of evidence for the celebration of such a festival in the 2nd millennium BCE, the time of Joseph. The Biblical narrator did not distinguish between the anniversary of the pharaoh's actual birth date (which might not have been a cause for celebration) and the anniversary of his birth date as a god-king (which we know was a cause for celebration).

What evidence should we still look for? I would be even more confident of this solution to Redford's challenge to the Bible's authenticity if we could find 2nd millennium BCE texts in which the pharaoh uses the anniversary of his coronation as an occasion for both forgiveness (in the case of the Cupbearer) and judgment/punishment (the execution of the Chief Baker). There are parallels in the ancient Near Eastern world, but it would be a stronger case if we had such evidence from 2nd millennium BCE Egypt.

In the meantime, we have at least defended the Bible against the charge of inauthentic-ness in the case of the Pharaoh's birthday in Gen. 40:20.

Exhibit IV: Who Were the Hyksos and What Was Their Relationship to the Biblical Story?

There is a popular theory that Joseph must have been Vizier under the rule of the Hyksos in Egypt. The Hyksos were Semites and would have been more likely to employ and trust a fellow-Semite than native Egyptian pharaohs.

Let us take a look at what we know about the Hyksos and see if this theory is plausible. The term Hyksos (Egyptian *heka khaswt* "rulers of foreign lands") refers to a group from Canaan, or perhaps the rulers of that group, who migrated to Egypt in the late Middle Kingdom period (c.1800-1650 BCE) and rose to power in the Second Intermediate Period (1650-1550 BCE). One theory was that the Hyksos conquered Egypt at the end of the 13th Dynasty (c.1650 BCE), but current theory, expressed by Donald Redford, is that there was "a peaceful takeover from within by a racial element already in the majority."[8] Did the Hyksos conquer Egypt from the

---

8 Redford E*gypt, Canaan and Israel in Ancient Times* (Princeton, 1992) 98-129.

outside or were they an internal part of the population who took over from the inside? Ironically, the internal-takeover theory sounds very much like the fear expressed by Pharaoh in Exodus 1 that the Israelites will rise up from the land and take over Egypt.

The Semitic names of Hyksos rulers of the 15th and 16th Dynasties (c.1650-1550 BCE) such as Khyan, Joam and JakBa`al seem to indicate their non-Egyptian origins. New Kingdom texts such as the *Papyrus Sallier I* (c.1220 BCE) say that the Hyksos period was an interruption of the rule of native Egyptians; it was in fact a ruthless imposition of foreign culture on the native Egyptians.

The period of the Hyksos seems to have left a mark on the national psychology of Egyptians, who were no longer confident of their security and were constantly afraid of invasions from the east. In c.1469 BCE, about a century after the expulsion of the Hyksos, Queen Hatshepsut left an inscription that includes the following:

> ...I have restored that which has been ruined. I have raised up that which had gone to pieces formerly, since the Asiatics were in the midst of Avaris of the Northland, and vagabonds were in the midst of them, overthrowing that which had been made. They ruled without Re, and he did not act by divine command down to (the reign of) my majesty. (Now) I am established upon the thrones of Re. I was foretold for the limits of the years as a born conqueror. I am come as the uraeus-serpent of Horus, flaming against my enemies. I have made distant those whom the gods abominate, and earth has carried their foot(prints).[9]

Why is there so little in Egyptian literature about the Hyksos? Egyptians never talked about their defeats. Neither did other ancient people, with the relevant and notable exception of the Israelites and Biblical literature. The credibility of the Bible is that much greater because it is willing to admit defeats and explore the reasons for those losses.

Here's what we can say. For two centuries ending in 1550 BCE, an Asiatic people called the Hyksos ruled Egypt. After their expulsion, the new pharaoh, Ahmose, extended his rule into Syria and Canaan, transporting many prisoners of war back to Egypt. Hoffmeier believes that after the expulsion of the Hyksos, Ahmose and his successors discovered large numbers of Semites, including the Hebrews, in the Delta. The Egyptian rulers forced these Semites to work alongside prisoners of war. If Exodus 1:8 speaks of a shift from accepted minority to an enslaved population, it may reflect the transition from the Hyksos period to the Eighteenth Dynasty. It is worth noting that the practice of using forced labor for building projects is only documented for the period 1450-1200 BCE, the very time most Biblical historians place the Israelites in Egypt. The realization that others were enslaved along with the Hebrews may explain who the "mixed multitude" was.

---

9 *ANET* 231.

This phrase refers to other slaves who escaped from Egypt with the Israelites (Exodus 12:38).

Exhibit V: Semitic Slaves in Egypt

Joseph's high ranking becomes even more plausible when considering the regular migrations and imperial transactions that occurred between Canaan and Egypt, as seen in the following discoveries:

The *Wisdom of Merikare* and the *Prophecy of Neferti*, ancient Egyptian documents, report influxes of thousands of Semites into the Nile Delta from 2200-2000 BCE. Similar patterns of settlement recurred over the next thousand years, creating a "significant Asiatic population" in the Delta region. The Merikare document explains that these Asiatic, Semitic-speaking peoples, like Jacob and his sons, had come to the fertile Delta area in search of food during times of famine.

Is there evidence of Semitic slaves in Egypt during this time period? A great deal. Semites came to Egypt as tribute from their rulers and as prisoners of war. They became *corvée* workers and miners among many other occupations. The scroll known as Papyrus Brooklyn,[10] which documents details of an estate in the late Twelfth or early Thirteenth Dynasty (ca.1700 BCE), lists over forty Semites who worked for this one estate. Since this does not seem to have been a time of Egyptian military conquest in the Near East, Semites may have been in Egypt because they had been traded and sold there.

Is there evidence of Semitic slaves who rose to become the overseer of an Egyptian house? Papyrus Brooklyn also mentions the trades and occupations of the Semitic servants, some of whom are called "he who is over the house" which would seem to be equivalent to the description of Joseph as "over the house" for Potiphar in Gen. 39:4b.

How much were they worth? According to Gen. 37:28, Joseph was sold into slavery for twenty shekels of silver. How does this price compare to the price of slaves in Egypt at the time? It compares perfectly. Tracking the price of slaves sold from 2400 BCE-400 BCE using extra-biblical sources, Kitchen finds that this amount matches exactly the going price in the eighteenth century. Steady inflation had driven it up to 30 shekels by the thirteenth century (which corresponds to Exodus 21:32), 50 shekels in the eighth century (which corresponds to II Kings 15:20), and to nearly 100 shekels soon after the Babylonian Exile in the sixth century.[11] By the time of the 1st millennium BCE, which the cons say is the time

---

10 William C.Hayes *A Papyrus of the Late Middle Kingdom in the Brooklyn Museum Papyrus Brooklyn* 35. 1446 (New York, 1955) 99.

11 Kenneth Kitchen "Joseph" in *New Bible Dictionary* 617-20; idem "Joseph" in *International Standard Encyclopedia* vol. 2, 1125-30; idem "Genesis 12-50 in the Near

period when the Joseph story was written, the price of a slave had gone up to fifty or sixty shekels. This point goes to the Pros. It is a casual detail. It is not as if the writer said to himself, "I am going to research the price of slaves in the time when I am saying the fictional Joseph lived. I am going to use an anachronistic price to show the authenticity of the story." No, the twenty shekels is a convincing piece of evidence for the defense of the Bible's historicity. In fact, all of this evidence points to the background of Joseph's sale into Egypt.

Exhibit VI: Matters of Life and Death

Death Customs – The Bible describes the mummification of Jacob and the Joseph. Joseph is placed in a coffin (Gen. 50:26). These are the only two cases of embalming in the Bible. The Bible here reflects Egyptian customs that were not practiced in Canaan; these details are mentioned because they are so unusual.

The Length of Joseph's lifetime – The Bible states that Joseph died at the age of 110. It matter less to me whether he really lived that long as that 110 is the ideal age for Egyptians in those times. The Israelite ideal was 70, the famous "three score and ten" of Psalms 90:10, or the 120 years of Moses' life. If the Biblical narrative states that Joseph lived 110 years, it reflects an authentic Egyptian ideal.

While there are other elements of the Joseph story that reflect authentic Egyptian history and culture, including the scene when Pharaoh rewards Joseph for his dream interpretation and makes him a high official, the points made here should suffice to make the case that the Joseph story, contrary to the Cons, is true to the period of New Kingdom Egypt.

Human Particles and Divine Waves:
The Dual Causality of Human Free Will and Divine Determinism[12]

Let us ask the question in the simplest way we can: Why do things happen? Certainly, our actions are instrumental in making things happen. If one believes that God acts in human affairs, how exactly does He do that? Why does He do it some times and not others? The study of Biblical theology is complicated because of historical evolution; ideas and concepts about the relation between God and human beings changed over the centuries of Israelite history. To understand these ideas is also a complex task because of the unsystematic nature of the texts involved. Certainly, the theology of Deuteronomy is very different than that of Ecclesiastes, and so on. The Biblical narrators, in attempting to discuss and analyze Israelite history, needed to articulate both the free will of the human characters and the Will

Eastern World" in *He Swore an Oath: Biblical Themes from Genesis 12-50* ed. by R. S. Hess et al (Cambridge, 1993) 77-92.
12 Yairah Amit "The Dual Causality Principle and its Effects on Biblical Literature" *VT* 385-400; Yehezkel Kaufmann *The Book of Joshua* (Jerusalem, 1959) 128 (in Hebrew); I. L. Seeligmann "Menschliches Heldentum und göttliche Hilfe: Die doppelte Kausalitat im alttestamentlichen Gesschichsdenken" *ThZ* 19 (1963) 385-411.

of God. To tell any story in this way is to meet extraordinary literary and ideological demands.

The great scholar Yehezkel Kaufmann coined the phrase "dual causality." Kaufmann, in analyzing the story of the battle at Ai in Joshua 7-8, states: "This is a typical biblical story. Events occur through dual causality, i.e., through both natural causes and divine guidance which determines a purpose for the events."[13]

The Joseph story is an excellent example of the phenomenon that Kaufman discusses because the reader is constantly asking the question of what is human and what is Divine. I will present the case that the very human actions of the characters in the story are part of a sequence designed by God as part of an overarching Divine plan and that every dream and famine is caused by a Divine act, a specific direct act performed by God to keep the sequence moving and the plan moving to its goal. Indeed, in this "novella" which has been considered relatively late Wisdom literature, there is intense Divine involvement.

As much as we've said about Joseph in this chapter, there is still more to say about him. I see Joseph as a man who is an outstanding model of faith in the Bible.

In order to understand Joseph's faith and his role in God's plan, we have to understand what the plan is. In Genesis 12, Abram is called by God to be His agent on earth and is sent to Canaan. Yet, soon after he gets to Canaan, a famine causes Abram and his wife Sarah to go to Egypt. We should be reminded that the famine is sent by God to force Abram to go to Egypt. All famines in the Bible are understood to be the work of God. Why God sends this famine is not immediately clear. After Sarah has been taken to serve in Pharaoh's harem (a foreshadowing of the enslavement of the Israelites in Egypt), and God has sent plagues on the Egyptians (a foreshadowing of the plagues in the time of Moses) Abram leaves Egypt some time later, a very rich man (a foreshadowing of the riches with which the Israelites leave Egypt). A few chapters later, in Genesis 15, God reveals His overarching plan to Abram:

> Know well that your offspring shall be strangers in a land not theirs, and they shall
> be enslaved and oppressed four hundred years; but I will execute judgment on the
> nation they shall serve, and in the end they shall go free with great wealth.... And
> they shall return here in the fourth generation, for the iniquity of the Amorites is not
> yet complete.

---

13 Amit penetrates Kaufmann's motivations when he points out that Kaufmann sees the battle at Ai as the first real battle. In order to express its historicity, Kaufmann disregards the direct intervention of God. In other words, the story of Ai actually may not be the best example.

By stating the plan, does it have an impact on human actions? Does Abraham later tell his son Isaac about their destiny? Is knowledge of the plan passed down to Jacob and then Joseph? Think about it in human terms: Would any parent not tell his child about such an extraordinary future? The revelation explains so much. Abram would tell Isaac: "This is why you do not have to be concerned about possessing the land now. You can live a peaceful life. Just get along with your neighbors. Do not go to Egypt now. If you do, the plan may swing into operation and our family may be enslaved. Know that someday, in the fullness of God's plan, the land will be ours."

There is an aspect of the Divine plan that involves time: "they shall be enslaved and oppressed four hundred years....And they shall return here in the fourth generation." Does God know when the enslavement will begin? Does He know how the Israelites will get to Egypt?

Let us move forward to the time of Jacob. In Genesis 37, Jacob and his family live in the land of Canaan. They do not rule the land, as predicted by the revelation to Abram in Genesis 15. Jacob, it seems, will live out the rest of his life in Canaan. God's plan, however, is still active. God wants the plan to move into the next stage. God's preferred method, however, is to work through human beings. The situation in Jacob's family is that there is a beloved son by a beloved wife. God sees that Jacob has made the mistake of favoritism; He sees the antagonism to Joseph's status and actions towards his brothers. So Joseph has two dreams. The dreams are sent by God, which is confirmed by the fact that there are two of them. If there would just be one dream, it could be Joseph's own wishes. Two dreams are from God and one reveals the other.

The way that I usually hear the story told is that Joseph is a spoiled braggart. He flaunts his "Technicolor Dreamcoat" and he snitches on his brothers. He brings his fate upon himself. He tells the dreams because he wants to flaunt his destiny at his brothers. He enjoys their displeasure. What if we say, on the contrary, that Joseph, not so much with arrogance but with a special kind of innocence, believes that God sent the dreams about his destiny and that they are true. Just for the record, they *are* true and they are sent from God; the proof is that everyone does wind up bowing before Joseph.

In my understanding of Joseph, Joseph sees his brothers' faults and reports them; he receives God's dreams and reports them as well; he does all of this because his reports and his dreams are true. He does not think about anyone's anger or any of the possible consequences. The brothers have now had it with Joseph. It is not that they do not take the dreams seriously; it is because they know that the dreams are from God that they know that they must act. They know, or at least think, that they have the power to do something to stop the fulfillment of the dreams. Jacob, at first personally miffed that he has to bow to Joseph in the dreams, "kept the matter in mind" (Gen. 37:11). Since Jacob may know the plan, and since he knows that the dreams are from God and must be taken with the utmost seriousness, Jacob may want to see if the dreams relate somehow to the plan God revealed to his grandfather Abraham.

When the brothers see Joseph coming, they say, "Here comes that dreamer! ... We shall see what comes of his dreams" (Gen. 37:19-20). The brothers are saying, "Here's our chance to wreck the fulfillment of those dreams." They are going to kill Joseph.

What would have happened to God's plan if the brothers had killed Joseph? The answer is that God would have found another way to get the Hebrews to Egypt. It just so happens, however, that Ishmaelite traders 'happen to be in the neighborhood' and pass by at precisely the key moment. Since there are no coincidences in the Bible, the Ishmaelites do not just happen by. They are there to give the brothers an idea: "Instead of killing Joseph, let us make some money on the deal." As crude as this is, it sounds quite human and plausible.

Joseph is now in Egypt. God's plan is beginning to move, but it has only taken one step toward fulfillment. God needs everyone, the whole family, in Egypt. Once there, they will eventually be enslaved. Once enslaved, they will eventually be rescued. Once rescued, they will come back and rule the Promised Land.

God now has the following task: To maneuver events so that Joseph's family comes down to Egypt. God keeps a close eye on Joseph even though Joseph is only a slave, hardly in a position to affect events. In Genesis 39, we see that God is with Joseph in Potiphar's house. Joseph is doing fine, but at this rate, will spend the rest of his life making money for an Egyptian courtier. Fortunately, God has made Joseph so good-looking that he's just irresistible to Potiphar's wife. Her accusation of Joseph's attempted rape, though unjust and false, creates a new and better field in which God can act. If Potiphar's wife does not accuse Joseph, he does not wind up in prison. If he does not wind up in prison, he might never meet Pharaoh. If he does not meet Pharaoh, the brothers might have visited but would not have lived in Egypt.

Again, God pays close attention to Joseph, protecting him in prison and waiting for the right opportunity. In Genesis 40, God sends dreams to the Royal Cupbearer and Chief Baker, who just happen to be in the same prison. Joseph knows where dreams come from. Instead of being reluctant to be involved in anything related to dreams because of how his life was affected by them, the faithful Joseph knows that the dreams are a Godsend. He gives God credit for his interpretations: "Surely God can interpret! Tell me [your dreams]" (Gen. 40:8). Again, two dreams reveal each other. The Chief Baker is eventually executed, as predicted, but the Cupbearer goes back into Pharaoh's service and eventually remembers Joseph two years later.

Why does he remember Joseph two years later? God makes him remember. In Genesis 41, Pharaoh has dreams; again, there are two dreams, one to confirm the other. Joseph says, "Pharaoh's dreams are one and the same" (Gen. 41:25). Joseph not only tells Egypt what to do but also creates a position for himself:

> Accordingly, let Pharaoh find a man of discernment and wisdom, and set him over the land of Egypt. And let Pharaoh take steps to appoint overseers over the land, and organize the land of Egypt in the seven years of plenty. Let all the food of these good years that are coming be gathered, and let the grain be collected under Pharaoh's authority as food to be stored in the cities. Let that food be a reserve for the land for the seven years of famine which will come upon the land of Egypt, so that the land may not perish in the famine."
>
> Gen. 41: 33-36

God does not tell Joseph anything directly. Joseph, understanding the direction of the dreams, and feeling the greatest God-moment of his life, acts in confluence with the moment and rides the Divine light wave into his destiny. That is the Biblical hero at his best: a person who gets on the Divine wavelength and rides it for all it is worth.

There is, however, something troubling in Joseph's interpretation and plan: It does not seem to be human lives that are to be saved but the land of Egypt. One can say that Joseph knows what worries Pharaoh and what does not. We will come back to this point below.

For now, let us remember that if there is a dream that predicts a famine, both the dream and the famine itself are sent by God. Egypt, under Joseph's foresight-full direction, is ready:

> Accordingly, when the famine became severe in the land of Egypt, Joseph laid open all that was within, and rationed out grain to the Egyptians.
>
> Gen. 41:56

The famine is not restricted to Egypt; it is regional. There is also a terrible famine in Canaan, where Joseph's family still lives Gen. 41:56b-42). This famine, sent by God according to the seven-year plan in Pharaoh's dreams, is a God-move, designed to get the whole family down to Egypt. Joseph has not been writing letters home; the family does not know he is alive. Without Joseph's forgiveness of his brothers for their treachery, the family will not be reconciled. Without family reconciliation, the family may not come to Egypt, the next necessary part of God's plan.

In the next few chapters, we see how the brothers come down to get food during the famine. We also see how Joseph learns that they are sincerely repentant for what they did to him. Once he is sure that they're sorry, he reveals himself to them:

> "I am your brother Joseph, he whom you sold into Egypt. Now, do not be distressed or reproach yourselves because you sold me hither; it was to save life that God sent me ahead of you.... God has sent me ahead of you to ensure your survival on earth,

and to save your lives in an extraordinary deliverance. So, it was not you who sent me here, but God; and He has made me a father to Pharaoh, lord of all his household, and ruler over the whole land of Egypt.

Gen. 45:4-8

Joseph means every word of this. He is not just trying to calm their fears now that they see how powerful their long lost brother is. Joseph, the man who has lived by his faith through the nadirs and peaks of life, sees that everything in his life has happened for a reason. He is God's instrument. He knew it when he was a teenager in Jacob's house, and he knows it now.

I am particularly interested in the verse cited above, "God has sent me ahead of you to ensure your survival on earth, and to save your lives in an extraordinary deliverance" (Gen. 45:7). The first part of the verse is obviously about saving the family from the famine, but I wonder if the second half of the verse is not about the Exodus, that someday, as part of God's plan, God will save the Israelites in "an extraordinary deliverance." At the end of the Book of Genesis, on his deathbed, we see again that Joseph is very aware of the Promise to the Patriarchs, the promise so clearly revealed to Abraham in Genesis 15. He knows the plan and is confident that someday it will be fulfilled:

"I am about to die. God will surely take notice of you and bring you up from this land to the land to the land that He promised on oath to Abraham, to Isaac, and to Jacob." So Joseph made the sons of Israel swear, saying, "When God has taken notice of you, you shall carry up my bones from here."

Gen. 50: 24-25

We thus see a connection between the Joseph story and the Exodus. However, there may be another connection as well.

I want to return to a vexing problem, the troubling, disturbing problem of Joseph's enserfment of the Egyptians.[14] The dreams give Joseph an opportunity to save a land and its people. In fact, the whole region is saved because there is food in Egypt. At the beginning of the seven years of famine, Joseph acts benevolently and beautifully (Gen. 41:56). As the years of famine proceed, however, Joseph's actions get morally questionable. After Jacob and sons are settled in the land of Goshen, however, we get a different picture of the dispersal of rations to the hungry masses:

---

14 See Benno Jacob *Genesis* 856-858 for a thorough discussion. Also see Ephraim Avigdor Speiser *Genesis* 353; Thomas Mann *Joseph the Provider* 247ff., 536ff.; Donald B. Redford *A Study of the Biblical Story of Joseph* (Leiden, 1970).

both the land of Egypt and the land of Canaan languished because of the famine. Joseph gathered in all the money that was to be found in the land of Egypt and in the land of Canaan, as payment for the rations that were being procured, and Joseph brought the money into Pharaoh's palace.

Gen. 47:13b-14

If this is not bad enough, Joseph's actions seem to get worse and worse:

And when the money gave out in the land of Egypt and in the land of Canaan, all the Egyptians came to Joseph and said, "Give us bread, lest we die before your very eyes; for the money is gone!"

Joseph does not say, as he had said to his brothers, "It was for this purpose that I am in this position. I will carefully ration out the provisions until the seven years of famine are over." Instead, he gives them bread for their livestock (Gen. 47:16-17). After another year, once they have traded Joseph all of their livestock, the famished Egyptians offer their land and themselves. They become serfs to Pharaoh. He transplants the people of Egypt from one region of the land to another (47:21), thus breaking down any local power and allegiance and centralizing all control. Joseph thus buys up all of the land of Egypt (except that owned by priests).[15] Joseph comes up with a system by which the Egyptian serfs will keep 4/5 of what they make for their sustenance and will give 1/5 to Pharaoh (Gen. 47:23-26): Then Joseph said to the people, "Whereas I have this day acquired you and your land to Pharaoh, here is seed for you to sow the land...." (Gen. 47:23)

It is not entirely clear whether the Egyptians become Pharaoh's bondsmen/slaves or feudal tenants. Whatever the case, the Egyptians are grateful:

"You have saved our lives. We are grateful to my lord, and we will be serfs to Pharaoh."

Gen. 47:25

The question is: How long did this gratitude last? Did the Egyptians look back and say that this is when they traded away their lives? Did they blame Joseph for this terrible exchange? Is this why the Pharaoh of Exodus 1 did not know Joseph; did they all hate him? Is this why the Israelites are later enslaved, an enslavement for an enslavement? If so, the enslavement of the Israelites is, in a sense, morally

---

15 The narrative pays a lot of attention to the subject of how the Egyptians become serfs. Why should the *Torah* be interested in this topic? Perhaps it is trying to teach a lesson to the Israelites. Probably traumatized by their hunger and insecurity, the Egyptians trade their freedom for food. Freedom is a higher ideal, however, than food. Later, the Israelites in the desert will show that they did not learn this lesson. They will murmur about food and water and rebel against Moses and God.

neutralized; the Egyptians are only getting the Israelites back for what Joseph did to them.

The interpretations of Joseph's actions have been presented in both positive and negative lights. One of the most negative and offensive interpretations comes from the German Bible scholar, F. J. Delitzsch:

> Joseph undoubtedly had in view no less the good of the country than that of the king when changing the disproportionately divided landed property into uniform parcels of copyhold liable to rent. The history of Joseph is a dangerous model for crafty ministers... in Joseph's financial speculation ... one of the unamiable sides of Semitic (Jewish) hereditary peculiarity comes to light...[16]

We see that anti-Semites can have a field day with what Joseph did. It is possible to defend Joseph, to say that he was merely doing what was best for the nation-state, for Pharaoh, and that he was merely responding to the requests and petitions of the people. It is an important debate. One of the other things at stake here is our evaluation of Joseph's character. Was he, as Jewish tradition says, a *tzaddik*, a righteous man, or not? However, there is much more at stake: If this is the plan, if the plenty/famine cycle is sent by God, it would seem that the enslavement by the Hebrew Joseph of the Egyptians may just be a means to lead the Egyptians to enslave the Hebrews. It may not be Joseph's morality that is at issue, but God's.

It all fits with the Divine plan that is expressed in Genesis 15 to Abraham. This plan is the overlying Cause of Joseph's descent to Egypt, of his rise to power, of the enserfment of the Egyptians and then the enslavement of the Israelites. Like it or not, morally comfortable with it or not, the Plan is one of the causes of the events that happen. I am not saying that the characters do not have free will. They have the free will to react to their situations. They have dreams and can choose to tell them or not, to act on them or not. Still, they are reacting to the situations created by the dreams and the famines, Divine signs. The Divine reality, which will, one way or another, be fulfilled, affects human realities.

There is dual causality; there are both Divine and human reasons for events. We can see what humans do and we can examine their motives. God does not force anyone to do anything. God's influence, the Divine cause, affects human actions whether we know it or not. In studying the historicity of the Bible, we can only see the evidence of human actions. Perhaps those actions are also a reflection of God's Will.

---

16 F. J.Delitzsch *A New Commentary on Genesis II* translated from the German (Edinburgh, 1888) 352.

Concluding Religious Postscript

What if we could be more like Joseph, understanding the light waves of Divine revelation and riding them into our futures? What if we saw prayer not as an endless litany of thanking God and, instead, as a means towards connecting with the waves of God? Is not that what attracts so many to New Age vocabulary and transient rites, the feeling of invisible lines of connection? The real lines of connection are emanating from God, if only, like Joseph, we can sense them and act in consonance with them.

Chapter IV

Gold or Coal:
Reimagining the Early Life of Moses

As strange as this may seem, knowledge of the Bible can be a problem.[1] Knowledge in this case means being versed in the scholarship and traditions about, and the interpretations of the Bible. After all that learning, how can knowledgeable people in our time possibly read the Book for themselves? If you're a knowledgeable Jewish or Christian person, you have heard all of the traditions of your faith, and you read the Bible with your tradition's glasses. We know too much to read for ourselves; we have lost a direct line from the Bible to us. We're told by many of the modern literary critics that every interpretation is just one reading, and that every reading is as good as another. That is such silliness and creates so much anarchy that those of us who reject it sometimes become afraid to read for ourselves because we do not want to do a reading as inane as some of theirs. All in all, reading the Bible for what it says is more difficult than we may realize.

The case I want to explore now is one of the most familiar of all, the early life of Moses. We all know the story, which in a sense, is the whole problem. Every time we heard the story told as a child, every movie we saw, every sermon we heard; we experienced an *interpretation* of the story. It becomes difficult to separate interpretation from the story itself. Still, that is exactly what I want to try to do here, to take us back to the Text itself and to use what we know from history and archaeology to present a picture of the first part of the life of Moses from what I think is a new perspective, one very different from the way we are used to thinking about it.

I am not a fundamentalist. I am a person of faith and I want to hear God's Word that I believe is embodied in the Bible. If I am going to hear that word, I have to use my own mind. I am not calling other interpretations incorrect. All those people heard the Word with *their* minds. It is my obligation, my duty as a person of faith, to listen to God.

While I am not a fundamentalist, I want to come to an understanding that is not at odds with what the Bible actually says and hopefully is true to what it says.

Before I discuss the early life of Moses, let me first draw a quick example from the life of Abraham. Who was Abraham? Why was he called for his great destiny? The Bible does not tell us anything but that he was descended from Noah; then

---

1 A version of this paper was presented as a lecture sponsored by the North Sinai Archaeological Project at Trinity International University on November 6, 2003.

again, so was everyone else. The *Midrash*, the body of Rabbinic discourse relating to the Bible, is anxious to explain why Abraham was "the one"; the one called to receive God's great revelation of monotheism and chosen-ness. If the Bible doesn't tell us why Abraham was chosen, the *Midrash* fills the hole by telling stories of how Abram as an infant already understands that there is only one God in the universe and that as a child little Abram righteously vandalizes his idol-making father's merchandise. The king throws young Abram into a fiery furnace. The *Midrash* comes to say: "Do you want to know why Abraham was chosen? Here's why. He was called because he was a great and special individual. In his childhood, he was the first iconoclast." Later interpretation elevates Abraham's importance in his younger years, a time about which the Bible says nothing.

The fact that the Bible doesn't say anything about Abraham until he is seventy-five years old highlights what we *do* know about Moses. The case of Moses is different because we *do* have data about his early life before the events of the Exodus. Even though we do have information about Moses' early life, there is a development that is parallel to what evolved about Abraham's life: Traditions developed around his early life that dramatically elevated the status of Moses during those years.

In the *Midrash*, the Pharaoh's soothsayers predict the coming of a man who will save the Israelites and destroy the great Egyptian king. The Pharaoh has a new adopted grandson named Moses. The soothsayers fear that he may be the subject of these prophecies because when Pharaoh would kiss and hug him, Moses would take the crown and place it on his own head. The soothsayers want to kill him, but one of the advisers (by the name of Jethro) constructs a test. Baby Moses is placed at a table on which there is a live coal and a gold vessel. If Moses goes for the *gold*, it means that he knows what he is doing and is indeed reaching for the crown; Pharaoh should kill him because Moses wants the crown and is indeed the predicted savior of the Israelites. If, on the other hand, Moses reaches for the *coal*, it means that Moses is not to be feared. Moses, like any normal child, reaches for the gold, but the angel Gabriel moves the child's hand towards the coal; Moses puts the hot coal in his mouth and stutters for the rest of his life.

Think about what the *Midrash* has done. It has not only explained why Moses has a stutter (a questionable notion to begin with) but has also placed Moses in the palace at a young age under the watchful gaze of Pharaoh. God is already heavily involved in protecting the child and sends an angel to save him. That both Pharaoh and God are paying close attention to little Moses is an assumption that the Bible does not share and that elevate the early life of Moses to a status that the Bible does not give him at this point.

"However," you may say, "I thought that God was protecting Moses from birth!" Indeed, the *Midrash* says that God was watching over Moses, that a Divine light was shining from the baby. The Book of Exodus, however, says only that his mother hid him when she saw "*ki tov hu*" which literally means that he was "good," probably meaning "healthy" in this case. Again, later interpretation elevates the status of Moses.

It is a pattern that continues at every point. The *Midrash* says that when Pharaoh's daughter sees baby Moses in the bulrushes; it is not her *hand*maid (the Hebrew word is '*amatah*) that reaches to pick up the child but her unnaturally elongated arms ('*amatah* can also mean "her *hand*") that draws him from the water. The *Midrash* here makes a miracle out of the simple (while important) act of drawing the baby from the water. If the salvation of Moses from the water is a great miracle, the *Midrash* creates a miracle inside the miracle.

The ancient historian Josephus says that when Moses is brought from his Hebrew nursemaid to the palace, Pharaoh does not have a son or heir. Moses is raised to be the next Pharaoh. So it is Moses, like any good Egyptian Crown Prince, who goes off as the general in a war against the Ethiopians. You may remember the first scene of the movie *The Ten Commandments* in which Moses is parading down Main Street in triumph after a great victory against the Ethiopians. You may also know that the popular opera and now-musical *Aida* is based on the Ethiopian adventures of Moses.

There's only one little problem: The Bible has nothing like this of any kind, no Moses as Crown Prince, no Ethiopian War, no great victory. Over and over again, later interpretation elevates the status of Moses.

In mentioning a movie, I have fast-forwarded to modern popular culture in order to show that the pattern holds. The first half of *The Ten Commandments*, the more entertaining half, is about Moses, played by the great epic actor Charleston Heston, building great monuments, vying for the princess and placing himself in a position to beat out the Crown Prince by blood, Ramesses, unforgettably played by Yul Brynner. Or think about the recent animated *Prince of Egypt*, a surprisingly delightful version of the Exodus story, that makes Moses the adopted son, not grandson, of Seti I, and the best friend and not the rival of Ramesses, in order to explore the emotional theme of brothers who are very close but become enemies. In two more realistic movies, *Moses* with Burt Lancaster and *Moses* with Ben Kingsley, Moses is the adopted grandson of Ramesses, the Pharaoh of the oppression and thus the cousin of Merneptah, the Pharaoh of the exodus. Even in these films, there is a special relationship or rivalry between the Prince and Moses. I am not even going to dwell on Sigmund Freud, not exactly an intellectual slouch, who, in a wild book called *Moses and Monotheism*, said that Moses was not an adopted Hebrew foundling but a native-born, non-Israelite, full-blooded Prince of Egypt.

The pattern of elevating Moses is a fact; the question is: "Why?" Why does interpretation from the *Midrash* to the movies go so far beyond what the Book of Exodus says about the early years of Moses? Different interpreters obviously have different motives, from seeing God's involvement and miraculous intervention at every turn, a theological motive, to those who change the Text in order to appeal to the modern masses, a financial motive.

In the process, we move further away from the Text itself. We are left with an impression, that Moses was, as the movie calls him, Prince of Egypt and he threw it all away, the palace and the dancing girls and the monuments, for what? A bunch of slaves? A desert kingdom filled with scorpions? A God you can't even see? Indeed, this is our modern Moses, who could have been a contender to be king and decided to be a servant of God and the shepherd of an oppressed, ungrateful people. What I want to explore is whether this is, after all, the real Moses of the Bible. Hollywood, and drama in general, try to unify and simplify action and characters to make the story more accessible. I understand this: There's no business like show business. However, the Bible is not business; it is eternal truth.

What the Book of Exodus Says

Looking at the Bible itself, which should always remain the precious *datum*, what do we really know? An unknown Hebrew baby is born to unnamed Hebrew parents at a time when an unnamed Pharaoh has decreed that all Israelite boys should be thrown in the river. An unnamed daughter of the unnamed Pharaoh takes pity on the baby, who is floating in the river in a little ark made by his loving and hopeful mother. The baby needs to be nursed; the baby's unnamed sister says she knows of a Hebrew woman who can supply what the baby needs. The princess pays the woman to nurse the child. The woman takes the baby back to her home and nurses him.[2] Exodus 2:10 states, v*ayyigdal hayeled*, "when the boy grew up, she brought him to Pharaoh's daughter, who made him her son." At what point did his mother bring him to Pharaoh's daughter? Was the child three years old, the usual age for weaning? Was he older? The Hebrew word *gadol* means "big." *Vayyigdal* means "and (or when) he got big." Dr. Moshe Greenberg points out that if the *vayyigdal* is only referring to the point at which he was weaned, the Bible would state, as it does elsewhere, for example, Gen. 21:8 about Isaac: *vayyigdal vayyiggamal*, "he grew and was weaned." *Vayyigdal* by itself indicates, "He grew up." Look, for instance, at Gen. 25:27 about when Esau and Jacob *vayyigd'lu* "when they grew up," one to become a skillful hunter, the other to be a homebody. Or see *vayyigdal* about Samson growing up in Judges 13:24, or how the son of the Shunammite woman grew up in II Kings 4:18. *Vayyigdal* by itself means, "He grew up." In the next verse, Exodus 2:11, the Text uses the word *vayyigdal* again: "Some time after that, *vayyigdal*, when Moses had grown up, he went out to his kinsfolk ...." Notice carefully what we do *not* have here. There is nothing about Moses

---

2 If the baby is taken back to a Hebrew home, he must have been under royal protection.

discovering to his shock and dismay that he is a Hebrew. In all four of the movies I mentioned, this is *the* dramatic turning point in the plot. Charleston Heston goes into shock; the animated Moses runs out into the desert with a terrible identity crisis, Burt Lancaster and Ben Kingsley are decimated to discover their true ethnicity. However, the Bible has no such turning point, because its assumption is that Moses had "*yigdall*ed," had grown up enough by the time he came to the palace that he knew who he was to begin with. Thus he goes out to see how the people that he has always known are his kinsmen are doing, only to see that they are being treated horribly. Verse 11 states:

> When Moses had grown up, he went out to his kinsfolk and witnessed their labors. He saw an Egyptian beating a Hebrew, one of his kinsmen. He turned this way and that and, seeing no one about, he struck down the Egyptian and hid him in the sand.

Moses thinks that this may be the end of the matter. He does not tell anyone what he has done. If he were a great and mighty prince, in a society ruled by Pharaoh-as-Law, he could have simply reported that he had an altercation with an official and had accidentally killed the official. In the film *Prince of Egypt*, Prince Ramesses wonders why Moses didn't just tell him what had happened so that they could clean it up with their father, the Pharaoh Seti. Why doesn't Moses in the Bible do something of the kind? He does not seem like such a mighty prince, does he? Instead, he seems like an ordinary Israelite, scared for his life as any slave would be after killing an Egyptian official. He learns the next day that the word is out on the street about what he did. Two Israelites are fighting, and Moses asks the offender why he's hitting his kinsman. The offender retorts, "Who made you chief and ruler over us? Do you mean to kill me as you killed the Egyptian?" If Moses were a prince of Egypt, would the Hebrew have dared speak to him in this way? How could he ask a prince of Egypt, who *was* a chief and ruler over the Hebrews, who put him in that position? What happened to the conqueror of the Ethiopians, the builder of monuments, and the possible heir to the throne? Moses was never any of those things.

Thus when Pharaoh hears about this, he seeks to kill Moses. This is an extremely significant moment- Pharaoh wants to kill Moses for killing an Egyptian taskmaster.

Where's the question: "Moses, why did you do this?" Where's the trial before the sentence? Couldn't Moses have come up with a reason (like "unnecessary roughness")? What was the life of a taskmaster compared to that of a prince? Instead, Moses immediately knows he's had it and flees the country. This confirms the theory that Moses was never a prince to begin with, that this foundling meant nothing to Pharaoh. After all of the murders of all the other Hebrew baby boys, what did Pharaoh care about the life of this one Hebrew when thinking about the security of the Dynasty and the state? Kill him. Pharaoh was the Law. Perhaps

Pharaoh wanted to execute Moses because he took the killing of the official as an act of rebellion that he needed to nip in the bud. "I should have killed that Hebrew boy to begin with." What if allowing baby Moses to survive in the first place was Pharaoh's clever plan: "I can always kill him, but maybe he will be useful." Perhaps Pharaoh had always known that Moses was a Hebrew baby and allowed the adoption for his own diabolical reasons.

Now think about Moses' early life. He was at the bottom of the totem pole. He had no chance to be Pharaoh. He was extremely lucky to be alive. Perhaps he had survivor's guilt. Moses hated what had been done to his brethren while he was being raised in the palace. He certainly strongly identified with his brethren.

Think if you will, of Moses as an ambitious young man, looking at his possibilities in the world. There was only one chance- to lead his brethren. His status did not give him pharaonic credentials, but it did give him a great resume compared to all the other Israelites. I do not mean that Moses was trying to agitate a revolution when he killed the taskmaster. I think that this happened spontaneously. Moses thought that his brethren who would hear about it from the near-victim would keep it quiet, at least from the Egyptians. Still, he had a right to think that they would appreciate his courage. They did not appreciate it, just as they would never appreciate anything Moses ever did. When the two quarreling Israelites mocked him, he realized that he was neither fish nor fowl and ran away. His act showed that Moses cared about his brethren and identified with them. Pharaoh, upon hearing the story, would not miss the point, and Moses knew it. So he ran out into the desert, to seek another destiny there. Little did he know what would happen next.

So far we have the Prince Theory, that Moses was a great prince of Egypt, and a simple reading of the Bible, which I would call the Counter-Prince Theory.

Here is a chart of the differences between the prince and the counter-prince theories:

PRINCE	COUNTER-PRINCE
• Mighty prince	• If a prince at all, the lowest
• A war hero	• Not a war hero
• Possible heir	• Not a possible heir
• Close in to Pharaoh #1	• Not close in; no day in court
• 2nd Pharaoh knows him	• No sign of recognition

Why is the popular conception so different from what the text actually says? We tend to read into Moses what we want to find:

1. Jewish commentators see God's salvation of Moses as prefiguring His salvation of the entire people. They may want to make God involved in the early life of Moses to answer the theological problem of God's inattention to the plight of the Israelites in bondage. The *Midrash* cites Rabbi Aqiba's tough questions to God about those who were immured in the buildings during the oppression: "Where was God? Why did He wait?" It is true that Genesis 15 predicted a long period of enslavement until the iniquity of the Canaanites would be complete. While God's considerations seem to also include finding the right moment in terms of the Egyptian situation as well, as I will discuss below, my point now is that Jewish interpretation may have tried to find God's involvement in Moses' early life in order to say: "God *was* doing something; He was preparing Moses for the Exodus." So that is why Judaism elevated Moses' status in his early life, to show that God was working on the problem.

2. Josephus the general sees Moses as a Jewish general like himself.

3. Christians see Moses as a type for Jesus. Look at a remarkable passage in Hebrews:

> By faith Moses, when he was born, was hid for three months by his parents, because they saw that the child was beautiful; and they were not afraid of the king's edict. By faith Moses, when he was grown up, refused to be called the son of Pharaoh's daughter, choosing rather to share ill treatment with the people of God than to enjoy the fleeting pleasures of sin. He considered abuse suffered for the Christ greater wealth than the treasures of Egypt, for he looked to the reward.
>
> 11:23-26

. Poverty instead of riches. Suffering abuse for the Christ. In this way the movie *The Ten Commandments* turns Moses the general into Moses the shepherd. It makes conscious choices and omits the war with the Amalekites in Exodus 17 and the civil war in the camp in Exodus 32. The only violence will come from God, not Moses. Moses becomes Jesus, a hero of non-violence. According to Christianity, Jesus did not want a political kingdom but the kingdom of God on earth. So in the Prince Theory, Moses could have been a contender for the throne but quite consciously threw it all away to seek a spiritual destiny as an agent of God. All of this is very beautiful and meaningful but it is a superimposition on the Book of Exodus.

We have seen that the Great Prince Theory has to read itself into the Biblical text. In judging between the Great Prince Theory and the Counter-Prince Theory, what can we learn from the evidence in Egyptian history?

Egyptian Evidence

The immediate problem for the Prince Theory is the fact that we cannot find the name of Moses in any Egyptian records. Think about this moment in the movie, *The Ten Commandments*. The pharaoh says, "Let the name of Moses be stricken from every book and tablet, stricken from all pylons and obelisks, stricken from every monument of Egypt, Let the name of Moses be unheard and unspoken, erased from the memory of men for all time."

Remember that *The Ten Commandments* was made in America in a time of explicit anti-Communism. So when Seti says that the name of Moses should be erased, he becomes a Communist erasing an inconvenient past. However, there's more involved: The movie is answering the Bible-deniers who ask why we can't find Moses' name anywhere in Egyptian documents. This is a question that seems important, but actually is only an important challenge if one interprets the Bible according to the Moses-as-Prince theory.

The Counter-Prince theory has a very different answer to the question of the absence of any record of Moses in Egyptian records: His name was not there because it had *never* been there. No one had to erase a name that had never been there in the first place. Moses was not the Moses of Josephus or the movies. So, you may ask, if we will not find Moses as Great Prince, how do we place Moses in the context of Egyptian history?

For those of us who respect the Bible, there is a difficult chronological marker. In I Kings 6:1, we learn that the Exodus occurred 480 years before the fourth year of King Solomon, which counting back from the mid-900s, puts the Exodus back into the 1400s. Indeed, there are many who try to place the events of the Book of Exodus in that earlier century. Scholars such as Bimson make a case for this earlier time. Recent popular culture, in novels like *Stone Tables* by Orson Scott Card and *The Midwife's Song* by Brenda Ray, follow this scheme. Many scholars find another way to understand the figure of 480 years between Moses and Solomon: If 40 years is a round number for 25, then 12 generations takes us from Solomon in the 900s back to Moses in the 1200s.

This takes us to the century that seems to fit with the time of the Exodus.[1] Why does the consensus of scholarship place the events of the oppression and the Exodus in that century? There are five important elements that scholarship believes point in this direction.

According to the Bible, Ramesses II enslaved the Israelites and built the cities of Pithom and Ramesses. Ramesses II would have named a new city after himself; that is what all good and modest pharaohs did. So Ramesses II, who lived in the 1200s, would be the pharaoh of the oppression.

---

1 It is a neat solution to the problem of the 480 years, and it may be right, but those of us who trust the Bible must be intellectually honest and admit that we're playing with the Book. Still, as a religious Jewish person, I must tell you that a verse in the second section of the Bible, in I Kings, is not of the same holiness as the evidence from the Book of Exodus, a book of the *Torah*, not only the first section of the Bible but the qualitatively more sacred section.

Archaeological evidence shows that Ramesses II used *'apiru,* who have some relationship to the Hebrews, as slaves for quarrying and building, exactly what we would expect from the Biblical portrayal of the way the Israelites were oppressed.

The Bible tells us that the Israelites lived in Goshen, and refers to this area as "the land of Ramesses" in Gen. 47:11. Ramesses II's capital was in the eastern delta, not far from Goshen. This fits the Biblical picture of the Israelites living close to the pharaoh.

Archaeology indicates that the Transjordanian nations of Edom, Moab and Ammon did not exist as such before 1300 BCE. Since the Israelites under Moses needed to deal with these nations on their way to the Promised Land, the nations had to be there. So a date for Moses before 1300 BCE does not fit.

The Merneptah stela, named for Ramesses II's son and successor Merneptah, has Merneptah, around the year 1207 BCE, attacking a number of nations and tribes in the land of Canaan including a reference to a people, but not a settled nation, called Israel. This would mean that the Israelites were in Canaan by that date, as we say in the trade, that date would be the *terminus ad quem* for the return of the Israelites from Egypt to Canaan.

These are the main reasons that the oppression and the exodus are put in the 1200s BCE. If we base ourselves on this assumption, then who was the pharaoh of the oppression and who of the Exodus? First, we have to establish that there were two different pharaohs for these two events. In trying to place Moses in Egyptian history, we need to know the names of the Pharaoh of the oppression and the Pharaoh of the exodus. Let us go over what we know about these pharaohs from the Bible.

The Pharaoh of the Oppression:
- was the builder of Pithom and Ramesses,
- enslaved the Israelites,
- committed infanticide.

The Pharaoh of the Exodus
- endured plagues,
- lost his first born son,
- let the people go
- chased them when they had left.

The text tells us that the Pharaoh whose daughter adopted Moses was dead before Moses returned from Midian to Egypt. A long time after that, the king of Egypt died. The Israelites were groaning under the bondage and cried out; and their cry for help from the bondage rose up to God.

The Israelites might have been expecting things to go better for them with a new ruler and are cruelly disappointed when things stay the same. Since it was established custom in Egypt for a new pharaoh to celebrate his accession to the kingship by granting amnesty to criminals, liberating slaves and releasing prisoners, the Israelites have reasonable hopes that a new king would mean a change for the better in their condition.[1] When things continue to be bad, and with the prospect of ongoing suffering, the Israelites cry out in desperation. God heard their moaning, and God remembered His covenant with Abraham and Isaac and Jacob. God looked upon the Israelites, and God took notice of them.

It is immediately after this, in the next two verses, that God appears to Moses in the "Burning Bush." God hears the cries of the Israelites and decides that it is time to send a prophet to help let them go.

While the fact of a new pharaoh does not seem to mark a change for the Israelites, it is specifically important for the call of Moses. The timing is interesting here. God commands Elijah to assassinate kings but waits for a generation until Elijah's disciple Elisha finally fulfills these actions after the death of the powerful King Ahab. Here, too, God seems to wait for the death of Ramesses II. While at the Burning Bush, Moses is told to "Let My people go," even a "Burning Bush" is not enough; Moses does not actually go to Egypt until God tells him that the pharaoh of the oppression is finally dead:

> The LORD said to Moses in Midian, "Go back to Egypt, for all the men who sought to kill you are dead." So Moses took his wife and sons, mounted them on an ass, and went back to the land of Egypt....
>
> Exodus 4:19-20

Timing is everything and the time is now right for the exodus. The point here is that the pharaoh of the oppression and the pharaoh of the exodus are two different people. If this weren't the case, our task in naming the single pharaoh involved in the 1200s BCE would be simple: it would be Ramesses II, the pharaoh from 1279-1212. BCE [2] Our task is more complicated because we need to separate the pharaoh of the oppression from the pharaoh of the exodus.

You may ask, since the Bible doesn't care about the names of the Pharaohs involved, why should I care? First, I want to connect Biblical facts with Egyptian historical facts. More specifically, I want to understand where an adopted Hebrew grandson of a pharaoh might fit into the political and succession picture. Josephus, an advocate of the Great Prince theory, says that Pharaoh didn't have an heir. *Could Moses have been an heir to the throne? Could he have been a great prince of Egypt?*

---

1 *Etz Hayyim* 326.
2 The relevant pharaohs and their reigns were:
   Ramesses I (1293-91 BCE)
   Seti I (1291-1278 BCE)
   Ramesses II (1279-1212 BCE)
   Merneptah 1212-1202 BCE (Ramesses II's 13th son)

We need to know the name of the pharaoh of the oppression in order to know where Moses might have fit in or not fit in. As the movies tell us, there are two choices, Seti I or Ramesses II. Seti I, as in the Ten Commandments or Prince of Egypt, had two daughters and a few sons.[3] If Moses were adopted by one of those daughters, that would seem to make him significant. While chronologically, I understand that the Seti I theory is a possibility, we can't forget that Moses would be the adopted *grandson*, not the adopted son, of Seti I.

We need to understand something very important about the Ramessides: This family prized its own blood. The idea of a dynasty may be what attracted Horemheb to make Ramesses I his successor in the first place. Horemheb, pharaoh from 1321-1293 BCE, made his vizier, close friend and confidant Ramesses his heir when Ramesses was probably already in his fifties. The idea was that while Ramesses himself would not last long (he only reigned for a couple of years before he died), he had a suitable heir, Seti, who in turn had a suitable heir, the boy who would become Ramesses II. Ramesses II was born in 1304 BCE, so Horemheb could see the Ramessside line in development. Ramesses II took his two principal wives, Nefertari and Istnofret, at least ten years before Seti's death. Thus Seti I would have seen at least five grandsons and two granddaughters just from those two daughters-in-law. Seti may have seen another 10 to 15 grandchildren from Ramesses' other ladies. Ramesses II was named co-ruler with his father Seti I early in his life. He accompanied his father on numerous campaigns in Libya and Nubia. At the age of 22, Ramesses went on a campaign in Nubia with two of *his* own sons. The succession was out there, in public, on the battlefield.[4]

Ramesses II made reproduction into a kind of art form; he literally wanted to become the father of his country. He wanted to spread his divine genetics and insure his bloodline. Remember that in the ancient world, populations were small. Infant mortality rates were high. Human fertility in general was of obvious importance; the Pharaoh was consumed with producing an heir before he moved on to his eternal life. I have seen statistics indicating that one third of all children did not survive past the age of fifteen. Even though pharaohs often had numerous wives, producing the right Crown Prince was not an easy task. The ladies of Ramesses' harem who were expected to produce potential heirs were often close family members, including daughters and full sisters. Ramesses II was proud of his prodigious feats of reproduction. He lived so long that it was a good thing that he produced so many heirs; twelve of his oldest sons would die before he did.

There are different estimates of how many children Ramesses II had. One guess is that he fathered one hundred children by his principal wives and consorts, and

---

3 The oldest seems to have died young, but this is irrelevant because it was the firstborn son of the pharaoh of the exodus, not the pharaoh of the oppression, who matters in the Biblical narrative.
4 When Seti I died, Ramesses assumed the throne and began a series of wars against the Syrians.

from fifty-to-a-hundred more by his other ladies. Another has seventy-nine sons and fifty-nine daughters. From Egyptian records,[5] we know the names of 29 of Ramesses II's sons and a number of his daughters. It is important to note that it is the names of almost all of the thirty sons of the principal queens that are known. They had the title, "King's Son of His Body," a title not conferred on the sons of lesser consorts. Many of the sons became priests and/or held high positions, influencing the administration and religion of the country for many years.

If Moses were born in the reign of Seti I, Seti hardly would have seen him as a potential heir. He was not a rival to Ramesses II, who was clearly "the man" in all sorts of ways. If, as I think, Ramesses II was the pharaoh of the oppression (the time of Moses' birth and adoption by a daughter of pharaoh), we should remember that he had between one and two hundred children including fifty to a hundred sons and obviously many more grandchildren than that. Moses would have had a lower status than *all* of those potential heirs. Adoption in ancient Egypt could be important when it was necessary[6]; in this case, nothing could have been more *unnecessary*. While incest was generally frowned upon in ancient Egypt, it was accepted in the royal family, where incest was used to safeguard the dynastic succession. The Ramessides weren't interested in an adopted Hebrew boy and they certainly didn't need an heir. If Moses were the adopted son of a *daughter* of Pharaoh, he would not have been

---

5 The names of Ramesses' children are attested to in many of his edifices around Egypt, not so much to boast of his incredible fertility but to pray to the gods for the sake of his children. We find their names at the Temple at Abu Simbel, the Temple of Derr, Luxor Temple (where a number of scenes are found including one with 25 sons represented), the Ramesseum (23 sons depicted), Wadi es-Sebua (scenes with from 25 to 30 sons and 8 daughters), and Abydos in the Temple of Seti I (scenes with 27 to 29 sons and from 16 to 22 daughters).
6 Just for the sake of discussion, it is interesting to note that an adopted son could be important in Ramesside Egypt. The dynasty began with Ramesses I Menpehtyra, a military officer from the eastern Delta who rose to the rank of Vizier under Horemheb and was adopted by that pharaoh. His adoption is recorded in the form of an inscription added to the granite interior coffin that seems to have been made for him while he was still Vizier. Everything we know about adoption in ancient Egypt attests to this possibility. In Ramesside Egypt, as always, children were considered a blessing to their parents, to care for them as they grew older; adults longed to have children to ensure their later care. If a couple was childless, adoption was an important option. Adoption was done legally, with formal papers drawn up in front of witnesses, all parties properly named, but it was also possibly done informally, as indicated by a letter from Deir-el-Medina that states: "He who has no children should get for himself some orphan to bring him up. Then he will be the person who pours water upon his hands, as a genuine eldest son." Rather than divorcing a sterile wife, a more publicly accepted way of solving the problem of sterility was adoption, and due to the short life expectancy and high birth rate, there was always a supply of orphaned children.

considered worthy of mention and obviously would have ranked far below any of these sons because he was not a "King's Son of His Body." Since Ramesses II's prodigious reproductive feats were partly the result of a political program to spread his seed and establish the dynasty forever with his blood, an adopted or foster son would not have fit this bill.

I do not reject the possibility that Seti I was the Pharaoh of the oppression and Ramesses II was the pharaoh of the exodus. In fact, there is the intriguing information that the first-born of Ramesses II died early. Remember that the pharaoh of the oppression lost his first-born son during the tenth plague, the plague that broke the back of Egypt and forced pharaoh to let the people go. Kitchen writes that Ramesses II was never the same again after the death of his first-born son, Amun-her-khepseshef, his first born son by Nefertari, born before Ramesses II's ascent to the throne, who was crown prince until his death between the age of 40 and 52. He was probably buried in the Tomb of Ramesses II's sons in the Valley of the Kings.

Again, if the pharaoh of the oppression is the pharaoh of the exodus, Ramesses II is that pharaoh. If there are two distinct pharaohs, then in seeking the pharaoh of the oppression, we should look to the long and powerful reign of Ramesses II. It would have been Ramesses II, secure in himself and in his power, who built the cities of Ramesses, naming it for himself, and Pithom. It would have been Ramesses who had the power and the resources to do anything he wanted. This would mean, however, that Moses was the adopted son of the *daughter* of Ramesses II, not Seti I. In this scenario, as in the Moses movies with Burt Lancaster and Ben Kingsley, Merneptah is the pharaoh of the exodus.

So what is the problem? Biblical chronology, as in the case of the 480 years, makes things complicated. If Moses were 80 at the time of the Exodus (as it says in Exodus 7:7), and if we use the Merneptah inscription to show that the Exodus could not be later than 1207 BCE, Moses would have been born in 1287 BCE at the latest and probably somewhat earlier. So it would seem that Moses was born during the reign of Seti I. This does not help much, because the Bible tells us that Moses lives 120 years. If he was not there at the Crossing of the Jordan, and the Israelites crossed the Jordan around by 1207 BCE, in the fifth year of Merneptah, then that would mean Moses was born before the Ramesside dynasty began. Again, we need to regard Biblical chronology, in this case the forty-year segments of the life of Moses, as symbolic and schematized. We need to put Moses' life within the century of the 1200s BCE.

Moses' Egyptian Mother

Let us try this from a different approach. Is there anything we can glean from the Biblical fact that the daughter of the pharaoh of the oppression was Moses' adopted mother? If the pharaoh of the oppression was Seti I, Tia might be the daughter who adopted the foundling. There may be a connection between Tia and Bithiah the daughter of Pharaoh mentioned in the Bible in I Chron. 4:17. Bithiah would be Bat (Melech) Tia, "the daughter (of the king), Tia. Jewish tradition identified Bithiah as the daughter of Pharaoh who adopted Moses (*Yalkut Shimeoni*, section 1074). Bithiah was the wife of a Hebrew man, Mered. Mered, in this view, is Caleb, a Kenizzite who joined the Israelites and became a Judahite. Caleb lived in the time of Moses and was one of the two scouts, with Joshua, who was allowed to enter the Promised Land. While I do not agree with Jewish tradition because the Bible mentions Caleb and Mered as different people, Caleb and Mered may, judging from the context in I Chron. 4, have been contemporaries. It is fun to think of Caleb marrying Moses' Egyptian mother, but Jewish tradition, by being so playful, is prejudicing us against a better possibility, that a different Egyptian princess, somehow related or connected to the characters in the Exodus story, left Egypt with the Israelites as the wife of an Israelite or left with the Israelites and later married Mered. I can't imagine any other circumstances in later Egyptian or biblical history that would allow a pharaoh's daughter to marry an ordinary Israelite named Mered. Again, I Chron. 4 tells us that Bithiah married an Israelite man named Mered. Mered is a son of Ezrah. We do not know who Ezrah was, but he seems to be from an ancient, scattered element within the tribe of Judah, or from an element that joined the tribe at a very early point, perhaps during the journey from Egypt to Israel.

The reference to Bithiah may refer to someone who lived too late to be Seti I's daughter Tia, but the reference still reflects a historical reality. We may focus on a document from year 53 of the reign (1226 BCE) where we find another Tia or Tuya, a daughter of Ramesses II and the Princess-Queen Nebttawy.[7] What if this Tia is the Biblical Bithiah? It is more than interesting that the daughter of Bithiah was named Miriam, the same name as Moses' older sister. Is it possible that the name Miriam is passed down in what may be one family?[8] If you say that I Chron. 4 must be wrong

---

7 Kitchen tells us, "Nebttawy is not often found upon the public monuments of the reign." *RITA* II, 630.
8 The name Bithiah is intriguing in another way. What if she was none other than BintAnath, the daughter and then wife of Ramesses II? BintAnath, who by assimilation is sometimes BitAnath, means the daughter of Anath, a Canaanite/Syrian goddess, a strange name for an Egyptian princess in the first place. What if her name has been changed to fit her new theology now that she's left Egypt and joined the Israelites? What if Moses was named _____ moses, like Ramesses, and that name has been changed as well? It wouldn't do to have the monotheist Moses with a name that included a pagan god, would it? We know that BintAnath had a daughter but we do not hear of her having any sons. What if adopting a boy was a perfect solution for this daughter of Pharaoh? Bent'anta (Bintanath, Bint-Anath, Bintanat) is buried in Tomb 71 in the Valley of the Queens. Queen Bent'anta may have become one of Ramesses II's consorts, perhaps after the deaths of the king's

when it says that a daughter of Pharaoh married Mered, because no daughter of a pharaoh ever married outside the family and certainly never married a foreigner, you are choosing an Egyptian tradition over a Biblical fact. If I were a cynic who was skeptical about many Biblical traditions, I would still accept the evidence of I Chron. 4:17 as historical. This is not a literary text. This is not poetry. No big point is made. It is not trumpeted as a sign of God's work. It is just a casual reference embedded in a set of genealogical lists. This same Mered married a daughter of Pharaoh and also married a Hebrew woman. No more is made of one marriage than the other; both the daughter of Pharaoh and the Hebrew women are happily Mered women. Bithiah who married Mered is not Tia, daughter of Seti I, and is not Moses' Egyptian mother. The dates do not seem to fit unless our chronological scheme is wrong, which, we should not forget, *is* possible. However, the text can be investigated and worked with in another way. Look at the daughter of Pharaoh as a minor daughter of Pharaoh who went along for the ride during the exodus, or who had fallen love with Mered, or whatever you might like to conjecture. I can speculate all I want, as long as by my speculation I do not detract from the Biblical fact that there was a daughter of Pharaoh who married an Israelite named Mered. Just as the *Midrash* plays with the Biblical fact and we need not assume that Bithiah is Moses' Egyptian mother, so we can play with the Biblical fact without assuming our speculations are correct.

What, you might ask, about the rule that an Egyptian princess couldn't marry outside the family? It is true that while outside the royal family there were no constraints on marriage (we know of Egyptian born women marrying both foreigners and slaves) there was a tradition of hypergamy within the royal family, which means that a prince or even a king may marry a commoner but the daughter of a king could not marry beneath herself. She could therefore not marry a non-royal because such a marriage was deemed degrading to the princess. Also, there was a more political consideration that marrying an Egyptian princess to the wrong person could lead to problems with the succession. In the absence of an obvious heir, an ambitious son-in-law might be tempted to claim the throne on behalf of his wife and children. The field of potential bridegrooms was therefore extremely limited for the Egyptian princess. Denied an Egyptian-commoner husband, Egypt's princesses were also forbidden to travel abroad and marry foreign kings who might with some justification claim to be equal status to pharaoh. The state propaganda that decreed all foreigners to be inferior effectively made such inter-state marriages inconceivable. The ban on non-Egyptian marriages was a long established prohibition, made explicit by Amenhotep III, who wrote to his brother-in-law, the King of Babylon (who had sent the Pharaoh a sister for his harem) to explain that

---

principal wives and specifically, the death of her mother who was probably Istnofret. We are uncertain of a statue of her, that might instead be of Nefertari, located at the feet of the colossal granite statue of Ramesses II in the first courtyard of the temple at Karnak.

'from time immemorial no daughter of a king of Egypt has been given in marriage to anyone'. This left the Egyptian princesses in a difficult position, their only possible bridegrooms being their fathers, their brothers, or their half brothers."[9] This is a strong tradition, but we're talking about real life, and real life is messy; real life breaks the rules. So perhaps there were some daughters of Pharaoh, some princesses, who were so low on the totem pole, who flew below the Pharaoh radar and were simply not important enough to care about one way or the other way. Maybe this Bithiah was a very minor figure, or the daughter of Ramesses II by a concubine, or whatever, or even an adopted Hebrew who left with her own people, a kind of female Moses in a certain way. The reference in I Chron. 4 is intriguing and may be a separate witness to the interrelationship of Egyptian and Biblical history. Perhaps I Chron. 4:17 can be seen as a quiet confirmation of the Counter-Prince Theory, for it says that there were minor daughters or sons or grandsons or adopted grandchildren who, in a sense, didn't count. Bithiah, whoever she was, knew that she didn't count and went off and became a Mered woman in Israel. Just as Bithiah, daughter of Pharaoh could marry Mered, so Moses could be hunted for killing an official because he really didn't matter. This was a world where you counted or didn't count depending on your birth. This would change until great people could rise from the masses, from humble births, and change the world. Moses was one such person.

Now for my weird theory. A daughter of pharaoh could only marry her father. A pharaoh's daughter at this time could not marry a foreign king. Imagine yourself a daughter of Ramesses II. You are what we call in Judaism an anchored woman. How do you become a mother? Your biological clock is ticking. Your maternal instincts are raging. Pregnancy was very important to ancient Egyptian women. A fertile woman was a successful woman. By becoming pregnant, women gained the respect of society, approval from their husbands, and the admiration of their less-fortunate sisters and infertile friends. However, you are a daughter of Ramesses II and you do not have a baby. You are bathing at the river and you find a healthy, good-looking baby boy. Here's your chance to be a mother. I am probably reading this in, but the princess' immediate acceptance of the plan to nurse the child sounds to me like a woman who wants to adopt but does not know what to do. If not, why not bring the baby to the palace and have her nursed there?

I tentatively conclude that Ramesses II is the pharaoh of the oppression, that one of his daughters adopted Moses, but that Moses was not even in the royal pecking order. Hence, no mention of him in the Egyptian texts and monuments; it is not that his name was erased as in the movie; he was nothing to begin with. As a young man

---

9 Joyce Tyldesley *Daughters of Isis: Women of Ancient Egypt* (London, 1994) 117-8.

without prospects in the Egyptian hierarchy, Moses went looking for his brethren. He found them, and the world has never been the same since.

I have tried to show that Jewish tradition, Christian tradition, Josephus and modern movies have all elevated the status of Moses in his early years in order to pursue their own agendas. However, I want to return to what the Bible itself says. We have to leap back over what all of these later works have done and let the Bible speak to us. I am convinced that I am listening to the Bible.

Frankly, I'd rather have Charleston Heston. I love the idea that Moses was a great Prince who left the palace and wealth and power to join with a motley group of slaves. I grew up with the Great Prince theory thinking that it was a fact. I have to back away from my own agenda and listen to the Eternal Text. I have taken the opposite position and tried to *lower* Moses' early status in our eyes. I am convinced that Moses was a "nobody" who became a "somebody" by being true not only to his identity and his people but to God's truth that none of us should be enslaved.

What is my biggest problem? It is trying to figure out a chronology that includes the Biblical data. I have not succeeded in doing this. However, I thank God for this. Because I am so convinced in my Counter-Prince Theory that I would think that I had all of this tied up in a neat package. The fact that I can't figure it out is oddly reassuring because I think that this is the way God wants it. He doesn't want us to figure everything out. What would faith be if we weren't challenged? The past would be a simple set of facts.

Instead, we're led into the mysteries of faith. We're challenged intellectually and spiritually. God gives us enough to be faithful, but not much more. God is wise, wise beyond our wisdom. We know what we want to know. He knows what we need. He knows what it means to have faith; it is something we need to remember in a world that substitutes cynicism and nihilism for the Word of God.

In the *Midrash*, Moses is offered gold or coal. The gold, for me, is the gold of interpretation, spectacular notions like the Great Prince Theory; it is what we want to reach for. It is what we want to hear. If we take the coal, on the other hand, it will make us stammer and stutter; we will be tentative in our judgments, careful in our approach. However, the words of our mouths will be the words of God and only the Words of God. You have before you the gold and the coal; choose the coal.

Chapter V

The Case for the Historicity of
The Israelite Exodus from Egypt

The historicity of the Exodus as it is described in the Bible is questioned on all fronts. Those who want to deny the early origins of the Israelites emphasize this kind of questioning. There are Jewish people, including some religious leaders, who, in their so-called sophisticated and liberal way, have added fuel to the fire. As I said in the Introduction, they want to observe Passover and say that they do not care whether the events that Passover commemorates happened or not.

The idea of this chapter is to evaluate just how strong the case against the historicity of the Exodus is. To sharpen the focus, I will use Donald B. Redford's "The Egyptological Perspective on the Exodus Narrative," [1] not only because he is a dean of Egyptian archaeology but also because he presents the strongest case I know of for a late date for the writing of the Exodus narrative. If the narrative were written centuries after the events happened, it may be inaccurate, exaggerated or just plain false. Redford says that there are clues that point to the lateness of this work.

The key word here is anachronism. To use an example from American history, if a writer reported a conversation between George and Martha Washington and George looked across the Potomac River and said, "There's a lot of traffic in D.C. today," that would be an anachronism. If the Biblical narrative describes the Israelites working at cities that did not exist during the New Kingdom period in Egyptian history, this would be anachronistic and would render the entire passage suspect. Just for the record, I want to make it clear that if a writer reported the conversation I just mentioned, I would not then assume that George and Martha were not historical figures. Still, I would have some questions about the writer's accuracy and historical knowledge.

Is the Biblical narrative about the Exodus anachronistic? I want to turn the tables on those who say it is. Instead of defending the Biblical text against the charges of anachronism, I want to review the critics' methods and findings to see if

---

1 Donald B. Redford "The Egyptological Perspective on the Exodus Narrative" in Anson F. Rainey *Egypt, Israel, Canaan: Archaeological and Historical Relationships in the Biblical Period* (Tel Aviv, 1987) 137-62.

they make their case. If the Bible is presumed factual until proven false, then let us see if critics such as Redford have amassed sufficient evidence to prove that the Biblical account of the Exodus must have been written at a relatively late date and thus may be legendary and not historical in character.

The Geography of the Exodus

Is the Biblical geography related to the Exodus anachronistic? The first thing that strikes Redford about the Biblical traditions of the Exodus is how little there is about the Egypt of the period (1200s BCE). Where, Redford wants to know, are the conquering Pharaohs, their armies and governors? There is no mention, he says, of "cities established in Pharaoh's name." One immediately wants to respond that the Bible is about God's relationship with Israel and that the might of a Pharaoh is only a foil at best for the might of God. In addition, what is the store-city of Ramesses if not a city established in a pharaoh's name? Redford admits, in an endnote, that "the plagues are in keeping with phenomena which *can* be witnessed in the Nile Valley,"[2] but he would rather send us to a Sumerian parallel about a plague of blood[3] than present this is as important evidence.

Evidence can be managed. Every attorney presents his/her evidence in a particular order, emphasizing some points, glossing over or ignoring others. I am sure that I am doing some managing of evidence here, even when I do not know that I am doing so. At least I am trying, however, to present the other side's case. At best, there are no sides; there is only the pursuit of the truth.

The battlefield on which Redford wants to fight concerns the toponyms (place-names) referred to in the Biblical account. Is it possible that these names are authentic reflections of the early period (2nd millennium BCE)? Redford's conclusion is that this is not possible. He chooses to dispense with source criticism that would posit both early and late traditions about the Exodus and its route. Instead, Redford systematically discusses the following toponyms: Ramesses, Goshen, Succoth, Pithom, Etham, Migdol and Ba`al Zephon. I will go through these names in the order they are presented in the Bible.

Pithom

So they set taskmasters over them to oppress them with forced labor; and they built garrison cities for Pharaoh: Pithom and Ramesses. (Exodus 1:11)

---

2 He mentions G. Hart "The Plagues of Egypt I" *ZAW* 69 (1957) 84ff. and "The Plagues of Egypt II" *ZAW* 70 (1958) 48ff. He means Greta Hort. The mistake is compounded in his Bibliography that is, as a result, out of alphabetical order. Everybody makes mistakes.
3 Kramer "Blood-Plague Motif in Sumerian Mythology" *Archiv Orientale* 17 399ff.

Pithom and Ramesses are mentioned as the two storage cities that the Egyptians forced the Hebrews to build. Since Pithom and Ramesses were cities found not out in the desert but in Egypt proper, it would seem that it would be easier to identify their locations. If we could identify them, we would then have the starting-places of the Israelites before they left Egypt. In Biblical archaeology, however, nothing comes easily. In trying to determine the location of this city, archaeologists and scholars have struggled to make a definitive case.

Pithom, in Egyptian, *pr-Itm*, means "House (*pr* = house as in the name Pharaoh, which means "Great House") of (the god) Atum." This name follows a name pattern that is often found in the New Kingdom, the period of the Exodus. Since *Per-Atum* is Pithom, and it is in the area that the Egyptians called Tjeku, Pithom is at the eastern end of the Wadi Tumilat. There are two sites, Tell el-Maskhuta and Tell er-Retabeh, which are near the eastern end of the Wadi Tumilat and are the two major candidates to be Pithom.[4]

---

4 Naville excavated Tell el-Maskhuta, fifteen kilometers west of modern Ismailiya and the Suez Canal, in 1883 (Edouard Naville *The Store-City of Pithom and the Route of the Exodus 3* (London, Egypt Exploration Society, 1883). Naville's evidence that this site was Pithom was that: 1. The Egyptian place-name Per-Temu is found at the site. 2. Along with a fortress, there were a number of rectangular brick chambers of different sizes, which Naville claimed were for storage. These buildings reflected the nature of the city's purpose as stated in Exodus 1:11. 3. He found bricks that were made without straw, just as in the Biblical story in Exodus 5. 4. A Latin inscription found there mentions Ero, the Greek equivalent of Atum. Ero =Atum and Per-Atum is Pithom.

At first glance, this evidence would seem to be convincing. As a lesson in why we cannot rush to identify a site with a Biblical place, we will evaluate each of these claims.

Claim #1: The Egyptian place-name Per-Temu and so the site should be identified with the similar name Pithom. Naville said that Per-Temu was the religious name for the city and Succoth (which relates to the Arabic name Maskhuta) was the civil name. (If this is true, it is ironic that Tell-el Maskhuta, which means "mound of idols/images", would reflect a civil and not a religious name.)

A Response: (Donald B. Redford "Exodus 1,11 *VT* 13 (1963) 401-18; idem "Perspective on the Exodus" in *Egypt, Israel, Sinai* 140-42; "Pithom" *Ld'ef* IV: 1054-58) Per means "house" and atum is the name of Atum, god of the sun. If we look at the reference to it in the *Papyrus Anastasi* VI passage, we realize that this text is actually rather complicated. It does not simply refer to the "house of Atum" but to the "pools of the House of Atum" and the place is qualified as being "of Merneptah-Content-with-Truth." The "House of Atum" referred to here may have been found elsewhere, not in the vicinity of these pools. Also, the Atum mentioned in this papyrus resided in a temple of Merneptah, probably at Pi-Ramesses. Succoth is a Hebraization of the Egyptian term Tjkw, the Wadi Tumilat as it was first designated in the New Kingdom. In the 19th Dynasty (the period of the Exodus), a large fortress at Tell er-Retabeh controlled the area and it is this fortress that is referred to in *Papyrus Anastasi* VI. By the 7th century, settlement was either in decline or abandoned altogether.

An important point about Tell el-Maskhuta is that aside from some early and brief occupation during the Middle Bronze Age, the site was only occupied in the 26th Dynasty, the 500s BCE. So it could not have been the Pithom of the time of the Exodus.

There are scholars and archaeologists who want to disprove the Bible. Sometimes they make identifications that are intended to make the Bible look like it is fabricated on falsehoods. So an interesting sidelight in the study of the identification of Pithom is that there are those who want Tell el-Maskhuta to be Pithom so that they can say that Pithom was not occupied in the right time period and is a later fabrication.[5] However, Tell el-Maskhuta is not Pithom so their attempt to diminish the Bible fails.

Tell er-Retabeh was occupied in the Ramesside period,[6] was contemporary with Ramesses/Piramesse (which I shall discuss immediately below) and is situated at the eastern edge of the lake in a dominant position overlooking the *wadi*.

So what is the problem? The Bible tells us the name of an Egyptian city. The name is a good Egyptian name that follows a pattern known from that period in Egyptian history.

Redford has a problem because of his insistence that while there are several places from the New Kingdom period that bear the name Pithom, only one of them

---

Claim #2: There was a building for storage; Naville found the evidence of a storage building along with a fortress; the storage building would reflect the nature of the city's purpose according to Exodus 1:11.

A Response: That there was a building for storage does not prove anything; many sites would need storage. Granary complexes are well documented in New Kingdom Egypt (Eliezer D. Oren "The Ways of Horus in North Sinai" in Rainey *Egypt, Israel, Sinai* 80). To make this evidence weaker, the so-called storage chambers may actually have been the foundation walls of a late period fortress.

Claim #3: Bricks made without straw were found on the site, relating to the Biblical story that the Hebrews were forced to make bricks without straw in Exodus 5: 6-10. By itself, this is not a convincing piece of evidence.

Claim#4: A Latin inscription found there mentions Ero, the Greek equivalent of Atum. Ero =Atum and thus Per-Atum is Pithom. A Response: The Latin inscription actually says something important (Alan H. Gardiner "The Delta Residence of the Ramessides" *JEA* 5 (1918) 267-69). It identifies Ero as being nine miles away from the site. Since Ero is nine miles away from the site, a site that is found at that distance, Tell er-Retabeh, may the site of Pithom.

5 Cf. John Van Seters *Hyksos and Israelite Cities* 28-34.

6 While Redford states that there was no Ramesside occupation at Tell el-Maskhuta, there was. Petrie discovered monumental temple-façade blocks of Ramesses II and an *in situ* foundation-deposit of Ramesses III. W. M. F. Petrie *Hyksos and Israelite Cities* (London, 1906) 30 pls. 32A, 34, 35C).

could have been the store-city that the Hebrews built. Redford says that the phrase found in the famous *Papyrus Anastasi* VI (4.16) is "the pools of pr-Itm which is (are) in Tjkw." Since it says that the "pools" are located in the Wadi Tumilat, but not necessarily "the House of Atum" itself, this is not, Redford says, a reference to Pithom at the time being discussed.

Now let us take another look at the very text Redford uses:

> "We have finished letting the tribes of the Edomite Shasu pass the Fortress (htm) of Mer-ne-Ptah Hotep-hir-Maat, which is in Tjeku, to reach the lakes/pools[7] of Pithom (Pr-Itm) which is/are (in) Tjeku for the sustenance of their flocks."[8]

This is a remarkable text for background about the Israelite sojourn in Egypt and the Exodus. It describes shepherds from the east coming into Egypt to a place where the Bible tells us the Hebrews worked and lived. It would be a fort in the Wadi Tumilat[9] (Tjeku).

The Shasu Bedouin may be the context for Proto-Israelites. We have a list of Shasu Bedouin toponyms that include a toponym with the name *T's'sw Yhw*, which may be the earliest written record (the reign of Amenhotep III date B) about a shrine to the LORD.[10] If the Bible is true, we would expect Bedouins such as Edomites or Hebrews to live at the eastern border of the Delta, the part of Egypt they would have come to when they arrived in Egypt from the desert.[11] This text fits.

As Bietak puts it, "So we have a Pithom in the right place at the right time in a parallel situation, blocking one of the two important entrances of the Eastern Delta."[12]

The historicity of the name Pithom has been established.

Ramesses

Let us move on to the other city, Ramesses. According to Exodus 1, the Israelite slaves were involved in the building of this great city and it was from this great city

---

7 Bietak states that the word translated by Redford as "pools" can be "lakes." We know from studies of ancient topography that there were lakes in the area.

8 *Papyrus Anastasi* VI 4.16. See *ANET* 259; Alan H. Gardiner *Late-Egyptian Miscellanies* (Brussels, 1937) 76-77; Caminos *Late-Egyptian Miscellanies* (London, 1954) 293-95)

9 Tumilat preserves the ancient name "Atum."

10 Raphael Giveon *Les Bedouins de Shosu de documents Egyptiens* (Leiden, 1971)

11 Herodotus, who visited Egypt in about 440 BCE, mentions Pathomus, a city of Arabians that lay at the Red Sea channel that passed through the Wadi Tumilat (Herodotus *The Histories* II:158).

12 Manfred Bietak "Comments on the "Exodus" in Rainey *Egypt, Israel, Sinai* 169.

that the Israelites set out on their escape from Egyptian bondage. Ramesses also is mentioned in Exodus 12:37 as the starting point[13] of the route of the Exodus.[14]

The city of Pi-Ramesses was, in its time, one of the grand cities of the world. Piramesse was founded by Seti I (1294-1279 BCE) and transformed into a new royal residence and governmental seat by his son and successor Ramesses II, the Pharaoh of the Exodus. Biblical Ramesses = Egyptian Piramesse. The site of this city is now[15] generally placed at Tell el-Dab'a at Qantir where excavators found the foundations of a royal palace and hieratic ostraca with the name Pi-Ramesses.[16] A mud-brick palace was also found, as were military barracks and workshops dating to the Ramesside period. While later archaeological work at a site often disproves earlier conclusions, in this case further excavation confirmed the earlier identification.[17]

Redford claims that all place names using the personal name Ramesses are compounded with either the prefixial element "house of ..." or "the town of..." Redford finds the name Ramesses in compounds in cultic and topographic use in the 1st millennium BCE, that is, hundreds of years later than the period of the Exodus. This makes him think that the use of the term Ramesses in the Bible is anachronistic. Redford says that the term Ramesses without a prefix, as it is found in the Bible, could not have been used at an early date and thus the narrative must be late.

---

13 Kitchen points out that just as Pithom is not mentioned as a stage on the route of the Exodus, Tell er-Retabeh is too far to the southwest to be on the route from Pi-Ramesses to Tjeku/Succoth. See Kenneth A. Kitchen "Egyptians and Hebrews, from Ra'amses to Jericho" in *The Origin of Early Israel - Current Debate* ed. Shmuel Ahituv and Eliezer D. Oren (London, 1998) 78.

14 The city diminished in importance by the end of the New Kingdom (c.1069 BCE) and much of its stonework was transferred to temples in Tanis and Bubastis. See E. Uphill *The Temples of Per Ramesses* (Warminster, 1984); Manfred Bietak Avaris and Pi-Ramesses 2nd ed. (Oxford, 1986). Since there was evidence of Pi-Ramesses at the latter sites, there was ample reason for confusion; many thought that Ramesses was to be equated with one of them. If the people living in Tanis thought that their city was the ancient Ramesses, it would be natural for post-exilic Jews to think the same thing. Thus Psalm 78 places Ramesses at Tanis and the Sea of Reeds "in the fields of Tanis."

15 After earlier theories that it was at Tell Farama and then that it was at Tanis. See Alan Gardiner "The Delta Residence of the Ramessides" *JEA* 5 (1918) 127-71; idem "Tanis and Pi-Ra'messe: A Retraction" *JEA* 19 (1933) 122-28.

16 Mahmud Hamza "Excavations of the Department of Antiquities at Qantir (Faqûs District) (season, May 21st - July 7th, 1928)" *ASAE* 30 (1930) 31-68.

17 William Hayes *Glazed Tile from a Palace of Ramesses II at Kantir* (New York: Metropolitan Museum of Art, 1937).

Let us examine what another prominent Egyptologist without a Biblical or religious axe to grind has to say about Ramesses.[18] Manfred Bietak shows that there is indeed evidence that the preceding Pi- of Pi Ramesses can be omitted when a phrase meaning "the town" is placed after it. In relating the name in Hebrew, especially (I would add) in a sentence describing the two places of Pithom and Ramesses as "store-*cities*," the name could simply be rendered "Ramesses." There are scholars who point out that the royal name Ramesses is only used in toponyms in New Kingdom times and then passes out of fashion. This means that the use of Ramesses in Exodus 1:11 is not an anachronism. If anything, this would show that the text is early. [19]

Manfred Bietak has been excavating Tell el-Dab'a/Avaris for decades; this Hyksos capital is near Qantir/Pi Ramesses. Bietak reviews how Qantir/Pi Ramesses, the capital of the Ramesside Pharaohs, lost its function and was abandoned. Its ruins were used as a quarry for the building needs of new towns in the 21st and 22nd dynasties, including the temples of the residences of the Bubastite kings in Tanis in the north and Bubastis in the south. All sorts of statues and monuments were transferred from the old city to the new ones.[20] In this later century, the people believed, not without reason, that Tanis was Pi Ramesses. Thus when the poet of the late, post-Exilic psalm (Ps. 78) states that the Israelites served "in the fields of Tanis," he follows what the Egyptians of his time thought.[21]

---

18 Manfred Bietak "Comments on the Exodus," the essay following Redford's in *Egypt, Israel, Canaan* 163-72.

19 Redford raises a problem with the identification of the Biblical Ramesses with Pi-Ramesses. Any toponyms that use the personal name Ramesses are compounded with a prefix such as pi "house of". So the famous Delta residence of the Ramessides is "the House of Ramesses Great-of-Victories." Earlier scholars such as Albright and Alt argue that this identification must be correct because the use of the royal name is only found in the New Kingdom and not afterwards. Redford, however, shows that these names are indeed used in later centuries. Moreover, he cannot understand why the Bible uses the name without the prefix, why the Bible refers to the city as Ramesses and not Pi-Ramesses. Bietak, following Gardiner and Helck, does not see the missing prefix as a problem. The preceding Pi- can be left out when there is an indication after the name that it is a town (p' dmj). So "Ramesses the town" might have become simply "Ramesses" in Biblical Hebrew, especially since there might be the association with the name of the pharaoh (Ramesses II) and the dynasty (the Ramessides) of that time (Alan H. Gardiner "The Delta Residence of the Ramessides" *JEA* 5 (1918) 137; W. Helck "Ikw und die Ramses-stadt" *VT* 15 (1965) 35-48).

20 Much later, in the 30th Dynasty (4th century BCE) there were secondary cults for the gods of Ramesses in Tanis and Bubastis.

21 In a similar manner, Josephus bases himself on a tradition from Manetho and thinks that Pi Ramesses is connected to Pelusium. The *Targumim* (the Aramaic translations) also think that Pelusium is Ramesses; they posit Tanis not as Ramesses but Pithom.

The people of the later centuries might have been confused by the fact that statues and monuments were moved from the original Ramesses, but we do not need to be. Certainly, Bietak is not confused by these later mistakes: Pi Ramesses is Ramesses and it is the archaeological site of Qantir. Redford is wrong; the city was given another name in the very time he claims it was named Ramesses.

Tell er-Retabeh, the site that seems to be Pithom, was occupied during the Ramesside period at the same time as Piramesse-Ramesses and stood at the eastern end of a lake in a position overlooking the Wadi.

Redford loses this skirmish on the toponymic battle map. He has not proven that the name Ramesses must have been written by a late Biblical writer. On the contrary, that the writer does *not* make the mistake of the psalmist of Psalm 78 reflects antiquity, not anachronism. Based on the Egyptological evidence, Redford has not demonstrated that an early writer could not have used the term Ramesses.

Listen again to Bietak's conclusion:

> So we have a Pithom in the right place at the right time in a parallel situation to the Ramesses-town, each blocking one of the two important entrances of the Eastern Delta. From this topographical and partly functional similarity we may understand the parallel quotation of Pithom and Ramesses in Exodus 1:11.

Remember that Bietak is an Egyptologist who does not have a Biblical axe to grind. He is simply making a statement that is common sense.

While Redford concludes that the Biblical traditions give us "palpably anachronistic geography," we have a Pithom and a Ramesses at the right place and the right time. We have evidence that supports the Biblical narrative's account of the Exodus.

Goshen

The Israelites lived in a part of Egypt called Goshen (Gen. 45:10 etc.). In Gen. 47:11, Goshen is called the land of Ramesses, the Egyptian name for a large part of the eastern delta after Ramesses II (c.1279-1212) built his capital there and gave it his name. Redford says that Goshen is a Semitic and not an Egyptian name. The Qedarite Arabs expanded into the eastern Delta by the Persian conquest. The term Goshen is an anachronism and could only be used by a later writer.

Hoffmeier's response is useful: The fact that later writers such as Jeremiah do not use the term Goshen implies that the name was *not* used in that later period.

We do not have any early uses of the name Goshen. This does not mean that the word is from a late writer or even a late glossator. Still, advantage Redford: If all of the toponyms he discusses only had late contexts like this one, he would have a much more impressive case.

Succoth

Succoth is the first Israelite stop on the way out of Egypt:

> The Israelites journeyed from Ra`amses to Succoth, about six hundred thousand men
> on foot, aside from children...
>
> Exodus 12:37-39

Succoth is a Hebraization of Tjeku, which is a name for a region, at the eastern end of the Wadi Tumilat, in the New Kingdom period. Tjeku was also the name of the capital of the eighth nome of Lower Egypt in the eastern part of the Delta.

In discussing Pithom and Ramesses, I cited the passage from *Papyrus Anastasi VI*, 54-61 describing the passage of nomadic Bedouin tribes looking for better pasturage with their herds:

> "We have finished letting the Bedouin tribes of Edom pass the Fortress (htm) of
> Mer-ne-Ptah Hotep-hir-Maat, which is in Tjeku, to reach the pools of Pithom (Pr-
> Itm) which is/are (in) Tjeku."[22]

Since the herdsmen are moving from east to west, the fort in Tjeku is east of the pools of Pithom.

Tjeku may be Tell el-Maskhuta. Naville discovered fragments from this site that mention Tjeku, sometimes with the determinative for "city." Some mention the priests of Atum of Tjeku and his temple.[23] In the 19th Dynasty the primary fort in the region was at the site we call Tell er-Retabeh. By the 600s BCE, a settlement named "Pithom of Tjeku" was built 13 kilometers to the east of Tell er-Retabeh; this is Tell el-Maskhuta.

The problem for Redford is that while Tell el-Maskhuta has Middle Bronze Age material, there is a gap in occupation until the 26th Dynasty. This would make the use of Succoth an anachronism.

To respond: Tjeku was a region, and Succoth in the Biblical references in Exodus 12:37 and Num. 33:5-6 could simply indicate the region that the Israelites passed through on their way out of Egypt, which would make perfect geographical sense. The Israelites would have wanted to avoid, not confront, the main fortress in the area.

The working hypothesis is that Tell el-Maskhuta is Succoth.

---

22 *ANET* 259; Alan H. Gardiner *Late-Egyptian Miscellanies* 76-77; Caminos *Late-Egyptian Miscellanies* 293-95.
23 Naville *The Store-City of Pithom* 16 pl. 5; 17 with pl. 7A. A statue speaks to "every priest who shall enter the temple of Atum residing in Tjeku."

Etham

After leaving Succoth, the Israelites proceeded to Etham[24] "on the edge of the wilderness" according to both Exodus 13:20 and Numbers 33:6-7. Numbers 33:8 states that the Israelites traveled in the desert of Etham for three days. While one can say that all of these toponyms are based on the knowledge of late Biblical redactors, I insist that the Biblical data must be respected as genuine and that there was a place called Etham on the edge of the wilderness. If Etham was at the southern end of the body of water, the Israelites could wander, somewhat aimlessly, in this area which was indeed wilderness, for three days, perhaps waiting further instruction from God (thinking theologically) or figuring out their next move (thinking historically).

Thus I am left to focus not on the name Etham but on the repeated reference to where it was located, "on the edge of the wilderness," that is, not near the Ways of Horus and its forts and canals.

Migdol

Redford states that Migdol is indeed a "common element in the toponymy of the eastern Delta in New Kingdom times" and can be used as the first element in a compound such as "the Migdol of ____(a royal name)." Migdol in the Exodus narrative, however, is not an element but stands by itself. It is therefore a reference to a city that only existed later. Redford thinks that the archaeological site Tell el-Herr is that city. Since Tell el-Herr was not occupied before Saïte times, we see anachronism at work. If one were to mention the use of a name Migdol in the Amarna Letters (14th cent. BCE, a century before the theorized date of the Exodus), Redford would claim that Migdol there only means "a tower."

This is all astonishing and tendentious scholarship. First, we know that the famous Seti I inscription about the Ways of Horus (the route from Egypt to Canaan) refers to Migdol as the third fort on the route. The Amarna letter Redford refers to, and cites in the original in a footnote, clearly designates Migdol, *without another element,* as a city in Egypt. Also, Tell el-Herr was not Migdol and there is no evidence to say that it was.

For all of the Migdols in different places and different times, there was a Migdol, in the northwestern Sinai, in the New Kingdom era, the period of the Exodus. There was also at least one Migdol, in the same area but not necessarily on the same site, in the sixth-fourth centuries BCE. Biblical references to Migdol, both early and late, should not be questioned and Biblical data on this subject should be respected and used.

---

24 Caminos *Late-Egyptian Miscellanies* (London, 1954) 298; E. Naville *The Store-City of Pithom* 28.

The North Sinai Archaeological Project, presently working at a site called Tell el-Borg, may have found Migdol, or the fort next to it on the route, The Dwelling of the Lion. The team has discovered and gathered abundant inscriptional, monumental and ceramic evidence to prove its New Kingdom date and is located exactly where it should be in relation to the first fort on the Ways of Horus (Tjaru=Tell Hebua I). Whether Tell el-Borg will prove to be the Migdol of the Exodus and the Ways of Horus remains to be seen, but it will probably make Tell el-Herr irrelevant. Thus there was a Migdol in the period of the Exodus; the term used by the Bible is not an anachronism but evidence of historical authenticity and veracity.

Let me review what we have so far:

• Both Egyptian texts and the Bible tell us that there was a place called Migdol in the eastern Delta/northwest Sinai.

• The Egyptian reliefs place it as one of the western forts on the Ways of Horus.

• We have used geology to prove that Tell el-Borg was on the Ways of Horus.

• We know what and where the first fort was: Tjaru, now called Tell Hebua; Tell Hebua is five kilometers west of our site.

• Our site was definitely inhabited at the time of the Exodus: We have New Kingdom pottery.

• Our site was a fort with walls that were built and re-fortified. The walls present a few stages of re-fortification, with one toward the end of the 18th Dynasty and one or two phases reaching back into the 1300s. *TBO* X 27, an inscription from the Weapon-bearer Kha of the Company of Amun, is a nameplate for a military company.[25] This company was part of the army division of Amun, probably based at or near Tell el-Borg. A company was made up of 200/250 men. The nameplate may have been set near the gate or door of the barracks-compound. The point here is that there was a garrison at a fort. This would fit the idea of a series of forts on the Ways of Horus in the New Kingdom period. It would also fit what I would like to call "the concept of Migdol" in its two or three manifestations, a garrison fort standing as a guardian-post at the entrance to Egypt.

• This fort, like other Egyptian forts, had a temple. Our site has a temple with granite blocks brought all the way from Aswan in the south. You should not take this granite for granted. The granite blocks were brought hundreds of miles from Aswan, in vivid illustration of the prophetic verses and the Migdol letter from Elephantine. When I sit near the granite blocks, I think about the verse in Ezekiel where he says "from Migdol to Aswan." If they were shipped hundreds of miles, it was for a very important reason such as the construction or rebuilding of an important temple in a significant fort.[26]

---

25 Schulman *Military Rank, Title & Orgnization*, Eg. NK (1964) 26-30.
26 *TBO* I 2A seems to be evidence of a small shrine in a border-fort in the time of Thutmose III, a king who reigned some two hundred years before Ramesses II. Since Thutmose III

Kenneth Kitchen, the foremost Ramesside scholar in the world, in one of the most interesting intellectual exercises I've ever seen, has reconstructed the temple at Tell el-Borg. Kitchen takes the bits and pieces of blocks and inscriptions and performs the archaeological equivalent of building a model of a dinosaur from a few bones. I do not know what is more exciting about it: the staggering knowledge of parallels or the ability to re-create the very size of the original blocks. Kitchen predicted that we would find a temple of eighty-by-thirty or thirty-five feet and that it would have plinths for idols. We have found what we think is that temple, very close to the huge granite block. So far, it is a little smaller than the reconstruction, but we may have found three plinths for the idols.[27] We have found a statue of a Pharaoh, and inscriptions from Ramesses II and other Pharaohs going back at least two centuries. In comparing the reconstructed triumph scene at Tell el-Borg with the scenes from Tel er-Retabeh, the one at our site is twice as big.[28] In short, this was a sizable temple. Only a few Egyptian temples are known from the Sinai in the New Kingdom period.[29] Since it was at least unusual to have a big temple in the Sinai, then our site becomes even more noteworthy and all the more likely to be known to the people of the Biblical period.

Tell el-Borg may indeed be the Biblical Migdol. Kitchen's says that Tell el-Borg may be a long-lost and forgotten temple and military settlement in the last Delta, possibly one hitherto wholly unsuspected. Whether it is a place of known name awaiting identification through more fragments bearing a name, or whether it is a settlement new to us, not previously reported in existing ancient sources, this is

waged many campaigns in Syria and Canaan, a fort like Tell el-Borg would have been an important post for staging a campaign. This shrine might have been rebuilt during the Amarna Period. Akhenaten (1353-1333 BCE) curbed the powerful cult of Amun and promoted the worship of the Aten solar disc; Aten was to supersede all other deities. The temples of other gods were closed and the scars of their desecration remained visible even after they were re-established. After "the heresy" ended, thousands of images and names of Amun and other gods had to be re-cut into the very temple walls from which they had been erased. The Ramesside period that followed was characterized by great growth and building. Ramesses II (1290-1224 BCE) built more temples than any other Pharaoh.

27 Ramesses II would have used any available stonework in building his temple. An additional note is that we have found animals buried in a pit right next to what may be the temple.

28 Petrie *Hyksos and Israelite Cities* (1906) pls. 29/30, 31 left.

29 "Egyptian Temples in Canaan and Sinai" in S. Israelit Groll (ed.) *Studies in Egyptology Presented to Miriam Lichtheim* (Jerusalem, 1990).

something we cannot know without future finds (if the right kind care to emerge!). However, finds so far are certainly evocative in their implications."[30]

I do not quarrel with this balanced view. I would say, however, that there is nothing wrong with speculation about site identification as long as we bear in mind that it is speculation to inspire us to continue working on developing our theories.

We are assembling facts. None of the facts here assembled contradict each other. Nothing here contradicts the Biblical facts. We have not proved that our site is Migdol. We have not found anything yet that says Migdol, and we want this very much, and we keep hoping, because that would lock up the identification.

We cannot prove, at least as of now, that Tell el-Borg is Migdol. However, there is no reason to say that it is *not* Migdol, which allows us to continue using this identification as a working hypothesis.[31]

Another point: How many Tell el-Borgs are out there, apparently trivial sites that do not seem worthy of excavation? How many promising sites have been bulldozed into rubble? Yet there are so many people in the scholarly and archaeological world who think that we have all of the evidence we need to make huge blanket statements about historical truth. Tell el-Borg, among other things, is a caution light: Do not think you know what is out there; do not jump to major radical conclusions while we are just assembling the facts.

Ba`al-Zephon

Ba`al-Zephon, "Ba`al of the North", is a Late Bronze Age name of a god that was worshipped in the Delta in Egypt in Ramesside times.[32] While Redford would seem to have trouble with this toponym that clearly reflects one of the names of Ba`al in the Late Bronze Age, he says that the name Ba`al-Zephon in the Exodus narrative relates to a cult that did not exist until later times. In later times, Ba`al-Zephon was transferred into Zeus Casius. There is a site on the Mediterranean Sea, Ras Qasrun, which may be Zeus Casios. Despite the fact that some scholars do not think that Ba`al-Zephon is Zeus Casios, Redford says it is. Another candidate to be Ba`al-Zephon, Tell el-Defenneh, went by the name Daphnae/Tahpanhes in later times. However, a Demotic text gives us both the names Ba`al-Zephon and Tahpanhes as apparently separate cities, so they cannot be the same place.

---

30 Kenneth A. Kitchen "Tell el-Borg: Preliminary Epigraphic Report 2: Further Ramesside Blocks" (August 2000) 8.

31 Other candidates to be Migdol such as Tell el-Herr, Tell Kedua and Tell Abu Sefeh cannot be part of this discussion unless we want to speculate about the Migdol of the prophets and classical times. What is important to remember about these sites is that there is not a shred of evidence that indicates anything about Migdol, even the Migdol of the later period. These identifications are made on the basis of circumstantial geographical evidence.

32 There was a cult of Ba`al-Zephon at Memphis in New Kingdom times; cf. Hoffmeier *Israel in Egypt* 190.

I would respond as follows: The connection Ba'al-Zephon=Daphnae is just a scholarly reconstruction. The absence of early evidence there does not render the name Ba'al-Zephon inauthentic as an early name. Just for the record, the site under discussion really never has been excavated and could very well have New Kingdom strata. Redford wants Ba'al-Zephon to be a site that only existed in later times so that he can say that the Biblical reference is anachronistic. Not so fast: Ba'al-Zephon is an authentic early name of a place that has not been found. There is no evidence here that the Exodus narrative must be late and legendary.

Ba'al-Zephon may be an important indication that we cannot separate the theological purpose of the event from the geography involved. Ba'al was the storm-god, an obviously appropriate patron god of ships and seafaring men.[33] There may have been a temple to Ba'al- Zephon on the Mediterranean in Syria and one on the coast of the Mediterranean in Egypt. These two temples would have been designed for the protection of their sailor-believers who were constantly crossing the sea between Egypt and the coast of what is now Syria/Lebanon/Israel.[34] In northern Egypt, three sanctuaries to Ba'al-Zephon are known; at Mt. Casius (at Ras Qasrun), Memphis, and Tahpanhes (Tel Defenneh). Manfred Bietak has discussed the possibility that one of the temples at Tel el-Dab'a, 2 km. south of Qantir, was devoted to Ba'al-Zephon. The fascinating cylinder seal found there has Ba'al-Zephon, the "protector of sailors," with each foot standing on a mountain. If the two mountains were on either side of the Mediterranean, we would have a witness to the theory that temples were built on both sides of the sea.[35]

One of the key texts about Ba'al-Zephon that speaks about "the Bark of Ba'al-Zephon" is the *Papyrus Sallier* No. IV.[36] The next deity in the list is Sopdu, god of the Asiatic marshes of Egypt. I am fascinated that this key text about Ba'al-Zephon has been dated to the period c.1270-1250 BCE, the exact period of the Exodus.[37]

---

33 Otto Eissfeldt Ba'al zaphon, Zeus Kasios und der Durchzug der Israeliten durchs Meer *Beitrage zur Religiongeschichte des Altertums*, Heft 1 (Halle: Niemeyer, 1932).
34 We know that sanctuaries were located in dangerous spots along the coast, say, at the tip of a cape where shipwrecks occurred frequently. An endangered sailor could invoke the divinity that would, it was thought, come to his rescue.
35 Manfred Bietak *Avaris and Pi-Ramesses: Archaeological Exploration in the Eastern Nile Delta* (London, 1981) 253; idem "Canaanites in the Eastern Delta" in Rainey *Egypt, Israel, Sinai* 43; E.Porada "The Cylinder Seal from Tell el-Dab'a" *AJA* 88 (1984) 485-88.
36 Gardiner *Late-Egyptian Miscellanies* 89.6-7.
37 A *migdol* that may be "of Ba'al-Zephon" is referred to in the *Cairo Papyrus* 31169. This may be near the Wadi Tumilat; see G. I. Davies *The Way of the Wilderness* (Cambridge 1979) 81.

Other Egyptological Evidence Supposedly Contrary to the Bible

Redford leaves geography/toponymy to look within Egyptology for other evidence that that could be brought to bear on evaluating the historicity of the Biblical account. He finds that there were indeed large numbers of Asiatics in New Kingdom Egypt, including many who were slaves and many who were Canaanites. He notes the fact that there were brickyards that were important at that time and place. What Redford does not understand is why, if the Bible is accurate, there is no evidence of the Hebrews living apart from others.

This is, I may say, a strange statement: The Bible tells us that Israelites and Egyptians lived side-by-side. As is commonly known, the Israelites "borrowed" from their Egyptian neighbors before they left; it is because they lived next to Egyptians that the Israelites had to put blood on their doorposts to avoid the Tenth Plague. Redford takes it as a negative against Biblical accuracy because he thinks that the Bible has Israelites and Egyptians living apart. Redford goes this far:

> One cannot deny the *possibility* that behind an historical allusion in New Kingdom texts...there lurk the ancestral Hebrews, but in sum it seems to me only plausible when the allusion is to a group already located in Canaan.

He is saying that the evidence is that the Hebrews may have lived in Egypt in New Kingdom times but that he will only take them seriously when they are no longer in Egypt.

Redford thinks that the Hyksos descent into, and conquest of Egypt is the background for the Biblical narrative. He says that there is evidence for the name Jacob in the Hyksos inscriptions. I will make a table of the Biblical account and what Redford says really happened:

THE BIBLE	THE HYKSOS
• Voluntary descent into Egypt by pastoralists, among them one Jacob.	• The Hyksos descended into Egypt, including one named Jacob.
• They prospered, multiplied, and became influential.	• They occupied Egypt.
• They were eventually hated by the native Egyptians. They left Egypt.	• The native Egyptians rose up and defeated them.
	• They had to leave and go home.

What the Bible does, Redford says, is to transmute the historical truth into a story that appeals to Israelite pride. "Ignominious expulsion" is transmuted into "salvation of innocents from tyranny." The Bible is the heir to the Hyksos version of the events.

What I think has happened here is that Egyptologists cannot help but see things through the Egyptian view of the period. The Hyksos are the bad guys, the foreign oppressors. It sounds eerily familiar, like modern anti-Israel, anti-Semitic rhetoric. Somehow, the Israelites are always the bad guys. It is uncanny.

The historical Minimalists won't even let Israelites be slaves just as the anti-Semitic revisionists won't let the Jews of modern times even be the victims of mass murder. It has been said that Jewish people invent their victimization to hide their own tyranny and oppression.

If anything, an ancient people would love to tell you if it had conquered mighty Egypt, even for a while. No ancient people would make up its enslavement,[1] any more than modern Jews would make up concentration camps. Such are the dangers of choosing negative scholarly theories about the Bible over the Bible. We follow this path at great risk.

Redford has not made his case. In fact, an examination of the evidence we have may reaffirm our confidence in the Biblical data. At the very least, a study of the evidence may serve as a caution light about jumping to conclusions before detailed study.

If history is actually what happened in the past and memory is that which seeks to infuse what is preserved with meaning, then many seem content to base their faith and observance on the memories recorded in classical Jewish texts. This is fine for some people as they seek to create their postmodern personal syntheses. For many of us, however, God is still He Who acts in history; we will not stop working to prove what is for some only a memory of fictitious events. Do not worry: After all of the Minimalists have had their day and their say, the Bible that they threw out with the bathwater will prove to be, by any definition, the truth.

Excursus: Pharaoh's Firstborn Son

In the ancient world, the first-born son will inherit from his father. The first-born[2] is both symbol and reality: the pride, the future and the might of the country. Pharaoh's first-born is the heir-apparent to the throne of Egypt. Before God sends Moses to Egypt, He tells him that the final blow to Pharaoh will be the destruction of the first-born of Egypt. Israel, God says, is God's first-born son; in retaliation for the untold suffering that God's first-born so has endured at the hands of the Egyptians, the first-born of Egypt will die. The tenth plague, the destruction of the

---

1 A formulation of this thought can be found in N. Sarna "Israel in Egypt: The Egyptian Sojourn and the Exodus" in H. Shanks ed. *Ancient Israel* (Washington, 2000) 38.
2 Kenneth A. Kitchen *Pharaoh Triumphant: The Life and Times of Ramesses II* (Cairo, 1990) esp. 39, 40, 67, 71 and 102.

first-born of Egypt including Pharaoh's first-born son, is, according to the Bible, what finally forces the Egyptian king to let the Israelites go from their slavery.

So let us ask an historical question as an experiment in discussing the veracity of the Bible: What do we know from extra-Biblical evidence about Pharaoh's first-born son? Do we know anything about his death that would contradict the Biblical account? Since scholarship thinks that Ramesses II is the pharaoh of the Exodus, do we know that Ramesses II's first-born son died in battle? Of old age?

Let us see what we know. Ramesses' principal wife was Nefertari. Nefertari's first son was Amen-hir-wonmef ("Amun is at his right hand").

Ramesses II lived by tradition. He was part and parcel of the new dynasty that began with his grandfather Ramesses I and became strong under his father Seti I (who reigned 1294-1279 BCE). Ramesses II was nine when his father Seti I succeeded his grandfather Ramesses I as pharaoh. Ramesses II was named for his grandfather. He always knew that the hopes of the new dynasty were focused on him. When he was ten years old, he was named "King's Eldest Son," which is especially interesting because his older brother, his only brother, was already dead. As a teenager, he was a participant in his father Seti I's Libyan campaigns (as portrayed in the Karnak reliefs) and Syrian campaigns against the Hittites. We see Ramesses II overseeing the cutting of obelisks from the granite quarries at Aswan. He was involved in Seti I's great building projects. He even built his own small temple to Osiris at Abydos. In the great dedication stele in Seti I's temple at Abydos, the longest inscription of his son Ramesses II's reign (running 116 lines), we read the following:

> The All-Lord [Seti] himself made me great, while I was a child, until I reigned.... I was installed as eldest son, as hereditary prince upon the throne of Geb [the earth god] ... [He, Seti, said] "Crown him as king, that I may see his beauty while I live with him"...

The event of becoming "eldest son" was one that stayed with Ramesses II for his entire life. Ramesses II was eternally grateful for his status and training as eldest son and raised his own eldest son, Amen-hir-wonmef, in the same manner.

In 1281 BCE, Ramesses II's first-born son was five years old. Even at this young age, he accompanied his father, Prince Ramesses, into a minor war to quell an uprising in Lower Nubia. With his father Ramesses leading the charge, Amen-hir-wonmef charged in a chariot (under the care of an adult charioteer) into battle. This is immortalized in the Beit el Wail temple.[3] When Seti I died in 1279 BCE; Ramesses II was twenty-five. He would reign for sixty-seven years until 1216 BCE. When Ramesses II became pharaoh, he gave Amen-hir-wonmef a new name, Amen-

---

3 H. Ricke, G. R. Hughes, and E. F. Wente *The Beit el-Wali Temple of Ramesses II* (Chicago, 1967).

hir-khopsef ("Amun is with his strong arm"). He gave his son the title and rank that he had had until he had become king. He became "General-in-Chief."

In the summer of 1272 BCE, Ramesses II embarked on a war of conquest to quell trouble in Canaan and the Transjordan. His crown prince led one column. He moved in a counter-clockwise fashion, striking through the hills of the Negev, across the rift valley south of the Dead Sea, up into Seir-Edom, conquering everything in his path. Prince Amen-hir-khopsef moved north across the Wadi Zered into Moab and along the King's Highway to conquer Butartu. Ramesses II moved in a clockwise route and met his son in Moab.

My thought is that to the world of the Israelites, the presence of Pharaoh's eldest son may have been well known. The crown prince leading an invasion force in that part of the world would have been big news. That the pharaoh's son is a successful military leader could not have been good news to Egypt's enemies. Their future looked bleak because Egypt's future looked so mighty. In 1275 BCE, after the famous battle at Kadesh, Ramesses II would not sign a treaty with the Hittites. He would only sign a temporary truce because he was so confident that he could eventually defeat anyone and everyone.

Something happened in the next years in the reign of Ramesses II. In 1259 BCE, he does sign such a treaty with the Hittite emperor Hattusilis III. According to the Hittite version found on clay tablets from Hattusas, the Hittite capital, it was Ramesses II who sued for peace.

There are many possible reasons that Ramesses II changed from a king who would only sign a temporary truce to a king that would sign a peace treaty with his enemies. Perhaps he had come to terms with the political realities and the limitations of his might.

Perhaps, to suggest a theory, Ramesses II had had the emotional stuffing kicked out of him by the loss of his heir apparent, Amen-hir-khopsef. We know that by that same year, 1259 BCE (year 20 of the reign), his son was dead.

What is so interesting about this is that Kitchen puts the Exodus sometime after year 15 of Ramesses' reign, around 1264 BCE.

Egyptians never spoke of a defeat. Here is Kitchen:

> For imperial Egypt the exodus was a fleeting, if unpleasant incident; for the Hebrews, it was epochal, and for the spiritual history of the world, of incommensurable effect.[4]

---

4 Kitchen *Pharaoh Triumphant* 71.

Chapter VI

If I Told You What Really Happened, You'd Never Believe Me: The Search for the Site of the Miracle of the Sea

"So what did they teach you at Hebrew School today?" her father asked.

"It was terrific, Dad," she said, "It was about how the Israelites got away from the Egyptians."

"Terrific," he said, "Go over it with me."

"The Israelite slaves got out of Egypt where they'd been for hundreds of years. However, as soon as the Egyptians let the people go, they changed their minds and chased the Israelites.

"Then what happened?"

"It was incredible," she said, "but I've got to do some homework."

"Just finish the story. What happened when the Egyptians caught up to the Israelites?"

"Ok, Dad. This rocket ship appeared out of outer space and little green men used lasers to build a huge suspension bridge over the sea. The Israelites were very happy and walked right over the bridge. When they got to the other side, the Egyptians started coming across the bridge. Once they were all on the bridge, the little green men blew up the bridge. And the Israelites lived happily ever after."

"That's what they taught you today at Hebrew School?" the father asked, incredulously.

"No, but if I told you what really happened, you'd never believe me."

It is true that the miracle of the sea has been questioned because it is a supernatural event. As we have seen in the last chapter, it is not just the miracle that has been doubted. Every aspect of the story, including the Israelite sojourn in Egypt, the enslavement, and the Exodus is questioned.

We know that there are those who would deny the enslavement in Egypt and the historicity of the Exodus, not to mention the miracle at the Sea. There are those who would say that the whole thing is a metaphor. There are those who see it as a kind of historicization of the myth of the combat with the sea-god.[1]

---

1 Norman Snaith "Yam Suf: The Sea of Reeds: The Red Sea" *VT* 15(1965) 395-98; Frank Moore Cross *Canaanite Myth and Hebrew Epic* (Cambridge, Mass.: Harvard University Press, 1973) 112-44; Frank E. Eakin Jr. "The Reed Sea and Ba`alism" *JBL* 86

There is no more crucial site than that of the crossing of the Sea; hence, the preponderance of theories. There are those, like Beke and some modern adventurers involved in a best-selling pot-boiler called *The Gold of Exodus,* who say that the Israelites crossed the Gulf of Aqaba, one arm of the Red Sea, into Arabia and went to a Mt. Sinai in that area.

There are those who would say that the Israelites crossed the Gulf of Suez, the other arm of the Red Sea, or a connected lake or tributary, and went into the Sinai Peninsula and a Mt. Sinai in the southern part of that region.

There are those, like Colonel Jarvis, Otto Eissfeldt, William Foxwell Albright and Eliezer Oren, who prefer a northern route, speaking of Lake Bardawil, the Gulf of Serbonis, as the site of the great miracle.

Before the North Sinai Archaeological Project was created, I was in the northern camp. I was long past the problem of the Red/Reed Sea. Since Numbers 33 distinguishes between the sea of the miracle and the Red Sea, the other sea in the area must be the Mediterranean. Indeed, to call the Mediterranean "the Sea" makes perfect sense; it was *the* Sea in the Biblical world. Notice carefully that the sea through which the Israelites pass is a different sea from the Sea of Reeds and is separated by at least a number of days and several stages of the Israelites' journey. The Red Sea is too far away from the places in Egypt from which the Israelites escaped to be the scene of the event. The sea of the event is the Reed Sea and is one of the lakes or bodies of water east of the Nile delta or may even be a body of water that no longer exists. Some translations, including *NJV,* have followed this logic and have replaced "Red Sea" with "Sea of Reeds."

The name of the sea in question, *yam suf,* does not literally mean "Red Sea" but "Sea of Reeds" or "reedy sea." *Yam Suf* does mean "Red Sea" in other Biblical texts; this had led to great confusion. Biblical parallelism demands that the poet use a poetic variant with the word "sea."

> Pharaoh's chariots and his army He has cast into the sea;
> And the pick of his officers are drowned in the *yam suf.*
>   Exodus 15:4

"Pharaoh's chariots and his army" has its parallel in "the pick of his officers." "Cast" has its parallel in "are drowned." "Sea" finds its parallel in "reedy sea." When, later, the Red Sea and its arms became known as the *yam suf,* the traditions grew that the miracle of the Sea had happened at the Red Sea.

(1967) 378-84; B. Childs "A Traditio-Historical Study of the Reed Sea Tradition" *VT* 20 (1970) 412-14.

It is important to emphasize that in the prose account of Exodus 14 the place of the famous crossing is not the *yam suf* but simply "the sea."

Exodus 13:8 states that the Israelites were led in a roundabout way "by the way of the wilderness *yam suf*." The syntax is terrible here; there is no preposition stating "to the *yam suf*" or "at the *yam suf*." The phrase seems to have been added by a later glossator.

Even if we do take *yam suf* here as "Red Sea," it could merely mean that the original route was to go on the highway south to the Red Sea. Indeed, those who have studied the names of ancient roads in the Sinai have found that if you were in a road going north, you would call it one name. If you were going south on the same road, you would call it by the name of a southern destination. So the Israelites were on a wilderness road going south.

I was also consumed, as I still am, with the fact that God instructs Moses to *shuv*, to have the Israelites "turn back." The Israelites, moving south, heading away from the Nile Delta and Mediterranean, are now told to turn around, that is, to come back north, to the *Yam*, the Mediterranean. After a trip to Egypt over fifty years ago (1948), William Foxwell Albright Jr., stated:

> In any case, the new discoveries prove conclusively that we must give up the now traditional southern crossing and separate the Red Sea completely from the Reed Sea in Exodus.[2]

I accepted this. To me, Lake Bardawil was just perfect for the spinning of a theory about the miracle at the sea. Lake Bardawil is a vast lake on the Mediterranean coast between Port Said and El Arish. It is a place where armies get swallowed up, an area that changes from land to sea and back to land because of periodic flooding. At certain points on the shores of this lake, there are big areas of rushes. If Lake Bardawil is the "Sea of Reeds," then, add the Mount of Lawgiving (Gebel Hellal), the quails and manna that could only be found in the north, the area with provisions for a large host, and the northern Sinai became, for me, a plausible context for the Israelites' wanderings. These various elements, Colonel Jarvis said, "fit into each other like the parts of a jig-saw puzzle."[3] I agree with him.

Certain elements in the argument, however, began to bother me. I became unsure that the so-called new discoveries, such as the speculation about Mt. Casius as Ba`al-Zephon, had proven anything. I really stopped believing in the northern theory when I started going to Egypt and saw the distances involved. I knew the Biblical story too well to think that the Israelites would have gone that far before the Egyptians pursued them and caught up to them.

Most of all, I wondered if the Mediterranean had come much further south than Albright and the other Northern proponents had thought. I kept asking, "What about

---

2 Albright "Ba`al-Zephon" 13.
3 Ibid. 155.

the Big Biblical Picture? What did the map look like?" To trace the route of the Exodus based on modern-day maps is incredibly unscientific. It is common knowledge that coastlines change, whether we are speaking of the site of ancient Troy, the harbor of Alexandria or the beach in New Haven, Connecticut. A map of the ancient Sinai was required so that we could know what the possibilities for the route of the Exodus were. In thinking about the area of the site of the miracle at the Sea, I became a man without a region.

Even though I was one who believed in the northern theory, I now must tell you that it was quite simply impossible to begin with.[4] In 1978, Israeli geologists had told us that the mound and lake of Sabakhat Bardawil rose up only in the 8th century BCE.[5] In Eliezer Oren's archaeological excavations at twenty sites in the northern Sinai, no evidence was found before the 6th century BCE, the Persian era.[6] Still, even Oren still backed Lake Bardawil as the site of the great event.[7] Why? Because it is hard to change the map in one's head.

Still, that is exactly what we need to do. Thanks to the geologist Steven Moshier, we have the Big Picture, or at least a fine, tentative approximation of it. The goal of learning what the Sinai looked like 3300 years ago is one that we now may have achieved. While there are some modifications to make, we basically know the map of the part of the Sinai relevant to the first stages of the Exodus.

---

4 Frankly, some people, like Jim Hoffmeier, knew this before Steven Moshier did his work. Bruno Marcolongo had presented an interesting reconstruction of the route of the Pelusiac Branch of the Nile, showing that, two thousand years ago, the coastline of the Mediterranean was further south than it is today. Bruno Marcolongo "Evolution du paleo-environnement dans la partie orientale du Delta du Nile depuis la transgression flandrienne (8,000 B.P.) par rapport aux modeles de peuplement anciens" *CRIPEL* 14 (1992) 23-31 and fig. 1.
5 D. Neev and G.M. Friedman "Late Holocene Tectonic Activity along the Margins of Sinai Subplate" *Science* 202 (1978) 427-9.
6 E.D. Oren "Migdol: A New Fortress on the Edge of the Eastern Nile Delta" *BASOR* 256 (1984) 7-44; idem "An Egyptian Fortress on the Military Road between Egypt and Canaan" *Qadmoniot* 6 (1973) 101-103 (Heb.); idem "Military Architecture along the 'Ways of Horus': Egyptian Reliefs and Archaeological Evidence" *Eretz-Israel* 20 (1989) 8-22; 21 (1990) 6-22; idem "Sinai, Northern" in *The New Encyclopedia of Archaeological Excavations in the Holy Land* vol. 4 (Jerusalem and New York, 1993) 1386-1396; idem "The Overland Route between Egypt and Canaan in the Early Bronze Age" *IEJ* 23 (1973) 198-205; idem "The 'Ways of Horus' in North Sinai" in *Egypt, Israel, Sinai: Archaeological and Historical Relationships in the Biblical Period* ed. by Anson F. Rainey (Tel Aviv, 1987) 69-119.
7 Eliezer D. Oren "How not to create a history of the Exodus: A critique of Professor Goedicke's theories" *BAR* 7:6 (1981) 46-53.

Using the new map, we must focus on one possible route out of Egypt. The map indicates a relatively narrow strip of land between the Mediterranean and the southern body of water, which may, for all we know, have been the Yam Suf. Perhaps our confusion about the Red/Reed Sea problem is that the Bible actually refers to both bodies of water. Perhaps the event involved the strip between them. Perhaps there was flooding at just the right point to inundate the Egyptians whereas the Israelites made it through.

What can we learn from Egyptological and archaeological evidence about this narrow area?

Tell Hebua

Tell Hebua is really four sites in some combination.[8] It is Tell Hebua I that interests us here. Mohammed Abd el-Maksoud has found New Kingdom pottery and parts of a huge fortress.[9] Maksoud has found a statue at Hebua I with an inscription at the base that states that the statue was a representation of the god at Tjaru. Tjaru was the first of the forts on the Ways of Horus. Tell Hebua can be identified as Tjaru/Sile, the first place on the Karnak reliefs. This is the Archimedean point of this discussion. Tjaru was a crucial point on The Ways of Horus, so crucial that it was sometimes called The Ways of Horus itself.[10] The identification of Tjaru gives us a legitimate right to claim that The Dwelling of the Lion and Migdol must be nearby to the east, following the order of the Karnak reliefs.

---

8 Mohammed Abd el-Maksoud "Fouilles récentes au Nord Sinai, sur le site de Tell el-Herr: Première saison, 1984-85" *Cahiers de Recherches de l'Institut de Papyrologie et d'Égyptologie de Lille* 8 (1986) 15-16; idem "Une nouvelle fortresse sur la route d'Horus: Tel Heboua 1986 (Nord Sinai)" *Cahiers de Recherches de l'Institut de Papyrologie et d'Égyptologie de Lille* 9 (1987) 13-16.

9 An important find is an inscription from King Nehsy in the Second Intermediate Period that demonstrates that the site goes back to the seventeenth century BCE. See Mohamed Abd el-Maksoud *Annales du Service des Antiquites de l'Egypte* 69 (1988) 1-3.

10 Gardiner was the first to suggest that "The Ways of Horus" was a town with a garrison by the period of a Tenth Century Herakleopolitan king. He cites the "Instruction of King Akhthoy" (King Khety Nebkaure providing instruction to his son Merikare) where the monarch states: "I drove in my (?) mooring-post in a region that I made to the east of the boundaries of..bn(?) at Way(s)-of-Horus, equipped with townsmen, and filled with people of the best of the entire land, in order to repel the arms of ...." When Sinuhe came back from Canaan after the death of Amenemhet, he stopped at a frontier town at the end of what was considered to be Egypt proper and the beginning of the road to the east. This town is referred to as "The Ways of Horus." See a translation of the relevant passage in Hoffmeier Israel in Egypt 167. See also Dominique Valbelle "La (Les) Route(s)-D'Horus" in *Hommages Jean Leclant* vol. 4 *Bibliothèque de l'École des Hautes Études 106* (Cairo: IFAO, 1994) 379-86 where she offers the theory that "The Ways of Horus" is a region of the northern Sinai.

Pi-Hahiroth

The Biblical toponym Pi-Hahiroth may be connected to the Eastern Frontier Canal. Hoffmeier's suggestion that Pi- Hahiroth describes an area where the Frontier Canal emptied into the Sea of Reeds is an interesting possibility. I would suggest, with our new map, that it might refer to an area where the canal and the southern body of water met the sea, near Tjaru, the Dwelling of the Lion and Migdol. There is a strong possibility is that the toponym Pi-Hahiroth is connected to the Hebrew stem *ḥ-r-t* "to dig,"[11] perhaps referring to one of the canals of the Nile.[12]

After initiating the modern scientific investigation of the remains of the Eastern Frontier Canal, Weissbrod and Sneh suggested that the name means "the mouth of the canals."[13] It would be located near the point where the channel of canals leads to an opening, a mouth as it were, at the sea.[14] The canal was built for several purposes, including defense. The canal or system of canals might have linked a number of forts that had been built and re-fortified for the defense of Egypt.[15] The canal seems to have been built from Lake Timsah to Lake el-Ballah and then northeast to the coast of the Mediterranean.[16] It certainly seems, but is not certain, that this canal is represented by the hieroglyphic phrase *ta denit* on the Karnak relief, which seems to mean "the dividing waters."[17] In the relief, there is a close relationship between the canal and Tjaru; it seems that the canal was a major moat for the fort.[18] One can even see a bridge going across the canal on the relief.

---

11 There is good linguistic evidence of Semitic parallels for this translation; see Hoffmeier *Israel in Egypt* 170.

12 W. Shea "A Date for the Recently Discovered Eastern Canal of Egypt" *BASOR* 226 (1977) 37.

13 Sneh, Weissbrod , Perath. "Evidence for an Ancient Egyptian Frontier Canal" 542-48.

14 So first Gardiner *"The Ancient Military Road"* 99.

15 Redford "Pi-Hahiroth" 371.

16 In Sinuhe's description of his journey from Canaan back to Egypt, he travels by boat, perhaps partly on canals, to a fort that may be Tjaru (Sneh and Weissbrod "Evidence for an Ancient Egyptian Frontier Canal" 546; Hoffmeier *Israel in Egypt* 167-68).

17 Redford "Pi-Hahiroth" in *ABD* V371.

18 It was Cazelles who first proposed a connection to "canals" (Henri Cazelles "Les localizations de l'Exode" 351); see Aharoni *Land of the Bible* 196. The Hebrew Pi-hahiroth may have an Egypytian analogue in *Papyrus Anastasi* III 2:9 where we see Pa-hir "the Hir-waters," a canal or lake which is placed in parallel to Shi-Hor "the Waters of Horus." Aly Bey Shafei states that the Pelusian branch of the Nile is mentioned in Egyptian inscriptions as "The Waters of Hor" or "The Waters of the Suns." An inscription of Seti I from Abydos calls the branch "The Waters of the God Ptah." Wine-jars excavated at Ramesses are "from the great orchards of Pi Ramesses at the River of the Sun." Herodotus speaks of Bubastis on the Pelusiac branch that flows out from

Even Redford suggests that Pi-Hahiroth is a Hebraized form of Akkadian origin, Pi-hariti "the mouth of the canal." Redford says that it would be "an appropriate toponym for the eastern edge of the heavily canalized Eastern delta."

The Biblical Passage
Let me review the key Biblical passage in order to try to understand the relationship between the key toponyms involved in the great event:

> The Lord said to Moses: Tell the Israelites to turn back and encamp before Pi-Hahiroth, between Migdol and the sea, before Ba`al-Zephon; you shall encamp facing it, by the sea. Pharaoh will say of the Israelites, "They are astray in the land; the wilderness has closed in on them.

The very specific geographical information makes it clear that the Biblical text is attempting to provide a precise set of referents. The unusually detailed identification, "before Pi-Hahiroth, between Migdol and the sea, before Ba`al-Zephon," makes the sentence somewhat awkward. Awkwardness may mean a gloss, but it may be an attempt to ensure identification. While, for instance, the Biblical writers do not have any interest in telling us where Mt. Sinai is, they are particularly interested in telling us where the miracle occurred. It is the challenge of the modern scholar and archaeologist to find a place that was known to the ancient readers of the Bible, the scene of the greatest event in Biblical history.

Exodus 14:2 provides four referents: The Israelites are to *šub*, to turn back. As we know from Joshua 19:12, *šub* in Biblical geography means to turn in the opposite direction. After the Israelites *šub*, they are to encamp before Pi-Hahiroth, the first coordinate, between Migdol (the second) and the sea (the third), before Ba`al-Zephon (the fourth). They are to encamp facing Pi-Hahiroth, by the sea. If the sea is *the* sea, the Mediterranean, then we need to know how far south the sea came. If Pi-Hahiroth is indeed the mouth of the diggings and is a reference to a site connected with the Eastern Frontier Canal, then we have two referents. If we could know, obviously, where either Migdol or Ba`al-Zephon is, we could know the location of the most famous miracle of them all.

What else can we glean from the details of the verse? One point is that Pi-Hahiroth is by the sea and another is that there is enough land between Migdol and the sea for a sizable, and I do not wish to go into how sizable, encampment. It would be helpful to have some idea how large an area these four landmarks form. In other words, do we need to think about the three place-names as being in tight

---

Heliopolis; he reports that Darius caused 120,000 Egyptians to die by forcing them to dig the Canal. A. B. Shafei "Historical Notes on the Pelusiac Branch, the Red Sea Canal and the Route of the Exodus" *Bulletin de la Societe Royale de Georgraphie d'Egypte* 21 (1946) 231-87.

geographical proximity? It is possible that the four coordinates create a large area. I will suggest that the verse describes a very precise and narrow area.

Here is the key verse in Exodus 14 and Numbers 33. I will emphasize what would seem to be the most insignificant word in the verse, *lifne*.

> Tell the Israelites to turn back and encamp (*lifne*) before Pi-Hahiroth, between Migdol and the sea, (*lifne*) before Ba`al-Zephon; you shall encamp facing it, by the sea.
>
> Exodus 14:2

> They set out from Etham and turned about toward Pi-Hahiroth, which faces Ba`al-Zephon, and they encamped before Migdol. They set out from Pene-Hahiroth and passed through the sea into the wilderness.
>
> Numbers 33:7-8

Naville thinks that Ba`al-Zephon was a place of worship and not a settlement. This remains an intriguing possibility. It is important here to emphasize that the cult of Ba`al-Zephon is well attested as early as the thirteenth century, the century of the Exodus. While it was Eissfeldt in modern times who underlined the significance of Ba`al-Zephon as a sacred pagan shrine, the ancient rabbis anticipated him by many centuries.[19] The Israelites are to *shuv*, to "turn back" to this place because God, according to the rabbis, has destroyed all of the idols of Egypt except those at the temple of Ba`al-Zephon. In the *Mekhilta* and elsewhere, Pharaoh is overjoyed at finding this untouched sanctuary and derives the inspiration from his experience there to pursue the Israelites into the sea.[20]

The rabbis may not be so far off the mark. Perhaps God wants the great destruction of the Egyptians to occur in front of the famous pagan shrine. God destroys the Egyptians, demonstrates his power to the Israelites, and humiliates the pagan gods, all in one immortal event. When the Israelites sing,

> *Mi chamochah ba'elim 'adonai*
> Who is like You, O Lord, among the gods?   Exodus 15:11a

---

19 See the *Targums* for this idea.
20 For full references, see Louis Ginzberg *The Legends of the Jews* Vol. VI 3-4. A partial parallel may be brought from Mesopotamian historiography. Sargon II of Assyria embarks on an important military expedition, leading his "army over the Tigris and Euphrates, at the peak of their flood, the spring flood, as (if to be) dry ground" (*ANET* 276). In short, nothing could stop him. In the Book of Exodus, God destroys Pharaoh and his army, and nothing, apparently, can now stop the Israelites from their goal, the land of Canaan; for them, the sea really does become dry ground.

Ba`al-Zephon would be powerful background. The rabbis, who attempt to discover meaning in every detail of the Bible, could not resist developing material on Ba`al-Zephon. However,, at least in this case, it is hard to believe that the Biblical writers themselves would not pause at the mention of Ba`al-Zephon, not with all of the Biblical texts that deal with Ba`al. In other words, *lifne* Ba`al-Zephon would be literally "in your face" to the Egyptian or pagan gods. If we have to deal with the question of why the route of the Exodus came so close to Egyptian forts, the answer may be theological.

If *lifne* means not only "near" but "to the east," as Redford thinks[21], then Pi-Hahiroth would be to the east of Ba`al-Zephon. If *lifne* is an indicator that the places are close to each other, we have a very helpful clue for the site identification of at least one of the relevant place names.

Tell el-Borg is at exactly the right place in a narrow space between the Mediterranean Sea and a lake. It was a perfect place for a fort, a strategically necessary one for the defense of Egypt.

An Hypothesis about the Route of the Exodus

So can we trace the route of the Exodus?[22] I think we can establish a working hypothesis. We follow the itinerary Ramesses, Succoth, Etham, Pi-Hahiroth. If Ramesses is Pi-Ramesses = Tell el-Dab'a, and Succoth is Tjeku which is Tell el-Maskhuta, the Israelites are moving out of Egypt. If Etham is place near or an area of wilderness as indicated by Num. 33, the Israelites are now outside of Egyptian control. A working hypothesis is that the Israelites started out from Ramesses/Tell el-Dab, made their way to Succoth/Tjeku/Tell el-Maskhuta, about twenty miles, went south to the wilderness of or near Etham south of the body of water on our new map, and then went back north to the vicinity of Tell el-Borg, where the great event happened.

If we use the Tell el-Borg-Migdol identification in our developing hypothesis, why would the Israelites turn back to this area? It is common sense to say that the Israelites would not have wanted to encounter the Egyptians at these forts.[23] Not only would most scholars agree,[24] even God agreed, when, according to the Book of

---

21 Redford in Rainey *Egypt, Israel, Sinai* 154.

22 E. Naville "The Geography of the Exodus" *JEA* X (1924) 18-39; A. H. Gardiner "The Geography of the Exodus: An Answer" *JEA* X (1924) 87-96; M. Haran "The Exodus Routes in the Pentateuchal Sources" *Tarbiz* XL (1971) 113-43 (Hebrew); idem "The Exodus" *IDB* Supp. 303-310.

23 Manfred Bietak *Tell El-Dab'a Vol. 2* (Vienna: Verlag Der Osterreichschen Akademie der Wissenschaften, 1975) 217-220, fig. 45.

24 See Aharoni (*Land of the Bible* 197), who claims that Exodus 13:18 means that the Israelites "moved southward quite rapidly to the desert interior, to areas that were outside of Egyptian control." However, the narrative and poetry of Exodus 14-15 follow this

Exodus, He reflects His knowledge of Egyptian highways and places in discussing the route of the Exodus:

> Now when Pharaoh let the people go, God did not lead them by way of the land of the Philistines[25] although it was nearer; for God said, "The people may have a change of heart when they see war, and return to Egypt." So God led the people roundabout, by way of the wilderness at the Sea of Reeds.
>
> Exodus 13:17

We now have a better understanding than ever of what the Bible means when it tells us that the Israelites did not take the quick way from Egypt to Canaan, right along the coast. That coast, which was then much farther south than the coast is now, had a series of Egyptian forts.

When we think about the Israelites "*shuv*ing" ("turning back") to the Migdol area, we tend to look for some rational explanation that has nothing to do with the theological. I suggest, for instance, that having gone around this body of water and thus to the south and east of the fort of Tjaru, the Israelites came north again, planning to follow the route of the Ways of Horus at this later point.

Perhaps, when the Israelites left Egypt, Pharaoh sent a message to Tjaru, to Hebua I. From that fort, the "Tjaru-oteers" chased after the Israelites. Perhaps the Tjaru-oteers were the Egyptians involved in the great event.

We basically know the map of the part of the Sinai relevant to the first stages of the Exodus. We have our new map of the area, and we can see how the Israelites might have gone, around a body of water that was probably a lake, and then back north to the area of Tell el-Borg.[26]

Minimally, we are able to say that, thanks to our new map of the area, we probably now know the area that the Bible points to as the area of the great event. Is this proof of the Exodus? No. Is this proof of the miracle? No. Is it even proof that the Israelites came through this area? No; however, it is progress towards all those

---

verse and according to Aharoni's site identifications, the Israelites move northward, not southward.

25 "The way of the land of Philistines" is the name for a well-known highway, the southern segment of the thousand mile international artery of transportation that went all the way to Mesopotamia. The Egyptian name for this highway was "the ways of Horus." Starting at the fort-city of Sile (Tjaru), the highway moved along the shore of the Mediterranean Sea.

26 Obviously, many scholars disagree with this. For instance, J. Simons *Topographical Texts of the Old Testament* 238, followed later by Har-El, states that the Migdol which the Israelites passed on their way out of Egypt, lay to the south of the Bitter Lakes and that the Israelites passed through the Red Sea near there.

questions. It shows that the Bible's geography of going south and coming back north and being near Migdol does make sense. It shows once again that the sea of the miracle was the Mediterranean or a Reedy Sea and not the Red Sea.

We now have a map by which to explore further. We're trying to find a key site in history. Even if we could prove Tell el-Borg as Migdol and the Biblical correlation were made, it still would not confirm the Exodus event or the great events involved. However, with the new map and that identification, we would be closer to a reconstruction of the area in the time of the Exodus.

We will not abandon the field for the doubters to run amuck. We will use every scientific and archaeological tool in an ongoing investigation concerning the greatest event in history.

Chapter VII

Did Joshua Fight the Battle of Jericho?
The Israelites in Canaan and the
Minimalist/Palestinian Denial of History

The Bible has always been a political text. One only has to think through the stories of Genesis to recognize their political impact. Ishmael, son of the first Hebrew, Abraham, is sent out into the desert to find his very different destiny than the one waiting for Abraham's son by his wife Sarah, Isaac. This reading is selected for the First Day of Rosh Hashanah, the birthday of the world, because it celebrates the birthday of the first Jewish child, Isaac. Ishmael is the father of the Arabs and Isaac the father of the Israelites. So when the Torah speaks about them, they are not just individuals but peoples. Think about this story as the reason for the division of the Jewish and the Arab peoples. If Ishmael is sent out into the desert, the Torah is saying that his descendants will live in the desert and not the cultivated land. This is a political statement. If the Torah says that God made a covenant to give the descendants of Isaac and not Ishmael the land of Israel, this also is a political statement.

Since the Bible was always a political text, it is no surprise that it still is. Thousands of years may have passed, but Jewish, Christian, and Muslim people are still busy, tailoring garments to superimpose on a very naked Biblical text.

So what is new? Whatever is new on the modern political front is bound to find its way into the Biblical text. We have the phenomenon of the recent Biblical revisionism, where the search for the origins of the Palestinians is in vogue in certain circles.

The Invention of Ancient Israel: The Silencing of Palestinian History by Keith W. Whitelam is an astonishing book. Whitelam is the Professor of Religious Studies and Head of Department at the University of Stirling. If it were just a crazy book by a radical professor, I wouldn't care so much but it is unfortunately representative of a trend in Biblical studies into which, even more unfortunately, some Jewish people, including some rabbis, have bought.

Whitelam says that because of the emphasis on the Bible and the Jewish people, the other side of the story, the other part of history, has been silenced. Everyone focuses on the Isaacs and not the Ishmaels. In ancient times, there were the Israelites but there were also other peoples who lived in the land that we now call the land of

Israel. The Canaanites were the most important of these peoples. The Canaanites, Whitelam says, were robbed of their land by the Israelites and Canaanite history was silenced.

In modern times, he says, the same thing has happened again. The heirs of the Israelites, the modern Israelis, have robbed the land of the Palestinians, the heirs of the Canaanites.

Factually speaking, there is no relationship between the Canaanites and the Palestinians. Palestinian history has not been suppressed. Let us say that we recognize the Arabs living in what is called Palestine as "Palestinians," as it seems we have to do in order to deal with the realities of our time. Still, these Palestinians have no more relationship to the ancient Canaanites than I do to the so-called Native Americans who, by the way, also came here from a different continent.

Hebrew is a dialect of Canaanite. The fact that Jewish people have maintained their ancient language (which, of course, has evolved) is an unmistakable sign of connectedness to the ancient land of Canaan. Arabic is a much later language that does not have its roots in Canaan.

Very few of the people who call themselves Palestinians today could prove that their ancestors lived in the land in, say, 1900. If they say that many of the Israelis of today are the grandchildren of people who came to the land from elsewhere, the same holds true for them. The irony is that Palestine, in the 1800s, was a land that was either barren or swampy. When the Jewish people started to reclaim and rebuild the land, it became interesting to the Arabs. Until then, they hadn't cared about the land at all.

Go back to 1966. You have never heard the term Palestinians. Arab refugees in Israel only began identifying themselves as part of a Palestinian people in 1967, two decades after the establishment of the modern State of Israel.

Give the Palestinian propaganda machine its due: it is clever and forceful. It does not shrink from bold statements simply because they are not factual. It skillfully manipulates those who would side with the innocent victims of the world.

If one says, "So what? There are crackpots who deny the Holocaust," I say that one should ever underestimate the power of a lie that sounds like a historical fact. Never underestimate the power of hatred, especially anti-Semitism. Anyone who does underestimate such things has not read a page of Jewish history.

The Minimalists deny the truth of the Bible while stating that they are seeking the truth of history. Ah, but you can falsify history. You can systematically destroy ancient Jewish places of worship. I have seen slides of what the Arabs are doing on the Temple Mount. They feel that if they get rid of the archaeological evidence, they can then claim that the Israelis were never in Jerusalem in early times.

Anti-Semites throughout history have accused Jewish people of the terrible things that they themselves are doing. So they say that Jewish people are silencing

Palestinian history. Who ever would have thought about silencing history, except the people who are doing it themselves?

Still, all of this constitutes much more than an argument about history. People are getting killed today because of the different versions of history that they believe.

Let us think about all this in terms of two individuals. Let uss say that there are two people who hate each other because of some things that have happened. A third person brings them to the table to talk. Before they can talk about where things go from here, they have to review what made them hate each other to begin with. Each version of the past is so different that they cannot agree on one basic fact. How can they go on from here in a positive manner if they can't agree on anything that has already happened?

As a rabbi, and as a person, I find myself in a lot of these situations. There are times that, as a third person trying to be objective, I cannot figure out what happened—that is how different the versions are. This is not just a matter of opinion; this is not just "different strokes for different folks." How can you talk about a problem if you cannot agree on what caused the problem or even what the problem is? So there are many times, in these personal situations, that we can simply not move forward because we cannot agree about the past.

At least we should know the truth. We should know the facts. So let us deal in facts. While the idea of a Palestinian people began in the last few decades, Israel became a people thousands of years ago. When exactly did they become a distinct people? One could say with Abraham, the first Hebrew, or with Jacob and his clan. A better argument could be made that people-hood seems to have been established when the Israelites left Egypt as a unity. When was this? As I have been saying throughout this book, I take the Biblical texts as data to be evaluated in developing historical reconstructions. Still, in order to convince others that the events recorded in the Bible are factual, it is helpful to introduce evidence from outside the Bible when it is available. So again, at one point can we say, for certain, that the Israelites were a defined people?

The Merneptah Stela

The Merneptah stele is very important extra-Biblical evidence that states that there was a people named Israel in the land of Israel before 1200 BCE. Merneptah, a Pharaoh in Egypt around 1210 BCE, left us this monument on which he says that he fought the Israelites in Israel. So even if you want to say that the Bible might have its political axe to grind, there was an Israel in the land over three thousand two hundred years ago.

The Merneptah stela is one of the most important archaeological finds in the field of Bible. This seven-foot high, black granite stone now stands in the Egypt Museum in Cairo. I have seen it; it takes my breath away because it contains the earliest extra-Biblical reference to the Israelites. I will present the important part of the passage and then explain it:

> The princes are prostrate, saying: "Mercy!"
> Not one raises his head among the Nine Bows.[1]
> Desolation is for Tehenu; Hatti is pacified;
> Plundered is the Canaan with every evil.
> Carried off is Ashkelon; seized upon is Gezer;
> Yanoam is made as that which does not exist;
> Israel is laid waste, his seed is not;
> Hurru is become a widow for Egypt!
> All lands together, they are pacified.

Since the importance of this stela cannot be overstated, some background about it is necessary. Merneptah, or as he is commonly called, Merneptah, became the pharaoh in June of 1223 BCE. He was the twelfth son of Ramesses II, the Pharaoh of the Exodus who died in the sixty-seventh year of rule. He was a king's scribe and participated in some of his father's wars. When his older brother, the heir apparent, died, Merneptah became the heir apparent and the commander in chief of the army. When his father died, he became king.

Merneptah was usually in poor health. We know from his mummy that he was obese, bald, arthritic, had suffered broken bones and didn't have many teeth. He only lasted about ten years as pharaoh. By the time of his seventh year, his men were already busy bringing burial goods into his tomb.

Merneptah preserved the borders of the empire and sent relief shipments of grain to his Hittite allies. The major event of his reign came in his fifth year of rule. Libyan tribes, allied with pirate tribes of the Aegean, attacked Egypt. Merneptah won a great victory and repelled the invaders. We possess a long hymn of victory about this, and the last section remembers some previous victories. We know that Merneptah went on a punitive campaign against the city of Gezer in the third year of his reign. We do not know if he and his army actually came into contact with all of the nations mentioned in this stela. It is this section that contains the important lines, which I will cite again as I explain them:

> The princes are prostrate, saying: "Mercy!"
> Not one raises his head among the Nine Bows.

"The Nine Bows" are a famous term used in Egyptian to speak of the enemies of Egypt. To "break the bow" of an enemy is to defeat and vanquish them. The "Nine Bows" usually refers to Nubians and Asiatics. The number nine is three times three,

---

1 See D. Tomimura "A propos de l'origine du mot égyptien "Neuf-Arcs"" *Oriento, Bulletin of the Society for Near Eastern Studies in Japan* 24 (1981) 114-24; Redford *Egypt, Canaan and Israel in Ancient Times* (Princeton, 1992) 87-93.

the plurality of pluralities, thus designating the entirety of enemies. Since it is a figure of totality, eight is as good as a literal nine.

Desolation is for Tehenu; Hatti is pacified;

Tehenu is Libya. Hatti is Asia Minor, which is Anatolia-North Syria. Tehenu and Hatti were the western and northern extremities of Merneptah's realm.
Now the writer talks about the victories involved.

Plundered is the Canaan with every evil.
Carried off is Ashkelon; seized upon is Gezer;

Notice how the text says "the Canaan." Redford says that it is not "the Canaan," which doesn't make sense, but Pakana`an, which is an Egyptian name for the city of Gaza.[2] Ashkelon and Gezer are also cities on the coast of Israel. These three cities, then, Gaza, Ashkelon and Gezer, make up a unit in what was later called Philistia.

Yano'am is made as that which does not exist;
Israel is laid waste, his seed is not;
Hurru is become a widow for Egypt!
All lands together, they are pacified.

Yanoam is an important town in northern Palestine, just south of the Sea of Galilee. Israel is obviously the crucial name for us, which I will explain at length. Hurru is a term for part of Syria.

So it would seem that just as the second three cities are in one geographical region, it would also seem that Yanoam, Israel and Harru are in the same general area. Archaeologists think that early Israel was concentrated in the Hill Country. This would fit.

I have to explain something about Egyptian writing. It used determinatives. Before the word, there would be a symbol indicating what the letters would mean. So here, Israel has the determinative for a people, not a land. None of the other toponyms, names of places, use the determinative for people. The determinative for people is used only for Israel. In hieroglyphics, all of this is very clear and pictorial. A crown is replaced by two figures of people. This is not a scribal mistake.

As John Wilson says, "Israel is not yet a settled people."[3] Earlier in the text, as Wilson points out in his note, the country determinative is used for a settled people (Rebu, Temeh, Hatti, Ashkelon) and the people determinative is used for groups that are not located (Madjoi, Nau and Tekten).

---

2 Redford "The Ashkelon Relief at Karnak and the Israel Stela" *IEJ* 36 (1986) 197.
3 *ANET* 378 n. 18.

Merneptah assumes the existence of Israel in Canaan. I am going to emphasize this: This stela refers to the Israelites in the land of Canaan. They are not a settled country but a people living in the land.

Another key piece of evidence is a set of pictorial carvings on a temple wall in Luxor, Egypt, which Egyptologist Frank Yurco believes depict the destruction of Ashkelon, Gezer, Yano'am, and the Israelites mentioned in the Merneptah Stele. If so, the first existing reference to Israel even comes complete with pictures of them.

What do the naysayers say and why do they say it? Minimalists downplay the significance of the Merneptah stela by claiming it simply refers to a trivial early nomadic tribe—a kind of proto-Israel. Still, the undeniable fact is that a pharaoh considered Israel's defeat to be worthy of mentioning and inscribing on stone. It is an undeniable fact that a people called Israel lived in Canaan by that time.

Ahlström says that "Israel" refers to a geographical region and not to the Israelites. Israel is a mixed population, basically Canaanite. Why does he say this? Because he doesn't want to admit that the Israelites were in Israel that early, or even existed as a people that early. Why not? Following his logic, all of Genesis, in fact the whole Torah, becomes a falsehood. It is all made up.[4] There is no Israel that early. If an extra-Biblical piece of evidence such as the Merneptah stela says that Israel was in existence in the land of Israel early, in the 1200s BCE, then it must not mean that at all; it must mean something else.

That is what Minimalists do. They reject not only the Bible but also archaeological evidence that supports the Biblical account.

If you're more objective, you have to say that someone, a people called Israel, was living in the land of Canaan in the time when the Israelites were supposed to be in the land of Canaan.

The importance of all of this is that it is an extra-Biblical record of Israelite people in Israel in 1220 or 1208 BCE. So here, archaeology can be helpful in giving us a date and helping us to fix Biblical chronology.

Indeed, this is what a lot of Maximalist Biblical historians have done. They have said, working backward from 1208 BCE when we know the Israelites were in Canaan, and assuming that the Israelites had been in the land for a while, and going back forty years to a date for the Exodus, the Israelites left Egypt in the 1280-1270 BCE range.

That does not mean that we can use this stela to be a Maximalist here. A Maximalist would say: This stela shows that the Biblical account is completely factual.

---

4 G. Ahlström *Who were the Israelites?* 39; idem "Merneptah's Israel" *JNES* 44 (1985) 59-61; idem *The History of Ancient Palestine* 282-88.

I would wait with this judgment. I would say that all but the most skeptical scholars agree that the Israelites were in Canaan by the year 1208 BCE.

Did Joshua Fight the Battle of Jericho? Israel in Canaan

A key argument of the Minimalists is that "Israel" emerged from indigenous peoples in Canaan. The whole idea of a conquest by Israelites coming in from Egypt is thrown out the window. This is another attempt to say that the Bible is not true. If the Bible says that there was a pan-Israelite conquest of the Israelites who had left Egypt and now conquered Canaan, the Minimalists will try to deny every part of the sequence. The Israelites were never in Egypt in the first place. There was no Exodus. They did not conquer Canaan.

There is a fascinating debate that is raging in recent Biblical scholarship. There are three main models brought to explain the history of early Israel in the land of Canaan:

Conquest Model - According to the Maximalists such as Albright, Bright, Speiser and Wright, the Biblical account of the conquest of Israel in the days of Joshua is true. They say that the Israelites were slaves in Egypt and came into Canaan, conquering part or all of the land. Albright did archaeological work at Tell Beit Mirsim and called it the Biblical Debir (Joshua 10:38-39; 15:15-17; Judges 1:11-13). Wright excavated Beitin and called it the Biblical Bethel (Joshua 8:17; Judges 1:22-28). They said that these cities were destroyed in the 13th century (1200s BCE) by the Israelites. They pointed out that fine Canaanite cities were replaced villages with poor straggly houses.

The problem with the Conquest model is that the evidence is uneven for different sites under discussion. Of the sixteen cities that the Bible says were destroyed by Joshua's forces, archaeology only has indicated that three were destroyed during a time period that would fit an Israelite conquest. Another problem is that we have nothing to indicate that the Late Bronze Age destruction levels were caused by the Israelites. It is not as if there are signs that say, "The Israelites did this." To respond, Hoffmeier makes the interesting point that while scholarship assumes that the Middle Bronze Age destruction levels at sites in Canaan are the result of an Egyptian invasion, there is nothing in the evidence to indicate that it was an Egyptian army that was the destroying force. Let me put it simply: If we have other data that says that there was a battle between certain forces at a site, and we find evidence of a battle at that time, it is reasonable to say that the battle was fought between those forces. If one says that the Biblical accounts cannot be taken as evidence, one is displaying one's own prejudices.

Peaceful Migration/Evolution Models - Scholars such as Alt and Noth questioned the conquest model, suggesting instead a peaceful gradual migration. They theorize that parts of what became the Israelites immigrated into Canaan from the east over time, eventually consolidating as "Israel."

The problem with this model is that gradual peaceful migrations do not explain the archaeological evidence that we do have of the destruction of Canaanite cities. Still, while all of this is just fascinating conjecture, I am not closed to the possibility that there is some truth in it. It is not so far-fetched to say that Israelites came into Canaan from the outside (I would insist Egypt) and that groups who were there merged with them to become the tribes of Israel. The tribal structure of Israel would seem to lend itself well to this model. Different groups became the various tribes of Israel. For instance, the Danites might have some relationship to Aegean peoples. It is interesting to remember that the Greeks in the Iliad were not called the Greeks but the Danaans. From the Biblical data itself, it is clear that the tribe of Judah evolved and was composed of clans and groups such as the Kenites, the Kenizzites, etc. Caleb, an important character in the Books of Numbers, Joshua and Judges, was a Kenizzite, yet became the leader of the tribe of Judah.

Thinking about the evidence of the Merneptah stela in this context, Israel would have been a primary group that then gradually grew bigger as more and more elements joined them. The fact that all of Israel at the end of the Book of Joshua assembles at Shechem, an ancient city that the Israelites had not conquered, would seem to indicate that other elements, including those who were living at Shechem, had joined with the Israelites to become a new and greater unity.

Peasant Revolt Model - According to this radical theory, the Israelites were never in Egypt and always lived in the land of Canaan. They were just people, call them Canaanites or Habiru, who became known as Israelites later on. This model posits the Israelites as peasants who revolted against their overlords and became "the Israelites." These peasants were originally an oppressed indigenous people who arose out of a socio/economic struggle and created their own religious identity and egalitarian society. If the archeological picture shows continuity of culture in the highland settlements, it is because the people there, "Canaanites" who became "Israelites," were the same people with a new identity. If this "peasant-revolt" model, presented by scholars such as Mendenhall and Gottwald, seems to have a Marxist bent, it does. It plays well in Third World liberation theology, inspiring the poor and downtrodden to rise up against their masters and the rich. The fine Canaanite houses with one big rich man and a lot of poor ones are replaced by a lot of meager houses.

This theory has many problems, especially in what it leaves out. There is nothing about the sojourn and slavery in Egypt. There is nothing about Mt. Sinai. The result is a people who had nothing of the history described in the Book of Genesis.

This contradicts beliefs and statements at the very heart of Biblical religion and literature. A very important text for modern Biblical scholarship is what is called "the Credo," a passage we find in Deuteronomy (and versions of it elsewhere in the

Bible such as Nehemiah 9). It is a summary of early Israelite history. When an Israelite farmer living in the land of Israel would bring his first fruits to the sanctuary and say:

> My father was a fugitive Aramean. He went down to Egypt with meager numbers and sojourned there; but there he became a great and very populous nation. The Egyptians dealt harshly with us and oppressed us; they imposed heavy labor upon us. We cried to the LORD, the God of our fathers, and the LORD heard our plea and saw our plight, our misery, and our oppression. The LORD freed us from Egypt by a might hand, by an outstretched arm and awesome power, and by signs and portents. He brought us to this place and gave us this land, a land flowing with milk and honey. Wherefore I now bring the first fruits of the soil which You, O LORD, have given me.
>
> Deuteronomy 26:5-10

The enslavement in Egypt is very basic to the history of the Israelites. While some scholars make a great deal of the fact that there is no mention here of Mt. Sinai, it is clear that the passage is about the relationship between the Israelites and the land of Israel; the revelation at Mt. Sinai does not really bear on that relationship. So the fact that Mt. Sinai is not mentioned is nothing to draw inferences from.

However, to imply, as the "peasant-revolt" does, that the entire early history of Israel, their early memories of originating in Mesopotamia and being enslaved in Egypt, were all fictions, begs the question of why they would make up such stories. If a people wanted to make the case that a land belonged to them, why say that they came from a different land? A wandering Aramean as your father/ancestor does not give you a very distinguished resume. A long stint as slaves in a foreign land hardly prepares you nor entitles you for kingships. The humble admissions of the Credo breathe the air of historical realism, not the lofty airs of fiction.

Notice how all of these models struggle over the most basic of questions: "Can we establish that the Israelites were in Egypt at all?" "Were the Israelites a distinct religious/ethnic group as opposed to the Canaanites?" "Is there any real archaeological evidence of a conquest?" We will take a brief look at these questions.

Israel in Egypt

We start with a common-sense argument: No ancient people would make up that they were slaves. The ancient world was about power and royalty. To be a slave was literally to be owned by other people. To be a subject people was to be lower than low.

The Minimalists state that there is not a shred of evidence of Israelite slaves. Yet there is a great deal of epigraphic evidence of Syro-Palestinians in Egypt from 1500 BCE on. Famous documents known as *Leiden Papyrus* 348 and 349 speak of the *'apiru. Papyrus* 348, from the reign of Ramesses II, mentions "the *'apiru* who are dragging stone to the great pylon of ... Ramesses II." [5] *Papyrus Leiden* 349 also mentions *'apiru* who serve the Egyptian state.[6]

This brings to mind Exodus 1:11, which says the Hebrews "built supply cities, Pithom and Ramesses, for Pharaoh" (a verse I will discuss at great length below). While hotly debated, *'apiru* is believed by some scholars to refer to the Hebrews, the *'Ibri*. In the Amarna Letters, the Habiru are often mentioned in connection with Labaya of Shechem. Even Ahlstrom, a naysayer, allows for a connection between these references to the *habiru* and the Biblical Jacob, who has dealings in Shechem in Gen. 34 (I would add the Joseph blessing in Gen. 49). If the luck of the archaeological draw would provide us with the discovery of an inscription that could link the term *'apiru/ habiru* to the Hebrews of the Bible, it would prove to be the first direct extra-biblical reference to the children of Israel in slavery in Egypt.

Do we have any evidence of Israelite enslavement in Egypt? We know that pharaohs took prisoners-of-war and made them slaves and workers. In the chapter on Joseph, I mentioned ancient Egyptian documents that report influxes of thousands of Semites into the Nile Delta between 2200 and 2000 BCE. Similar patterns of settlement recurred over the next thousand years, creating a significant Asiatic population in the Delta region. Many of these Semitic-speakers came to the fertile Delta area in search of food during times of famine.

I also presented evidence of Semitic slaves in Egypt during this time period. Semites came to Egypt as tribute from their rulers and as prisoners of war. They became *corvée* workers and miners among many other occupations. *Papyrus Brooklyn* lists over forty Semites who worked for this one estate. Semites may have been in Egypt because they had been traded and sold there.

What about the Biblical narrative about the Israelites in Egypt? There is internal evidence, items in the Biblical narratives, which ring true against the Egyptian background. These details are arguments for the narrative's authenticity. Much of it fits with the details of what we know about New Kingdom Egypt. Kenneth Kitchen[7] and others have provided us with some interesting examples:

The close oversight of the Israelite workmen reminds us of the close supervision by the Egyptians of workmen and especially of foreign labor as we see at Deir el Medina. The two-tier structure of taskmasters reflected in the Biblical text (Exodus 1:11; 3:7, 5:6, 10, 13) is also to be found in Egyptian documents.

---

5 *Papyrus Leiden* I, 348, verso 6, 6-7; Gardiner *Late Egyptian Miscellanies* 134; English translation in Caminos *Late Egyptian Miscellanies* 491.
6 Caminos *Late Egyptian Miscellanies* 493.
7 Kenneth Kitchen "From the Brickfields of Egypt" 145-46.

Moses asks Pharaoh to hold a three-day religious festival (Exodus 5:1). At Deir el-Medina, work rosters report men who are recorded as being allowed to miss work "to offer to their god."

After the request to hold the festival, the Israelites are punished with the requirement that they double their quota of bricks without being given the straw with which to make them (Exodus 5:7-8). In *Papyrus Anastasi* VI, an Egyptian official indicates that men are necessary to both gather the straw and make the bricks. The idea of a quota of bricks is well known as early as the Old and Middle Kingdoms.[8]

We see here, as we do in the chapter on the historicity of the Exodus, that the Bible's account of the enslavement of the Israelites in Egypt seems, at the very least, historically plausible.

The Conquest

The Minimalists claim that the Book of Joshua paints the conquest as one of burning every city to its foundations. The Book of Joshua itself, however, only indicates that three cities were burned with fire, namely, Jericho, Ai, and Hazor. So when an excavated city does not have a thirteenth-century destruction level, it is important to remember that to lay siege to a city or to defeat its army does not necessarily mean to destroy the city.

This raises an essential point: When we use words such as "conquest model" it is because this is the presentation by scholars; it is one reconstruction of what happened as articulated by students of the Bible and history. The conquest model and the Biblical record are two different things. This point cannot be overestimated. The way I read the Book of Joshua, and the way that I compare it to the record of Israelite conquests and battles in the Book of Judges, is very different from the way that proponents of the Conquest Model speak of the entrance of the Israelites into Canaan. The Bible is so much more complex than what some of us call the "Sunday School Version" of the Book of Joshua. In the "Sunday School Version," Joshua and all of the Israelites defeated Jericho and then, with brutal extermination, in battle after battle, completely defeated and wiped out the Canaanites. Wright states that "the books of Joshua, Judges, and Samuel carry the story from triumph to triumph, until even the greatest of Canaanite walled fortresses were destroyed (Lachish about 1220 BCE, Megiddo, Beth-Shan, Jerusalem and finally Gezer shortly after 1000 BCE").[9]

There are two huge problems with this statement. First of all, the Biblical text is much more complicated. For example, after the Book of Joshua tells us of the "conquests" and draws the lines of the boundaries of the tribes, it says this about the tribe of Ephraim:

---

8 Charles F. Nims "Bricks without Straw" *BA* 13 no. 2 (1950) 22-28.
9 G. Ernest Wright *Biblical Archaeology* (Philadelphia, 1957) 69.

However, they failed to dispossess the Canaanites who dwelt in Gezer; so the Canaanites remained in the midst of Ephraim, as is still the case.

Joshua 16: 10

Secondly, the archaeological picture is also much more complicated than Wright's statement would have it. An objective look at the archaeological finds at Hazor, Lachish, Ai/Bethel, and Jericho yields an interesting and varied picture.

Hazor was inhabited and destroyed during the time of Joshua. Excavations have uncovered a palace with a small chapel area with the heads of decapitated statues of Canaanite deities littered across the floor and an Egyptian sphinx with a pharaoh's name hacked away. Israelites would have been the only ones who would have done these things. Joshua 11:11's reference to the Israelites burning "Hazor with fire" fits the evidence.

At Lachish, the destruction of the Level VI city fits the evidence of Joshua 10:31-32:

> From Libnah, Joshua proceeded with all Israel to Lachish; he encamped against it and attacked it. The LORD delivered Lachish into the hands of Israel. They captured it on the second day and put it and all the people in it to the sword.... At that time King Horam of Gezer marched to the help of Lachish; but Joshua defeated him and his army, letting none of them escape.

The archaeological data presents us with the destruction by fire of a large Canaanite city. The fact that there were no fortifications would allow the Israelites to defeat the city in a sudden attack. The fact that the city, after it was razed, was completely deserted would be explained by the complete annihilation of the people.[10]

While Wright based part of his enthusiasm for the conquest model on his excavations at Beitin, what we learn from that dig is very confusing indeed. Wright thought that Beitin was the Biblical Bethel; the destruction layer found at Beitin was the destruction of the Canaanite Bethel by the Israelites under Joshua. If he Bible does not say, however, that the Israelites destroyed Bethel, the theory is that the tradition was transferred from Bethel to Ai because it was an impressive ruin. Ai means "ruin"; the idea of calling a town "ruin" is intriguing in itself. Thus the Biblical record of a victory at Ai (Joshua 7 and 8) really describes the victory at Bethel. The Bible often describes Bethel as being close to Ai. The archaeological site of et-Tell, close to Beitin, has been identified as Ai. At et-Tell, there is no

---

10 W.F. Albright "Further Light on the History of Israel from Lachish and Megiddo" *BASOR* 68 (1937) 22-26.

evidence of occupation from Early Bronze III 2400 BCE to Iron I 1200 BCE; it was not inhabited during the time of Joshua and was not destroyed at that time by fire.

Let me tell you what we do not know. We do not know if Beitin is Bethel and therefore we do not know if et-Tell is Ai. The identification of Ai has been based on the proposed identification of the site that we think is Bethel. We may be looking in the wrong area altogether.

This sounds like special pleading. "Sure, you do not find what you're looking for so you say it is not the right site." As someone who is very involved in an archaeological excavation at an ancient site the name of which we are not certain. I want to testify to the fact that site identification is much more difficult than most people think. There are 475 place names in the Bible.[11] Only 262 (55%) have been identified with any degree of certainty. Most of these are based on the preservation of the name at the site. 158 are places that still bear the name of the ancient site. In the case of 32 other places, the name was found near the ancient site. Without the preservation of the name, only 72 places have been identified, and only about half of these carry a degree of certainty; the rest are conjectures.

If we think about these statistics, we realize that without toponymic evidence, without evidence that says, "This was Place X," we will have a hard time establishing any identification. If you are in the business of writing an encyclopedia of the Bible and part of your task is to identify places, you may make it seem that the place has been identified, when, in reality, we do not really know. Some editors will say, "Place X has been identified with the modern Tell El-XXX," which, in a sense, is true: some archaeologists or scholars may have identified the place as such. That word "identified" is ambiguous and the unsuspecting reader may not understand that the correlation is anything but certain. Often, that apparent certainty masks confusion and difficulty. A central dilemma of Biblical archaeology remains balancing the need to identify the geographical contexts of Biblical events with the standards of evidence required by modern archaeology. The truth is that there are very few sites indeed that yield the kind of evidence required to make the site identifications that we need in order to do historical reconstruction.

Thus it is not just special pleading to say, "The fact that there is no destruction level at the site that we think may be Ai does not necessarily mean that the Israelites did not defeat the people of Ai because the place may not be Ai to begin with."

Most famous of all, of course, is the archaeological case of Jericho. Jericho, so well known to the general public, is certainly the most famous conquest of the Israelite in Canaan. It is also a great story about archaeology and how its evidence and answers can change over time. We know that Jericho was destroyed by violence at some point in the second millennium BCE; it was occupied briefly and partially during the period of the Judges. The question is exactly when that first destruction occurred, and who destroyed it.

---

11 Y. Aharoni *The Land of the Bible: A Historical Geography* (Philadelphia, 1979) 129.

In the 1930s, Garstang excavated Jericho, Tell es-Sultan, and concluded that there was massive destruction and burning in 1400 BCE. City IV would then fit I Kings' date of 1447 for the Exodus and 1407 for the Conquest.

Kathleen Kenyon excavated Jericho from 1952-58. City IV was at the end of the Middle Bronze Age ca.1550 BCE. Kenyon believed the site was uninhabited from 1500 BCE to about 800 BCE. Israel could not conquer a city that was not there during the Late Bronze Age. Kenyon dated Jericho's destruction to 1570 BCE, when the Egyptians threw the Hyksos out of their land and pursued them north to Jericho and beyond. Thus the destruction of Jericho would not have been by the Israelites at all. So this would not fit with the Bible and rejects Garstang's proof of the Biblical account.

While Kenyon's discoveries were published in journals and a popular book, it was only much later that a technical report of her excavations was completed and published. Bryant G. Wood researched her findings and discovered evidence that contradicts her conclusions. He goes back to Garstang's dating and redates Kenyon's ceramics from the Middle Bronze Age to the Late Bronze Age, which fits the Biblical account.

Kenyon discovered a type of pottery that was only made for a limited time in the late 1400s, a century and a half after 1570 BCE, which was Kenyon's date for the destruction. Seals were found for pharaohs from 1570 BCE to as late as Amenhotep III, who died in 1349 BCE. These artifacts make it plausible to date the destruction of Jericho between the fifteenth and thirteenth centuries when the Maximalists, those who follow the Biblical chronology, think that the Exodus occurred.

In Joshua 3-4, the Israelites cross the Jordan River on dry ground. They then besiege Jericho, marching around it for seven days, and eventually watching as its walls fall. Wood finds a natural cause in the seismological activity in the region. In an intriguing article in *Biblical Archaeology Review*, he cites Stanford University geophysicist Amos Nur, who mentions a 1927 earthquake and mudslide in this century "that cut off the flow of the Jordan." Other cutoffs, typically lasting one or two days, occurred in 1160, 1267, 1546, 1834 and 1906 (all CE). In the 1927 quake, a section of a cliff 150 feet high fell into the Jordan River near the ford at Damiya. The Jordan was blocked for twenty-one hours. Wood's interesting suggestion is that the collapse of Jericho's walls resulted from an aftershock from the earthquake that blocked the Jordan River and allowed the Israelites to cross into Canaan.

This fits the model of dual causality, a natural cause that fits God's immediate purpose. In this line of thinking, geological or meteorological or historical phenomena happened. The question of causation can be explained through an examination of these phenomena. A further interpretation can be that the will of

God was involved in the timing of these events; they did not just happen but happened for a Divine reason.

Very often, scholars will state that we do not have any evidence, say, about the Israelites in Egypt. This really means we do not have the exact kind of evidence that they happen to demand on a particular topic. A fairer judgment would be that when we do not have sufficient evidence to make a definitive conclusion, we should refrain from saying anything with certainty. In the meantime, the Biblical data on the Israelites in Egypt clearly fits what we know about ancient history writing; a people would never make up the enslavement of its ancestors. In addition, we continue to see that the Biblical record of events, if evaluated openly and fairly, fits what we know about the ancient society of New Kingdom Egypt.

Concluding Unabashedly Political Conclusion

The Palestinians never existed until recent decades when Arabs living in certain areas began to call themselves by this name. These people are not descendants of the ancient Canaanites. If the Palestinians of today see the Israelis as an enemy, as the Canaanites of ancient times might have seen the Israelites as an enemy, then there is a commonality of animosity between the Canaanites and the Palestinians. That commonality is based on the historical fact that the Israelis of today are indeed descended from the Israelites of old.

The three scholarly models of the rise of the Israelites, the conquest of the land, the gradual immigration into the land, the revolt by groups within the land, all agree on one basic fact. The Israelites were a significant political and ethnic group in the land of Canaan/Israel/Palestine well over three thousand years before anyone called themselves Palestinians.

If one wants to say that the current realities are what they are, and that the political situation must be dealt with as it is, one is quite correct. However, the opponents of the modern Israel should leave ancient history out of it. History, to be perfectly blunt, is on our side.

Chapter VIII

Why Is Elijah the Prophet of Waiting?
Or
How Archaeology Illuminates
A Great Assassination Plot

Most Jewish people have heard of Elijah the prophet. In Jewish tradition, Elijah visits Seder tables around the world every year on Passover; people go to the door and open it for him; he even gets his own special glass of wine. Elijah is sung about as the Sabbath melts into the week and comes to the *berit milah*, the circumcision, of every baby boy. He comes every Passover to see if it is the right year for the Messiah to come. Since the Sabbath is a taste of the world as it will be when the Messiah comes, we invoke Elijah's name as we re-enter the week. Elijah checks out every baby boy to see whether the child is the one for whom we're waiting.

Why is Elijah accorded such incredible respect? If you say that it is because Elijah ascended to Heaven in a fiery chariot and never died, you're begging the question: Why did he rate the fiery chariot? Why is not it Moses who gets to come for Passover? After all, he's the prophet of the Exodus from Egypt. What is it about Elijah that merits such honor and attention?

In the process of exploring the answer to this question, I will examine the relationship with what would seem to be myth and that which is fascinating, real-life history.

You may have heard the phrase "a still, small voice." It comes from a passage (I Kings 19) in which the prophet Elijah finds himself on Mt. Sinai and hears the still, small voice of God. The passage is usually quoted to show that God is not to be found in great demonstrations of supernatural power but in the voice that motivates us to fulfill the tasks of our lives. You would never guess where this passage goes. By the time the still small voice has finished speaking, Elijah will embark on a radical political program that will last twenty years and result in the assassinations of three kings and the violent and bloody deaths of many others.

Historically speaking, archaeology will provide the context for the revolutionary agenda initiated by the still, small voice. Archaeology and the Bible will work hand-in- hand to explain the dramatic and graphic events of one of the most turbulent eras in the history of ancient Israel.

Elijah at Mt. Sinai

Let me set the scene. Ahab and his pagan wife, Jezebel, are the king and queen of the Northern Kingdom of Israel. They have happily taken the religion of the Israelians[1] and merged it with Ba`alism, the religion of the Canaanites.

It is at this time that one lonely man, Elijah, emerges from obscurity to protest and rebel against the powerful and successful monarchs. His task is formidable and overwhelming. Even after a great triumph over Ahab at Mount Carmel (I Kings 18), or because of it, Elijah finds himself in the greatest personal danger; the future of the religion of Israel is at the lowest possible ebb.

In I Kings 19, Elijah flees, first to the Southern Kingdom of Judah, then out into the desert. He literally prays for death. Those who are familiar with the Book of Jonah will see remarkable resemblances between Elijah and Jonah and their despair. God sends an angel with food and drink; Elijah is restored to such an extent that he is able to walk forty days and forty nights. We see forty days and forty nights and we think about Moses on Mt. Sinai. The allusion is purposeful: Elijah is, whether he knows it or not, on his way to Mt. Sinai. When he arrives there, Elijah is granted a new revelation. Like Moses, he stands in the entrance of a cave, the cleft of the rock. Like Moses, he witnesses God passing by. However, *this* time at Mt. Sinai, God is not in the power of nature; He is not in the mighty wind or the earthquake or the fire. God is in a still small voice, a soft murmuring sound. God in the still small voice is such a sublime thought that most of us stop reading at this point.

If there is a voice, there must be a message. There is indeed a concrete, historical, political message that has dramatic implications for Elijah's time. God tells Elijah that even though things have gone very badly in the kingdom of Israel and Elijah had run away for fear of his life from the evil King Ahab, God will now tell him what to do. He gives Elijah three tasks:

> The LORD said to him: "Go back by the way you came, [and] on to the wilderness of Damascus. When you get there, anoint Hazael as king of Aram. Also anoint Jehu son of Nimshi as king of Israel, and anoint Elisha son of Shaphat of Abel-meholah to succeed you as prophet. Whoever escapes the sword of Hazael shall be slain by Jehu, and whoever escapes the sword of Jehu shall be slain by Elisha. I will leave in Israel only seven thousand—every knee that has not knelt to Ba`al and every mouth that has not kissed him."
>
> I Kings 19:15-18

---

1 I will use this term, coined by my late teacher H. L. Ginsberg, to distinguish the Northern Israelites from the Israelites in Judah. The Israelians are the people of Israel (the northern Israelite kingdom), the Judeans the people of Judah, the southern Israelite kingdom; cf. *The Israelian Heritage of Judaism* (New York, 1982).

God says to Elijah that he should go back the way he came and on to the wilderness of Damascus. In Syria, then called Aram, he will anoint Hazael as king. Elijah will then go to the Northern Kingdom on two other missions. He will anoint Jehu, son of Nimshi, as King of Israel, and will make Elisha, son of Shaphat of Abel-Meholah, his successor as prophet.

There are three kingdoms that concern us here. As I explained, there are two Israelite kingdoms, Judah to the south, Israel to the north. In addition, Aram is a kingdom north of Israel,[2] in what we would now call Syria. After the decline of the kingdom of Solomon, the kingdom of Aram Damascus moved into the political vacuum. The Bible mentions eight wars between the Israelites and the Arameans over a period of 150 years. The three kingdoms had a complex set of relationships, a kind of triangular diplomacy, for the two hundred years of Northern Israel's existence (c.920-721 BCE).

To review the passage, God tells Elijah to:

• Anoint Hazael to be king of Aram. The interesting point here is that there was a king of Aram, Ben-Hadad. Hazael was a general of Aram but not the prince. To anoint Hazael is to say that he will be the next king of Aram. Why would God give Elijah these instructions?

• Anoint Jehu to be king of Israel. The interesting point here is that there was a king of Israel, Ahab. Jehu was a general of Israel but not a prince or heir to the throne. To anoint Jehu is to say that he will be the next king of Israel. Considering how King Ahab has persecuted Elijah, it does not take much to understand that God and his prophet would be anxious to get rid of Ahab and his dynasty.

• Anoint Elisha as his successor. God might have give Elijah this unusual command in order to make sure that the program was carried out. Since this was all so dangerous, Elijah, whom Ahab wanted to kill in the first place, might be killed in the process of keeping his appointments for anointments.

Now I do not know about you, but if I were granted such an incredible demonstration of God's power, if I were granted such a magnificent revelation, I would rush to fulfill the commands of that revelation. The first command is quite clear: Go to Damascus. I, personally, would go to Damascus. I would then anoint Jehu as King and then make Elisha my successor.

Elijah does not do so. Instead, he goes to Abel-Meholah and makes Elisha his disciple. We may say to ourselves: Abel-Meholah is in the north, closer than Damascus. Elijah fulfills this command first. Maybe it is not such a bad idea. In case Elijah should be killed, Elisha will fulfill that which is undone.

However, Elijah does not go to Damascus to anoint Hazael at all, ever. Neither did he ever anoint Jehu to be King of Israel. This is very strange. When Elijah

---

2 *Aram* is the root word in the word Aramaic, as in the language in which some Jewish prayers, such as the *Kaddish*, are recited to this day.

ascends to Heaven most of a generation later, he has not fulfilled his missions to anoint the new kings.

The question of why Elijah does not follow God's commands fascinates me and I will come back to this question below.[3] At this point, it is sufficient to say that nineteen or twenty years go by until Elisha, as Elijah's successor, finally does what his master was supposed to do. In II Kings 8, Elisha goes to Damascus when King Ben-Hadad is ill. Hazael, apparently a general or high-ranking official, is sent to ask the prophet Elisha, in his role as seer, if Ben-Hadad will recover. Elisha tells Hazael to lie and report to his king that he will recover, while telling Hazael that the king will die and that Hazael will succeed him. Hazael goes, lies and adds to the command by assassinating Ben-Hadad himself (II Kings 8). In the next chapter, II Kings 9, Elisha sends one of his disciples to anoint Jehu and gives him strict instructions that he should say: "Thus said the LORD: I anoint you King over Israel." The disciple does so and gives Jehu very complete instructions about the killing he is supposed to do.

A skeptic might say: "I know that there was an assassination and *coup d'état* in Aram and Israel at about the same time. That does not mean that these events had anything to do with each other and it certainly doesn't mean that God or His Israelite prophets had anything to do with this. What kind of thing is that for a prophet to be doing? What proof do you have that the prophets were involved?"

I now turn to archaeology with the question: Is there any extra-Biblical corroboration of these events? There is an intriguing inscription that is just that.

The Tel Dan Inscription

During the summer of 1993, an archaeologist named Avraham Biran discovered a fragment of a basalt stela at Tel Dan[4] that mentions the "King of Israel" and the "House of David."[5] Tel Dan is in very northern Israel. In the Bible there is an expression, "from Dan to Beersheba" which means from north to south. Tel Dan is way up north, near what was then the border between the northern kingdom of Israel and the foreign kingdom of Aram.

---

3 Benjamin Edidin Scolnic "The Flexible Word of God: Thoughts on the Other Pole of Biblical Authority" *Judaism* 36:3 (Summer, 1987) 331-38.
4 The importance of The Tel Dan Inscription (a.k.a .The *Bytdwd* Inscription) is reflected by its large bibliography. A few examples are: E. Ben Zvi "On the Reading 'bytdwd' In The Aramaic Stele from Tel Dan" *JSOT* 64 (1994) 25-32; A.Biran and J. Naveh "An Aramaic Stele Fragment from Tel Dan" *IEJ* 43 (1993) 81-98; A.Biran and J. Naveh "The Tel Dan Inscription: A New Fragment." *IEJ* 45 (1995) 1-18; N.P.Lemche and T.L. Thompson "Did Biran Kill David? The Bible in the Light Of Archaeology" *JSOT* 64 (1994) 3-22.
5 Biran and Naveh "An Aramaic Stele Fragment from Tel Dan" 81-98.

Here is the inscription:

...my father...
...and my father lay down (died) he went to...
rael formerly in the land...
I . Hadad went before me...
...my king and I slew of (them...[cha?])
riots and two thousand horsemen...
the king of Israel and (?)...
...House of David and I...
(?) land of Ham(?)
other...
(ru)led over Is(rael?)...
siege upon(?)...

I want you to see how little archaeologists often have to work with, fragments of inscriptions that they must reconstruct. While this inscription is broken, the first thing that pops out at you is the phrase "House of David." It is not just a reference to the dynasty of kings that descended from David in the Kingdom of Judah. It is also the earliest, most ancient, extra-biblical attestation of King David ever found.

That may not seem like a big deal if you assume that there was a historical person named King David.

What you have to remember is that there are many people who think that everything about the Bible is fictitious. So to find an inscription from another culture that has the name David, or his dynasty "The House of David," is, as hard proof that everyone must accept, pure gold.

This does not mean that everyone accepts it. The clear reference to the House of David here does not stop some scholars from denying the validity of this conclusion.[6] They say that *bytdwd* does not indicate "House of David" because there is no division between the word for "house," *byt*, and the name "David," *dwd*. They are wrong about this: Aramaic inscriptions are filled with this phraseology and often do not use word-dividers. This is indeed how an Aramaic scribe would write it.[7]

Why would anyone argue against the reference to the House of David here? It is simply because such scholars do not want to recognize anything as evidence of King

---

6 Philip Davies "House of David' Built on Sand: The Sins of the Biblical Maximizers" *BAR* 20 no. 4 (1994) 54.
7 Anson Rainey "The 'House of David' and House of the Deconstructionists" *BAR* 20 no. 6 (1994) 47; Baruch Halpern "The Stela from Dan: Epigraphic and Historical Considerations" *BASOR* 296 (1994) 63-80; Gary Rendsburg "On the Writing *bytdwd* in the Aramaic Inscription from Tel Dan" *IEJ* 45 (1995) 22-25.

David or the House of David. They are Minimalists, trying to say that the Bible is made up. They are as orthodox in their thinking as fundamentalists.[8]

Think about it. This stela was discovered in northern Israel almost three thousand years later. An Israelite did not write it. It is not a legend or a story. It is an inscription by an enemy of Israel referring to a victory over Israelites. All that a reasonable person wants to say is that there was a Davidic dynasty. The Minimalists do not want even to say that.

Beware scholars who do not want to see the truth. Their scholarship takes a backseat to their anti-religious prejudices.

From What Time Period Is the Tel Dan Inscription?

In order to place this inscription in a historical context, scholars naturally turned to the Bible, looking for a passage that would fit. Since both the kingdom of Judah and Israel are mentioned, the Biblical passage has to be in the time of the two kingdoms, which narrows down the time to c.920 to 722 BCE. The time would have to be when there was a conquest of Dan by the Arameans. Scholars developed a theory that a particular passage about the history of Israel in the 800s BCE fit these parameters. In this passage (I Kings 15:16-22 = II Chron. 16:1-6; the full text is cited in the footnote[9]), King Asa of Judah and King Baasha of Israel are continually fighting a war that lasts their whole reigns.

It may seem strange that two Israelite kingdoms would fight each other, but that, unfortunately, was not so unusual. Notice again how the Bible does not leave out

---

8 James Hoffmeier "Of Minimalists and Maximalists" *BAR* 21 No. 2 (1995) 20-22; idem "The Recently Discovered Tell Dan Inscription: Controversy and Confirmation" *Archaeology and the Biblical World* 3 no.1 (1995) 12-15.

9 There was war between Asa (king of Judah) and King Baasha of Israel all their days. King Baasha advanced against Judah, and he fortified Ramah to prevent anyone belonging to King Asa from going out or coming in. So, Asa took all the silver and gold that remained in the treasuries of the House of the LORD as well as the treasuries of the royal palace, and he entrusted them to his officials. King Asa sent them to King Ben-hadad son of Tabrimmon son of Hezion of Aram, who resided in Damascus, with this message: "There is a pact between you and me, and between your father and my father. I herewith send you a gift of silver and gold; Go and break your pact with King Baasha of Israel, so that he may withdraw from me." Ben-hadad responded to King Asa's request; he sent his army commanders against the towns of Israel and captured Ijon, Dan, Abel-beth-Maacah, and all of Chinneroth, as well as all the land of Naphtali. When Baasha heard about it, he stopped fortifying Ramah and remained in Tirzah. Then King Asa mustered all Judah, with no exemptions; and they carried away the stones and timber with which Baasha had fortified Ramah. With these King Asa fortified Geba of Benjamin, and Mizpah.

I Kings 15:16-22 =. 16:1-6

such uncomfortable facts. The Bible does not just tell us what we want to hear. So if I cannot stand the idea of two Israelite kingdoms fighting each other, that is my problem. No matter what the skeptics say, the Bible lets the truth fly openly.

King Baasha of Israel is winning the war and King Asa of Judah is so desperate that he does something drastic. He takes all of his gold and silver and all of the gold and silver from the Temple in Jerusalem and sends them to King Ben-Hadad of Aram in Damascus. Ben-Hadad was only too happy to take the money and oblige; he attacks Israel and occupies some of its northern cities and areas (which he wanted to include in his country anyway). Now Baasha of Israel is in trouble, so he leaves Judah alone and worries about protecting his own capital.

This passage seemed to be connected to the events described by the stela in that it has the Arameans conquering Dan.

Critics pointed out, however, that this passage states that Asa bribes Ben-Hadad into attacking Israel, whereas the Tel Dan Inscription indicates that this Aramean commander attacks both the kings of Israel and Judah. The critics were right.

There seemed to be a contradiction between the Bible and archaeology. What happens when the Bible says one thing and archaeology presents something else? It would never occur to anyone that the Bible would be right in such a case. It would not enter anyone's mind, say, that the Aramean commander was bombastically saying that he had attacked two kingdoms when he had only attacked one.

So archaeology won and the Bible lost. The Bible, it seemed, had been disproved. It never occurred to anyone that perhaps the scholars had come up with the wrong period, that the contradiction between the facts underlying the Tel Dan Inscription and the passage from Kings was a result of selecting the wrong passage and wrong time period.

That would have been the end of the story and the skeptics would have won a battle against the Bible. Later, in the summer of 1994, however, more fragments of the stela came to light:

> [...] my father went up [against him when] he fought at [...]
> And my father lay down, he went to his [ancestors] (viz. became sick and died). And the king of I[s-]
> rael entered previously in my father's land. [And] Hadad made me king.
> And Hadad went in front of me, [and] I departed from [the] seven
> [...-]
> s of my kingdom, and I slew [seve]nty kin[gs], who harnessed
> thou[sands of cha-]
> riots and thousands of horsemen (or: horses). [I killed Jeho]ram son of [Ahab]
> king of Israel, and [I] killed [Ahaz]iahu son of [Jehoram kin-]
> g of the house of David. And I set [their towns into ruins and turned]
> their land into [desolation...   ]
> other [...   and Jehu ru-
> led over Is[rael...   and I laid]
> siege upon [...   ]

These fragments have the names of two different Israelite kings, Jehoram, King of Israel, and Ahaziah, King of Judah, who lived in a later period. In this later period, the Bible states, the kings of Judah and Israel were allies against another, later King of Aram also named Ben-Hadad. This Ben-Hadad had a general named Hazael, whom you will remember from the stories of Elijah and Elisha. Jehoram and Ahaziah fought a major battle at Ramoth-Gilead in a battle against Hazael:

> Ahaziah son of Jehoram ... marched with Jehoram son of King Ahab of Israel to battle against King Hazael of Aram at Ramoth-Gilead, where the Arameans wounded Joram. He returned to Jezreel to recover from his wounds inflicted on him at Ramah when he fought against King Hazael of Aram. King Ahaziah ... went down to Jezreel to visit Jehoram.... During his visit he went out with Jehoram to Jehu son of Nimshi, whom the LORD had anointed to cut off the house of Ahab. In the course of bringing the house of Ahab to judgment, Jehu came upon the officers of Judah and the nephews of Ahaziah, and killed them. He sent in search of Ahaziah, who was caught hiding in Samaria, was brought to Jehu, and put to death.
>
> II Chron. 22 = II Kings 9:14-15

This changes the whole picture. The objection raised by the Minimalists was as follows: In I Kings 15, the King of Judah was not allied with the northern king but had, in fact, set up the attack. In the first inscription, however, Judah and Israel are allies. The objection is now removed completely. Scholars simply had the wrong time period. Instead, the second inscription tells us what we could not get out of the first inscription, namely, the correct time period.

What is of general interest is that what was wrong was the theory, not the Bible. It is also interesting to see the prejudice: If the inscription were in disagreement with the Bible, everyone's inclination would have been to say that the Bible is wrong. Why couldn't the inscription be making something up or exaggerating?

So we can now understand the stela. Hazael or one of his generals or people probably erected this monument to commemorate the victory over the allied Israelite kingdoms.[10]

Let us review. There seems to have been a plot to assassinate the kings of Israel and Aram and replace them with non-dynastic military types who would listen to their prophetic backers. When Hazael, in the Tel Dan inscription, says that he killed Ahaziah of Judah and Jehoram of Israel, and that now (perhaps his ally) Jehu rules Israel, he is not idly boasting. He was part of an alliance that did all that.

So this is what archaeology can do: bring us into the real-life, historical framework of the Biblical period and allow us to see what the Biblical narrators were talking about and evaluating.

---

10 Biran and Naveh "The Tell Dan Inscription, A New Fragment" 115.

The Radical Politics of Prophets

Some might say, "I believe that the *coups d'état* happened and the Tel Dan Inscription does suggest that Hazael and Jehu acted in some kind of conjunction.[11] However, to think of Israelian prophets as the initiators and instigators (or at least the messengers and go-betweens) of such a plot seems like so much after-the-fact special pleading, trying to make the case that God and His prophets are involved in history for the purpose of punishing the evil and the faithless.

Why would God speak to Elijah, so early in the game, and not wait to speak to Elisha in the right generation? Why does God set up a program for a scenario that will not exist for another generation?

What we do not have here is a profile in prophetic courage with Elisha proclaiming to Ahab that Jehu will usurp him. We do not even have Elisha go directly to Jehu himself. We have Elisha send a disciple with a sneaky, frightened message to Jehu. It makes the story extremely believable because of the reality of that fear factor.

This is, obviously, not a very pretty picture. We have trouble thinking about our houseguest Elijah as the radical terrorist of his time, masterminding one of the most amazing assassination conspiracies of history. All of this is fine if you believe that the prophets are only messengers of God who are merely carrying out God's plans. Thus there are those who read about the actions of prophets such as Elijah and Elisha and are terribly disturbed by the idea that prophets are involved in war and assassination. They do not understand that there is a time when violence is necessary. The prophets, under God's direction, understood this.

Do not think of prophets as tame old men and women who were kind to everyone. They were full of zealous and jealous rage for God. When they faced moments of crisis, when the life of the faith and the people were at stake, the prophets would do absolutely anything to resolve the crisis.

The early prophets were very involved in the politics of their times. We see, for instance, the prophet Gad who is at the right hand of a young brigand named David in his early years of fleeing from the legitimate king, Saul. If one follows the chronology of David closely, one finds that Gad is already with the outlaw David, claiming his kingship before Saul is dead I Samuel 22:5; I Chron. 29:29). Gad's association with David is a radical, revolutionary step.[12] Other examples may be culled at will. When Nathan, in close alliance with Bathsheba, is involved in the politics of succession at the end of King David's reign, he subverts the logical and legitimate successor (I Kings 1). When Ahijah the Shilonite surreptitiously

---

11 We know that such alliances existed. See, in my chapter on Hezekiah and the Assyrian crisis below, how kingdoms act in concert against their overlord Assyria.

12 Gad is not working on his own if we assume that he knew of Samuel's anointment of David as in I Samuel. If, however, the story of that anointment is a text written after the fact in order to legitimize David, as so much of I Samuel and I Chronicles is intended, it may be that Gad's association is a radical step of his own making.

proclaims Jeroboam king over Israel while Solomon is still alive and Rehoboam the heir, he is involved in the demise of the United Kingdom (I Kings 11).

We also know that the three kingdoms of Aram, Israel and Judah were in constant interrelationship. Thus the Aramean leper general Naaman comes down to Israel to Elisha to seek healing. This passage alone demonstrates, in a casual way, that the Aramean generals had contact with and respected Israelian prophets. Thus the idea that Elisha had contact with and influence on the Aramean general Hazael is not so strange at all.

Disappointment with an Anointment

Something bothers me. Jehu turns out to be a bloodthirsty cutthroat. He murders every royal personage he can get his hands on (between seventy and eighty by my count, including all of Ahab's descendants). He kills both Jehoram of Israel and Ahaziah of Judah. Just as Elijah had prophesied that Ahab would be punished in the very place, Jezreel, that he had had Naboth the Jezreelite killed, Jehu assassinates the kings in the field of Naboth (II Kings 9:25ff.).

Jehu is so violent that another prophet, Hosea, who came a century later in Israel, states that God has condemned the dynasty of Jehu:

> ... I will visit the blood of Jezreel upon the house of Jehu, and will cause to cease the kingdom of the house of Israel.
>
> Hosea 1:4

Hosea takes Jehu to task for what he has done. It seems that Hosea vehemently disagrees with his fellow prophets who had created Jehu. The prophet Hosea condemns the actions of King Jehu, which had been previously given praise in II Kings. This would seem to be a remarkable example of a prophet condemning the prophecy of another prophet.

> Know, then, that nothing that the LORD has spoken concerning the House of Ahab shall remain unfulfilled, for the LORD has done what he announced through His servant Elijah. God has now fulfilled the prophecy of the prophet Elijah. And Jehu struck down all that were left of the House of Ahab in Jezreel—and all his notables, intimates, and priests—till he left him no survivor.
>
> II Kings 10:10-11

After further massacre,

> The LORD said to Jehu, "Because you have acted well and done what was pleasing to Me, having carried out all that I desired upon the House of Ahab, four generations of your descendants shall occupy the throne of Israel."
>
> II Kings 10:30-31

Notice the conflict. In one Biblical passage, God says "Well done!" to Jehu. It is said that everything Jehu did was prophesied and commanded by the great prophet Elijah. In the other passage, God speaks through Hosea and says, I will soon punish the House of Jehu for the bloody deeds at Jezreel and put an end to the monarchy of the House of Israel.

What we seem to have here is a remarkable example of dueling prophecies. Both prophecies are in the Bible; both are the Word of God. Yet they would seem to be mutually exclusive. How can this be? How can two prophets, both spokesmen for the Word of God, contradict each other? Doesn't this mean that God has contradicted Himself?

I do not think that there is a contradiction here at all. It is interesting that God does not give Jehu's dynasty the monarchy in perpetuity; they will only hold the throne for four generations. Is there a hint here that God is concerned that Jehu and his successors will be evil? The evil will be punished unto the fourth generation, God says in the Ten Commandments.

Jehu may be selected by God to do a mission and rid the land of the evil rulers. If he will turn into an evil man himself, he will be punished. Jehu still has free will and he doesn't do the right thing with his mission.

How could Jehu have done this? The answer is that people are not chess pieces that God moves around at will. Jehu was a big disappointment to God and the prophets, as Hosea expresses.

God would say: People are surprising in both directions.

What God chooses to do is to select people, prophets and politicians and warriors, to fight evil. If the people who are given the power to fight evil become evil themselves, that is their exercise of free will.

The Great Assassination Plot

Take God out of the equation and you have the following possibility: What if Elijah and Elisha hatched and carried out a radical, incredibly bold plan to change the course of politics and history in their country? The Bible, at least as represented by I and II Kings, certainly seems to be on the side of Elijah and Elisha. The fact that Elijah receives the command to carry out these actions at Mt. Sinai is very striking; Elijah is the only person in the Bible who went back to Mt. Sinai. The fact that Elijah is transported to Heaven in a fiery chariot is clearly the greatest possible affirmation of what Elijah has done.

What we have in the Bible is an account by which the prophets are involved in, and in fact instigate, a double *coup d'état* in Aram and Israel. The Bible gives us a connection between Hazael and Jehu, a connection that now seems to be corroborated by our Tel Dan inscription in which Hazael states that he killed Jehoram of Israel. If Hazael and Jehu were in an alliance, created by the prophet Elisha as messenger not only from God but also between the two assassins, then Hazael could indeed claim credit for the killing of the northern king.

Elijah and the Elisha participated in a great, bi-national plot of assassination that brought down two dynasties.

The Biblical account is historical.

Religious Postscript – The Prophet of Waiting

I return now to a question set at the beginning of this chapter. Why does Elijah deserve the honor of ascending to Heaven in a fiery chariot? He delayed fulfilling God's commands! Perhaps, I muse sometimes, because God saw that Elijah was the perfect candidate to be what I like to call "the Prophet of Waiting." Just as Elijah waited for the right time to bring salvation to his people, he would be the right prophet to wait and herald the beginning of salvation for humankind when the Messiah comes. Perhaps God was testing Elijah, seeing whether he could wait for decades. Perhaps God was saying to a despondent Elijah at Mt. Sinai: "You think you're all alone? You think you want to kill them all? Fine, here's the program: Go create a political context for the destruction of all of the people that you are calling wicked." At that moment, Elijah is transformed from a prophet of zealous and jealous rage to a prophet who is even willing to let an evil king repent and live happily ever after.

Thus Elijah is the prophet who waits. We who have hope for the world wait with him.

Author's Note

In the Talmud (Mishnah *Eduyyot* 7), there is a series of statements about what Elijah will do when he comes. In one statement, it is said that Elijah will solve all the contradictions and disputations. Sometimes, when I cannot reconcile the tension between history and the Bible, I decide just to wait for Elijah.

Chapter IX

Why Amos Was Famous

While you've heard of the prophets of the Bible, you may not have considered the fact that there were a great many prophets who did not make it into the Biblical canon. That is, we only have a small representation of the prophets of ancient Israel; we may only have the most famous prophets and their work. The process by which certain prophets were included and mentioned in the Bible is a fascinating one, much more understandable than the process by which literature was selected for what Harold Bloom calls "the Western Canon." In the latter process, why a particular book or and writer survives is a complex question involving such aspects as the uniqueness and uncanny nature of the work.

In studying the Biblical canon, the question is: Why did the prophets that are included in the Bible make it?

I want to make the case that one of the main reasons that some of the prophets made it into the Biblical canon was that they accurately predicted historical events.

What made Amos famous was that he predicted a terrible earthquake that hit the land of Israel.

Isaiah predicted the salvation of Jerusalem, and Jerusalem was miraculously saved against all odds.

Jeremiah predicted the fall of Jerusalem in 587/86 B.C.E, and Jerusalem fell, traumatically.

Biblical prophecy is based on predicted historical events coming true.

As opposed to those who say, "It doesn't matter if it really happened," the Bible often seems quite concerned with establishing the veracity of its events.

That is, it is not enough to say that a prophet is great because he gave poetic and meaningful speeches. For the Biblical mind, what made a prophet great was the fact that he made historically verifiable predictions.

This definition of prophecy begins with the greatest prophet of all time. In Deuteronomy 18:15-22, Moses gives part of one of his three farewell speeches to the Israelites. Looking into the future, Moses tells the people that there will be other prophets in later generations. Just as the Israelites at Horeb (Mount Sinai) did not want to see and hear the revelations of God, and asked Moses to be their intermediary, so the Israelites of future generations will welcome prophets who will be able to see the future and will be the media for communicating that future. If the

Israelites are heading for trouble, the prophets will warn them. If things are going to get better, the prophets will inspire them.

> The LORD your God will raise up for you a prophet from among your own people, like myself; him you shall heed. This is just what you asked of the LORD your God at Horeb, on the day of the Assembly, saying, "Let me not hear the voice of the LORD my God any longer or see the wondrous fire any more, lest I die." Whereupon the LORD said to me, "They have done well in speaking thus. I will raise up a prophet for them from among their own people, like yourself: I will put My words in his mouth and he will speak to them all that I command him; and if anybody fails to heed the words he speaks in My name; I myself will call him to account. But any prophet who presumes to speak in My name an oracle that I did not command him to utter, or who speaks in the name of other gods—that prophet shall die."

There will be false prophets; they will get theirs. They will be punished for pretending to be something that they were not. For my purpose here, the most important part of the passage is what comes next:

> And should you ask yourselves, "How can we know that the oracle was not spoken by the LORD?"— if the prophet speaks in the name of the LORD and the oracle does not come true, that oracle was not spoken by the LORD; the prophet has uttered it presumptuously: do not stand in dread of him.

The proof of prophecy is in its ability to predict events that actually happen. It is not enough for prophets to give righteously indignant denunciations of immorality. It is not enough for them to stress the importance of living by the covenant with God.

Predicted historical events were a signature of prophecy, an authenticating sign that the prophets were an expression of the Will of God.

People who do not believe in the possibility of prophecy insist that Amos might have falsely claimed that he had prophesied that an earthquake was coming.

Contradicting this claim is the fact that Amos prophesied that Jeroboam II would die by the sword:

For Amos has said, "Jeroboam shall die by the sword, and Israel shall be exiled from its soil (Amos 7:11). Instead, Jeroboam seems to die a natural death as recorded in II Kings 14:29:

> Jeroboam slept with his fathers, the kings of Israel, and his son Zechariah succeeded him as king.

If the Bible is a fake, if its predictions are all after-the-fact pretense, its editors would have left out a prediction that did not come true.

If, on the other hand, Amos makes a prediction that comes true, the prediction is recorded and its fulfillment recognized. What makes all of this even more believable is that the Bible records predictions that do not come true.

Which makes me believe that we have accurate records of Amos' prophecies and that he prophesied two years before the earthquake.

The Earthquake in Amos
Look at the first verse of the Book of Amos:

The words of Amos, a sheepbreeder from Tekoa, who prophesied concerning Israel in the reigns of King Uzziah of Judah and Jeroboam son of Joash of Israel, two years before the earthquake.

Amos 1:1

Amos 1:1 gives us a historical context for Amos' prophecies: the years of King Uzziah of Judah (783-742 BCE), and King Jeroboam II of Israel (786-746 BCE). Amos, a man of the southern kingdom of Judah, went on a courageous prophetic mission to Bethel in the northern kingdom of Israel.

The Bible is even more precise in dating the prophecies "two years before the earthquake."[1] This was a very severe earthquake in the reign of Uzziah that was remembered for all time to come. As a result of this information, most scholars date his prophetic work somewhere between 760-755 BCE.[2]

There is something marvelously understated about the notice that Amos prophesied two years before the earthquake. It takes someone else to draw out just how important this notice is. On the other hand, it is right there, in the first verse. Amos prophesied two years *before* the earthquake. Thus when the earthquake actually occurred, people remembered his predictions. They remembered how he emphasized the warnings:

Shall not the earth shake for this
And all who dwell on it mourn?
Shall it not all rise like the Nile
And surge and subside like the Nile in Egypt?   Amos 8:8

---

1 W.G. Dever "A Case-Study in Biblical Archaeology: The Earthquake of ca.760 BCE" *Eretz-Israel* 23 (1992) 27-35; D.N Freedman and A.Welch "Amos's Earthquake and Israelite Prophecy" in *Scripture and Other Artifacts: Essays on the Bible and Archaeology in Honor of Philip J. King* ed. by M.D. Coogan, J.Exum, and L. E. Stager (Louisville, Kentucky, 1994) 188-98; N. Shalem "The Earthquakes in Jerusalem" *Jerusalem* 2 (1949) 22-60.
2 While earlier generations of scholarship tended to read 8:8 as a later addition (added after the earthquake mentioned in 1:1 had already happened), I understand 1:1 as indicating that the earthquake two years later was seen as confirmation of the prophet's words.

I saw my LORD standing by the altar, and He said:
"Strike the capitals so that the thresholds quake,
and make an end of the first of them all."

Amos 9:1

It is my Lord the GOD of Hosts
At whose touch the earth trembles
And all who dwell on it mourn ...

Amos 9:5

For I will give the order
And shake the House of Israel—

Amos 9:9

It was not only the kingdom of Israel that was affected by this catastrophe; Judah would feel its impact as well. Uzziah, the longest-reigning King of Judah, had become proud of his great buildings and the strength of his army (II Chron. 26). God also afflicts Uzziah's kingdom and buildings with the great earthquake.[3]

Earthquakes in the Prophetic Books
The image of the earthquake became an important one in prophetic literature. Isaiah 2:10-21 uses it in his vision of the Day of the Lord. Everything, people, large human-made constructions like towers and ships, large aspects of nature such as mountains and trees, will all fall. Isaiah 5:25 seems to be a direct reference to Amos' earthquake:

That is why
The LORD's anger was roused
Against His people.
Why He stretched out His arm against it
And struck it.
So that the mountains quaked,
And its corpses lay
Like refuse in the street.

Amos predicted the earthquake, but Isaiah is speaking towards the end of Uzziah's reign with its effects vivid in his mind. He sees the dead bodies in the street. Isaiah uses the image of the earthquake in other speeches as well:

---

3 God also strikes Uzziah personally, giving him incurable leprosy (II Chron.26:16-21).

Terror, and pit, and trap
Upon you who dwell on earth!
He who flees at the report of the terror
Shall fall into the pit;
And he who climbs out of the pit
Shall be caught in the trap.
For sluices are opened on high,
And earth's foundations tremble.
The earth is breaking, breaking;
The earth is crumbling, crumbling.
The earth is tottering, tottering;
The earth is swaying like a drunkard;
It is rocking to and fro like a hut.
Its iniquity shall weigh it down,
And it shall fall, to rise no more.
                    Isaiah 24:17-20

The latter citation is frightening. There is no escape. The language is so graphic that one sees the victims fruitlessly trying to flee, scratching at falling soil. If there is anything certain in our lives, it is the ground beneath our feet. If one cannot assume the solidity of the earth, what can one assume? No wonder that Isaiah would keep referring to the great earthquake of his time.[4]

The prophets who lived in subsequent generations used the fear of earthquakes to warn the people of impeding doom. Joel 4:16 seems to parallel Amos 1:2:

And the LORD will roar from Zion,
And shout aloud from Jerusalem,
So that heaven and earth tremble.
But the LORD will be a shelter to His people.
                    Joel 4:16

The LORD roars from Zion, shouts aloud from Jerusalem;
And the pastures of the shepherds shall languish,
And the summit of Carmel shall wither.
                    Amos 1:2

---

4 There are even more passages in Isaiah that refer to earthquakes:
 Therefore shall heaven be shaken,
 And earth leap out of its place,
 At the fury of the LORD of Hosts
 On the day of His burning wrath. (Isaiah 13:13)
 She shall be remembered of the LORD of Hosts
 With roaring, and shaking, and deafening noise,
 Storm, and tempest, and blaze of consuming fire.   Isaiah 29:6
 By the fury of the LORD of Hosts
 The earth was shaken.   Isaiah 9:18

Nahum 1:5,[5] Jeremiah 4:23-26, Ezekiel 38:17-20 and Haggai 2:6-7 all refer to God's power through earthquakes.

Of all of the references to earthquakes, the most relevant to our concerns here is Zechariah 14:5, which is an explicit reference to the earthquake of King Uzziah's time centuries earlier.

> Then the LORD will come forth and make war on those nations as He is wont to make war on a day of battle. On that day, He will set His feet on the Mount of Olives, near Jerusalem on the east; and the Mount of Olives shall split across from east to west, and one part of the Mount of Olives shall shift to the north and the other to the south, a huge gorge. And the Valley of the Hills shall be stopped up as it was stopped up as a result of the earthquake in the days of King Uzziah of Judah— And the LORD my God, with all the holy beings, will come to you.
>
> Zechariah 14:3-5

God fights for Israel and then stands upon the Mount of Olives, demonstrating His authority. It is at the conclusion of the battle of Jerusalem that we see God establishing His kingdom. The mountain is cloven into two parts—half moving toward the north and half toward the south, leaving an east-west valley between the halves. The valley was to provide a safe passage for the refugees from Jerusalem.[6] The ensuing flight for refuge is compared to the flight that happened in the days "of the earthquake in the days of Uzziah." Remember that the speaker is Zechariah, in post-Exilic times, after the return to Judea from Babylonia, around 520-515 BCE. Thus well over two hundred years later, a prophet can put forth a vision that reminds his listeners of the effects of that great earthquake. In the United States, the San Francisco earthquake of 1906 might be a suggestive parallel; it is the earthquake that people always refer to a century later. Many centuries later than this, in post-Biblical times, the earthquake of Uzziah's time was certainly not forgotten.[7] For instance, in referring to Uzziah, Josephus combines the outbreak of the king's leprosy with the cataclysm:

---

5 The mountains quake because of Him,
  And the hills melt.
  The earth heaves before Him;
  The world and all that dwell therein. (Nahum 1:5)
6 It was a valley of blessing, stretching from Jerusalem to Azal. This Azal is probably to be identified with Beth-Ezel (House of Azal) of Micah 1:11, a village 30 miles southwest of Jerusalem (see also 1 Chronicles 8:37, 38). Beth-Ezel is situated in the highlands just west of the Judean mountains and thus is as far as any valley could go. Once reaching Azal, one is free from mountain terrain and has a clear passage to safety.
7 For later rabbinic discussion, see N. Shalem "The Earthquakes in Jerusalem" *Jerusalem* 2 (1949) 22-60 (in Hebrew).

... a great earthquake shook the ground, and a rent was made in the temple, and the bright rays of the sun shone through it, and fell upon the king's face, insomuch that the leprosy seized upon him immediately; and before the city, at a place called Eroge, half the mountain broke off from the rest on the west, and rolled itself four furlongs, and stood still at the east mountain, till the roads, as well as the king's gardens, were spoiled by this obstruction.

Antiquities 9:222-27

One scholar has suggested that the earthquake caused a landslide that temporarily obstructed the Kidron valley. As a result, there is a short depression between Mount Scopus and the Mount of Olives. [8]

I understand that earthquakes are often used figuratively in the Bible as a token of the Presence of the Lord (Judges 5:4; II Samuel 22:8; Psalms 77:18; 97:4; 104:32). I insist that the use of a real-life image or event as a metaphor does not deprive the event of its reality.

For all of the references that we have discussed, the fact remains that the earthquake in Uzziah's time is the only one specifically identified in the Bible. The rational question at this point is: "Is there evidence of an earthquake at the time of Amos?" Indeed there is.

Archaeological Evidence of the Earthquake in Amos' Time

This earthquake is a scientifically verifiable, historical event. The evidence of the earthquake provided by archaeology is substantial.

Israel lies on a major fault-line that forms the Jordan Valley and continues on south to form the African "Rift." Earthquakes are not uncommon in the region.

N. Shalem, in studying earthquakes in the region, does not find evidence of any period of extended seismic activity. He also shows that the danger and effects of a quake were greater because people did not prepare for them. Along the mountainsides, "the shock set houses on the move, threw them one against the other, rolled them over like an avalanche, until the destruction was total."[9]

Earthquakes are mentioned among the extraordinary phenomena of the land (Psalms 18:7; and see Hab. 3:6; Nahum 1:5; Isaiah 5:25). The evidence that we have already seen in later prophetic passages shows that the quake in Uzziah's day was especially memorable; the later prophets are still talking about it long after it happened.

What is interesting is that even though it is far from the epicenter of the earthquake, evidence of an earthquake has been found at Hazor. In Stratum VI,

---

8 J.A. Soggin *The Prophet Amos* (London, 1987) 25.
9 N. Shalem "Seismicity in Palestine and in the Neighboring Areas" (unpublished MS cited in J.Milgrom "Did Isaiah Prophesy during the Reign of Uzziah" *VT* 14 (1964) 179).

walls were cracked and bent; some courses just fell.[10] Yadin's excavations at Hazor showed two unusual features on the boundary of strata V and VI. Level V buildings were reconstructions of the previous level and many had two layers of floor. Some walls in stratum VI were "tilted" and the floors had ceiling fragments on them. In a well-excavated house owned by one of the wealthier citizens of the city, the pillars and walls were found "askance"; "all of the floors were littered with hundreds of pieces of ceiling plaster." Yadin describes these phenomena as "unusual" and explains them as the result of destruction by earthquake.[11] Level V dates from the reign of Pekah Ben-Remaliah, king of Israel (737-732 BCE), so the one destroyed by earthquake is very likely from the time of Jeroboam II (789-748 BCE) and Uzziah (785-733 BCE). The pottery is typical of the eighth century. Thus the date 763 BCE fixed by Biblical evidence accords with the archaeological evidence as well.

Dever has collected other evidence of the earthquake of 763 BCE. Fallen courses and split walls have been found at Gezer; the "Outer Wall" collapsed.[12]

Stratum III at Beer-sheba may show the destruction of an earthquake.[13] Stratum IV at Lachish and Deir 'Alla may be sites with earthquake damage.[14]

The prediction of a major earthquake, then, was, if made by a human without Divine inspiration, quite a daring prediction. That Amos would have predicted the one major earthquake of Biblical times is, if one takes God out of the equation, quite a coincidence.

God and Earthquakes

We have seen that God spoke to Elijah at Mount Sinai (Horeb) after the occurrence of an earthquake (I Kings 19:11). Elijah, who had been hiding in a cave, realized that God does not need to use a mighty earthquake to speak, but can, in His restraint, reveal Himself simply in a still, small voice. This does not mean, however, that God will not or cannot speak through an earthquake.

In the Bible, earthquakes and the Flood and other "natural" calamities are seen as having been used by God at special times, with special people, for special purposes. Like other miracles, Biblical earthquakes were employed infrequently when no other human or physical agency could inflict judgment on the wicked,

---

10 Y.Yadin, Y.Aharoni, T. Dothan, I. Dunayevsky and J. Perrot *Hazor II: An Account of the Second Season of Excavations, 1956* (Jerusalem, 1960) 24.
11 Yadin *Hazor: The Rediscovery of a Great Citadel of the Bible* (New York, 1975) 150.
12 Dever "A Case-Study in Biblical Archaeology" 28-30.
13 King *Amos, Hosea, Micah—An Archaeological Commentary* (Philadelphia, 1988) 21.
14 Dever "A Case-Study in Biblical Archaeology" 28-30.

redeem His righteous people from difficult situations, or gain human attention so God's Word could be considered.

An interesting Biblical reference to an earthquake is found in Korah's rebellion in the Book of Numbers. When the Israelites were in the desert, a rebellion (or set of rebellions) led by Moses' cousin Korah (and leaders of the tribe of Reuben) was a very serious revolt against the authority of Moses and therefore God. Moses responds by saying that if the rebels die natural deaths, it will mean that Moses is not the prophet of God. If, however, the rebels die catastrophic, unusual deaths, it will mean that Moses was indeed sent by God.

> And Moses said, "By this you shall know that it was the LORD who sent me to do all these things; that they are not of my own devising: if these men die as all men do, if their lot be the common fate of all mankind, it was not the LORD who sent me. But if the LORD brings about something unheard-of, so that the ground opens its mouth and swallows them up with all that belongs to them, and they go down alive into Sheol, you shall know that these men have spurned the LORD." Scarcely had he finished speaking all these words when the ground under them burst asunder, and the earth opened its mouth and swallowed them up with their households, all Korah's people and all their possessions ... the earth closed over them and they vanished from the might of the congregation. All Israel around them fled at their shrieks, for they said: "The earth might swallow us!"
>
> Numbers 16:28-33

Moses sets up a kind of scientific test of the validity of his Divine authority. One might think that after everything the people had witnessed, the plagues, the miracle at the Sea, the manna in the wilderness, the people might have believed that Moses was the prophet of God. Unfortunately, being human, the Israelites needed constant reminders of God's power. So Korah and all his men were killed, and all of their possessions taken, as the land on which they were camped split apart and closed back upon them.[15] In fact, the purposes of communication, judgment, and salvation are all important in understanding the Biblical view of earthquakes. When nothing else works, the idea seems to be that God shakes us up and makes us consider His control of nature.

This is, however, and no pun intended, a slippery slope. Theologically speaking, do we want to think that God sends earthquakes?

If one believes in God, one believes that God has the power to do anything He wants to do. If He wants to use an earthquake to punish human evil, He can. If He wants to warn the people by speaking through prophets, He can. In a certain way, one's attitude toward the historicity of the Bible comes down to the nature of one's

---

15 See also the earthquake near the Philistine camp near Geba` in I Samuel 14. The Israelites of King Saul's time defeated the Philistines near Geba` after an earthquake occurred in their camp (I Samuel 14:15). Jonathan and his armor bearer were separated from their army and might otherwise have been killed by the Philistines.

beliefs in God. If one does not believe in God, there is no possibility of a miracle. If one believes that God is a great Power Who created the world but Who has had little to nothing to do with it since, miracles are probably not in the picture.

If, however, one believes that God is a force in human history, the Cause of certain great events, it becomes possible to look at events, then and now, and at least wonder if God, as a Cause along with a human or natural cause, was involved in a miracle.

My reading of the Bible forces me to understand that God does things that may upset or anger me. God does not need my permission or approval to act. Belief in God does not mean being happy and excited with everything God does or allows.

Thus as difficult as it may be for me to think about God being involved in an earthquake in the time of Amos, or in my own time, I am forced to struggle with such thoughts. If the Bible is going to be at the core of my beliefs, I must not put my preferences before the Word of God. I can rail and scream against Divine justice or injustice, but I have to have the faith to believe that I am not God and that God is.

Amos the Prophet

Amos was a great prophet who took on the political and social structure of his time. At the very apex of the prosperity of the northern kingdom of Israel during the time of Jeroboam II[16], Amos had the courage to denounce the corruption of Israel's upper class.

Amos seems to have given the coming earthquake as the sign that his words were from Yahweh. The political and religious world hated his words. When his words came to pass, they all knew that a prophet had spoken to them, and that God had truly shown His mercy to them by trying to avert their punishment. God had been in their midst but they had not known it.

Amos spoke before the earthquake. So we should not say that it was the earthquake that started the classical age of prophecy. Prophecy began as a response to the monarchy and its failure to live up to the Israelite covenant with God.

Still, condemnations of excesses will not make a prophet well known. It was the earthquake that made Amos famous.

---

16 For examples of their opulence, see J. W. Crawfoot and G. Crawfoot *Early Ivories from Samaria* (London, 1938).

Chapter X

Like A Bird In A Cage:
Why Isaiah Is #1 on the Prophet Parade

Picture the scene: It is 701 BCE.[1] The mighty Assyrian army, the greatest military force in the world known to the Israelites, is besieging Jerusalem. The prophet Isaiah promises the frightened inhabitants of the city that God will save them from the fearsome host outside their gates. Isaiah tells them that the king of Assyria will go back the way he came and return to his own land (Isaiah 37:33-5; cf. I Kings 19).

Imagine being a person in Jerusalem at that moment. Even if you wanted to believe what he was saying, even if you believed in God, even if you had been raised on the idea that God had promised King David that his city would not be conquered because it was the center of the world and the link between heaven and earth, it would take all your faith to believe in Isaiah's prophecy.

Then one morning you wake up, happy to be alive, and you hear that the Assyrians are gone. You rush to the walls and look out; you say to yourself, in a disbelief that strengthens your belief for the rest of your life: "They're gone, they're really gone."

They really were gone. This event happened. It sounds too good to be true; it sounds like a fairy tale. It is, nevertheless, historically accurate.

The Historical Context
The evidence includes:

- The Biblical passages on the subject
- Archaeological finds.
- The ancient Near Eastern texts

---

1 A. R. Millard "Sennacherib's Attack on Hezekiah" *Tyndale Bulletin* 36 (1985) 61-77; Kenneth A. Kitchen "Egypt, the Levant and Assyria in 701 B.C" *Fontes Atque Pontes: Eine Festgabe für Helmut Brunner ÄAT* vol. 5 (1983) 243-53; R. E. Clements *Isaiah and the Deliverance of Jerusalem* (Sheffield, 1980).

First, some historical background. Isaiah prophesied during the reign of three kings: Jotham (742-735 BCE), Ahaz (735-715 BCE) and Hezekiah (715-687 BCE). After Jotham's death, Isaiah became the advisor to the new king, Ahaz, telling him to have faith in God in the face of attacks from the northern kingdom of Israel. Instead of depending on God for protection, Ahaz got Assyria to help. This was not a very good idea, as we shall see.

When Ahaz died, Hezekiah succeeded his father and enacted many positive changes in Judah. He conducted religious reform, including the destruction of the bronze serpent from the time of Moses (see Numbers 21:4-9), which the people were worshipping, referring to it as Nehushtan. Hezekiah wins the admiration of the Biblical writer:

> He trusted only in the LORD the God of Israel; there was none like him among all the kings of Judah after him, nor among those before him. He clung to the LORD; he did not turn away from following Him, but kept the commandments that the LORD had given to Moses. And the LORD was always with him; he was successful wherever he turned.
>
> II Kings 18:5-7a

This statement about Hezekiah's monotheism follows the theology of reward and punishment. If one follows God, one succeeds. If one departs from God's ways, one will fail. Two verses later, we read about the defeat of the northern kingdom of Israel by the Assyrians. Israel suffered this defeat, according to the Bible, because of its rebellion against God:

> [This happened] because they did not obey the LORD their God; they transgressed His covenant —all that Moses the servant of the LORD had commanded. They did not obey and they did not fulfill it.
>
> II Kings 18:12

The contrast is clear. Hezekiah is rewarded for his faith and actions and the Israelians are punished because of their lack of faith and disobedient actions. This whole scheme, however, will be put to the test. If the Assyrians will also defeat Hezekiah, despite his faith, then the theology of reward and punishment will fall apart.

Hezekiah had been a loyal, tribute-paying vassal of Assyria for many years. The Assyrians, the great empire of Mesopotamia at that time (following the ancient kingdoms of Sumer, Akkad, and Babylonia), had many such vassal-states. Hezekiah became a puppet of the Assyrians. When another vassal tried to lure Hezekiah into a rebellion in 714 BCE, Hezekiah did not join the rebellion against the Assyrian emperor Sargon II.

The situation changed, however, which made Hezekiah re-think his loyalty to Assyria. A new Assyrian king, Sennacherib, ascended to the throne after the death of his father Sargon II in battle in 705 BCE and the Assyrians were involved in putting down a rebellion of a coalition of Chaldeans, Arameans and Elamites led by Merodachbaladan in Babylon. To the south, Egypt was a rising power that could help Judah rid itself of Assyrian domination.

In 701 BCE, Hezekiah[2], inspired by nationalistic dreams of independence and a renewal of the kingdom of David, revolted against Assyria: "He rebelled against the king of Assyria and would not serve him" (18:7b). The kings of Sidon (in modern Lebanon) and Ashkelon further south also revolted against Assyria (perhaps in coordination with Hezekiah).[3] Despite what had happened to the northern kingdom, it seemed like a good time for a rebellion.

The question is, what happened next?

The Biblical Evidence

The Biblical evidence presents us with a confusing picture. Before I try to straighten out the confusion, I will just cite the passages and explain what they're saying. We will need the extra-Biblical evidence to understand them completely.

The first part of the passage seems clear enough. In the fourteenth year of his reign, 701 BCE, Hezekiah of Judah rebels against Sennacherib of Assyria and gets defeated badly. He is forced to pay a fearsome tribute.

> In the fourteenth year of King Hezekiah, King Sennacherib of Assyria marched against all the fortified towns of Judah and seized them. King Hezekiah sent this message to the king of Assyria at Lachish: "I have done wrong; withdraw from me; and I shall bear whatever you impose on me." So the king of Assyria imposed upon King Hezekiah of Judah a payment of three hundred talents of silver and thirty talents of gold. Hezekiah gave him all the silver that was on hand in the House of the LORD and in the treasuries of the palace. At that time Hezekiah cut down the doors and the doorposts of the Temple of the LORD, which King Hezekiah had overlaid [with gold], and gave them to the king of Assyria.
>
> II Kings 18:13-16

All of this is clear enough. Hezekiah sends the tribute to the king of Assyria who is at his headquarters in the city of Lachish, southwest of Jerusalem. The defeat was a difficult and humiliating one. For a religious king such as Hezekiah to strip the

---

2 Hezekiah reigned c.715-687 BCE. The dates are confirmed by II Kings 20:20 and especially II Chronicles 32:30.

3 There also seems to have been some form of coordination with the forces led by Merodachbaladan. II Kings 20:12-13 (and see Isaiah 39:1-2; II Chronicles 32:31) speaks of a visit of the ambassadors of Merodachbaladan to Jerusalem. There is a problem with the position of this passage, but I will get to that below.

Temple of all its silver and gold must have been heart-rending. If Hezekiah has been so good, why are things going so badly?

Still, historically speaking, all of this would be simple. The confusion begins because the passage goes on for pages (II Kings 18:17-19:37). We are surprised to read that Sennacherib sends a large force under the command of several of his top officers to besiege Jerusalem. Sennacherib's representative, the Rabshakeh, the Royal Cupbearer, a persuasive speaker, delivers a great oration in Hebrew. He knows that the people are hoping that the Egyptians will come and fight the Assyrians. He says that Egypt is an unreliable ally who will not be able to help. He also points out that the northern kingdom of Israel has fallen before the Assyrians and that there is no god to protect them from the great might of the empire. He lists cities that the king and his predecessors have taken.

So why do not the Assyrians just take the city? Why all the oratory? It seems that Sennacherib has to resort to such tactics because he is unable to take Jerusalem; he uses psychological warfare to try to convince the people to turn against King Hezekiah. We wonder why Jerusalem was so difficult for these conquerors to defeat.

More important is the fact that none of this makes any sense. We have already read that everything is resolved. The Israelites have already lost. They've given him all of their silver and gold. Why does Sennacherib send this force when Hezekiah has already given him everything there is to give?

We begin to wonder if we are not reading about a second invasion, another invasion. It begins to seem that Sennacherib sends this force at some other point in time.

Hezekiah and his ministers are very upset. Hezekiah goes into mourning at the Temple. This man of faith turns to God in this, his hour of trial. His ministers turn to the prophet Isaiah. Perhaps the Assyrians will be struck down because they have questioned the power of God? Will Isaiah pray on their behalf? Isaiah tells them to tell their king not to fear:

> "... Thus said the LORD: Do not be frightened by the words of blasphemy against Me that you have heard from the minions of the king of Assyria. I will delude him; he will hear a rumor and return to his land, and I will make him fall by the sword in his land."
>
> II Kings 19:6-7

While all of this is going on inside the besieged city of Jerusalem, the Rabshakeh hears that his king Sennacherib has left the headquarters in Lachish and is attacking another Judean city. Sennacherib hears that King Tirkahah of Nubia is on his way to fight the Assyrians, so he tries sending messengers to Hezekiah to get him to surrender. Again, he says that the God of the Judeans will be powerless before the might of the Assyrian army.

Hezekiah goes to the Temple again and prays to God for deliverance from these blasphemous enemies. Isaiah sends a beautiful, poetic message to Hezekiah, saying that Sennacherib will fail in his attempt to take Jerusalem. The conclusion of the long passage is important:

> He shall go back by the way he came;
> He shall not enter this city
> declares the LORD.
> I will protect and save this city for My sake,
> And for the sake of My servant David.
> II Kings 33-34

These words are immediately fulfilled:

> That night an angel of the LORD went out and struck down one hundred and eighty-five thousand in the Assyrian camp, and the following morning they were all dead corpses.
> II Kings 19:35

Isaiah earlier prophecy, that Sennacherib will go home and will be killed there, is also fulfilled:

> So King Sennacherib of Assyria broke camp and retreated, and stayed in Nineveh. While he was worshipping in the temple of his god Nisroch, his sons Adrammelech and Sarezer struck him down with the sword. They fled to the land of Ararat, and his son Esarhaddon succeeded him as king.
> II Kings 19:36-37

Some scholars, resisting the idea that this miracle could be true, say that these verses about the deaths were just tacked on. I think, on the contrary, that these verses are where the whole story was going all along, they are what the story is about, they are the reason the whole story of Hezekiah and Isaiah is told here in the Bible. Against all odds, he predicted that Jerusalem would be saved and the enemy king killed in his own land.

The might of God is proven once again. Just as in the story of the Exodus, where God brings down the mightiest human power in the world, so here the mightiest empire is struck down by the power of God.

If you've heard of Isaiah, it was this event that made him #1 on the list of the classical prophets (his book comes first out of fifteen).

Archaeological Finds

There is remarkable archaeological evidence to bolster our sense of the historicity of the Biblical account.

Hezekiah planned well. He knew that the Assyrians would come and besiege Jerusalem. In a siege, the water supply is a major issue, so Hezekiah built an underground tunnel from the spring of Gihon (the city's main source of water) outside the city to the pool of Siloam inside the walls of the city (II Kings 20:20; Isaiah 22:9-11; II Chron. 32:4). The Gihon, which was outside the city, confronted King Hezekiah with a dilemma: while he needed to ensure water for the besieged city, he also needed to deny the source of the water to the Assyrian forces. The Bible describes Hezekiah's solution: "It was Hezekiah who stopped up the spring of water of Upper Gihon, leading it downward west of the City of David" (II Chron. 32:30). The waters of the Gihon were diverted into the Gai wadi by means of a tunnel 581 yards long, which was hewed from both ends simultaneously, probably along the course of a natural cleft in the rock. The inscription in the rock at the end of the tunnel describes the completion of the project.

> When Hezekiah saw that Sennacherib had come, intent on making war against Jerusalem, he consulted with his officers and warriors about stopping the flow of the springs outside the city, and they supported him. A large force was assembled to stop up all the springs and the wadi that flowed through the land, for otherwise, they thought, the king of Assyria would come and find water in abundance"
>
> II Chron. 32:2-4

We have evidence of this tunnel besides that found in the Bible. The famous "Siloam Inscription"[4] actually gives us some of the details about the tunnel. A boy bathing in the waters of the Gihon Spring (we should remember the Gihon from our long discussion of the rivers of Eden) in 1880 discovered a major find.[5] The luck of the archaeological draw accidentally gave us this inscription that was found in the wall of the lower entrance to the tunnel of Hezekiah south of the area of the Temple in Jerusalem. Engraved in the rock, the inscription describes the meeting of the two groups of hewers who had begun digging from opposite ends of the tunnel. The first half of the inscription is missing. The type of script used fits the period; so does the language, that of classical Hebrew prose.

Here is the inscription:

> [... when] (the tunnel) was driven through. And this was the way in which it was cut through:—While [...] (were) still [...] axe(s), each man toward his fellow, and while

4 *ANET* 321
5 It was first studied by Conrad Schick, one of the first explorers of Jerusalem.

there were still three cubits to be cut through, [there was heard] the voice of a man calling to his fellow, for there was an overlap in the rock on the right [and on the left]. And when the tunnel was driven through, the quarrymen hewed (the rock), each man toward his fellow, axe against axe; and the water flowed from the spring toward the reservoir for 1,200 cubits, and the height of the rock above the head(s) of the quarrymen was 100 cubits.[6]

When I read these lines, I am one of the men; I am in the tunnel. I am in Jerusalem, digging a tunnel so that my people will have water during the siege. I can hear my fellow worker shouting. I feel a strong sense of camaraderie, even joy, from being part of the important task at hand. I am just a workman, but I am part of the salvation of my people. Remember, no one wrote this inscription to prove an element of the Bible.

Another important archaeological find is a section of a well-built city fortification wall that may have tripled the area of the walled city of Jerusalem.[7]

In general, and as I will explain further below, the archaeological excavations that have been conducted in the territory of ancient Judah have give us a large amount of data that corroborates the witnesses of Sennacherib and the Bible.

What the Skeptics Say

Those who do not believe in the Biblical account say that Hezekiah surrendered to Sennacherib at Lachish to prevent the total destruction of his kingdom.[8] By his abject submission, Hezekiah dodged the final bullet. That, they say, is all that really happened. There was no miraculous deliverance of Jerusalem.

This theory follows the first part of the account, II Kings18:13-16, but does not do justice to the long narrative of II King 18:17-19:37. To contradict the Bible, to deny the historicity of the deliverance narrative, never bothers the skeptics. They want to ruin the sacred truth and take pleasure in doing so. So, for them, to reject the second part of the account is not a problem.

Since the skeptics often rule simply by being skeptical, this would probably be the end of the story if it were not for the other evidence. The skeptics have to deal with the Assyrian evidence, which, because it is not Biblical, they do take seriously.

The Assyrian Evidence

The important passages from Sennacherib's annals[9] tell the story of his third campaign. His first two campaigns were devoted to settling matters to the east in

---

6 The inscription is now in the Istanbul Museum.

7 Nahman Avigad *Discovering Jerusalem* (Nashville, 1980).

8 Clements *Isaiah and the Deliverance of Jerusalem JSOT* Supp.13 (Sheffield, 1980).

9 Sennacherib reigned 704-686 BCE. His name means, "The god Sin has substituted the dead brothers." While he was the third son of his father Sargon II, he was the first child to live past childhood, hence, perhaps, his name.

order. In 701 BCE, Sennacherib moved to the west to put down a widespread rebellion. He laid siege to Ekron. From the south, a large ("an army beyond counting") force of Egyptians and Ethiopians attacked. Sennacherib was victorious in a fierce battle. The annals tell us that Sennacherib conquered 46 Judean cities.

> As to Hezekiah the Jew, he did not submit to my yoke, I laid siege to 46 of his strong cities, walled forts and to the countless small villages in their vicinity.[10]

Sennacherib mentions many cities in his account, but does not mention the city of Lachish. If all the Assyrian evidence we had were from these annals, many scholars would say that the Biblical account, which refers to the Assyrians in Lachish several times, is inaccurate. Fortunately, archaeologists excavating the ruins of Sennacherib's palace in Nineveh found reliefs depicting the siege of Lachish. In addition, excavations at Lachish itself yielded more reliefs.[11] Not only does the ceramic corpus found in Level III of that site fit comfortably with the end of the eighth century, but there are many details on the Assyrian frieze that are confirmed. These details include: the citadel's many-towered wall, the supplementary outer defense wall, the location of the Assyrian earthen siege wall to the right (east) of the main city gate as it would have been seen from the perspective of the Assyrian camp and a defensive counter-ramp inside the city wall opposite the Assyrian camp.

Thus the Biblical references to the Assyrians at Lachish are corroborated by Assyrian evidence. Sennacherib goes on to detail what he conquered in Hezekiah's land. He deported (he says) 200,150 people. He took huge numbers of animals as booty; however, he did not conquer Jerusalem nor kill Hezekiah for his rebellion. Sennacherib does put the best possible face on this failure. Referring to Hezekiah, he says:

> Himself I made a prisoner in Jerusalem, his royal residence, like a bird in a cage. I surrounded him with earthwork in order to molest those who were leaving the city's gate. His towns which I had plundered, I took away from his country and gave them (over) to Mitinti, king of Ashdod, Padi, king of Ekron, and Sillibel, king of Gaza.

Notice what even this bombastic statement does *not* say; Sennacherib did not conquer Jerusalem. Something prevented the conquest of Jerusalem.

> Hezekiah himself, whom the terror-inspiring splendor of my lordship had overwhelmed and whose irregular and elite troops which he had brought into

---

10 *ANET* 288
11 David Ussishkin *The Conquest of Lachish by Sennacherib* Publications of the Institute of Archaeology 6 (Tel Aviv, 1982).

Jerusalem, his royal residence, in order to strengthen it, had deserted him, did send me, *later*, to Nineveh, my lordly city, together with 30 talents of gold, 800 talents of silver, precious stones, antimony, large cuts of red stone, couches (inlaid) with ivory, nimedu-chairs (inlaid) with ivory, elephant-hides, ebony-wood, boxwood (and) all kinds of valuable treasures, his (own) daughters, concubines, male and female musicians. In order to deliver the tribute and to do obeisance as a slave he sent his (personal) messenger.

I am intrigued by two details of this section. First, Sennacherib claims that some of Hezekiah's troops deserted him. This seems to correspond to the Biblical account of the Rabshakeh's speech and its attempt to get Hezekiah soldiers and people to desert him. The fact that Hezekiah is in such despair that he runs to the Temple and sends his ministers to see Isaiah would seem to indicate that there were deserters. This also just makes sense, in terms of normal human behavior. A great many people would be very afraid if the mightiest army in the world was pounding at the gates.

I am even more interested in the word later, which I have italicized in the citation. What does this mean? Why would Sennacherib take an IOU? The time to receive the tribute was while he was in the country. Promissory notes do not make for a triumphal return to Nineveh. If he needed to return home to quell uprisings, a great procession carrying the riches of a conquered country wouldn't hurt his standing. Still, if the Bible says that Hezekiah sent tremendous tribute to Sennacherib, and Sennacherib's account agrees, why not accept this simple fact?

We know from Assyrian evidence that after[12] Sennacherib returned to Assyria, he was assassinated, under dramatic circumstances. According to his grandson Ashurbanipal, Sennacherib seems to have been smashed alive with the idols of protective deities.[13] Sennacherib's son and successor Esarhaddon won a victory over his rebel brothers and chased them out of the country, which seems to be an exact parallel to the Biblical passage:[14]

Thereupon, my brothers went out of their senses, doing everything that is wicked in (the eyes of) the gods and mankind, and (continued) their evil machinations. They (even) drew weapons in the midst of Nineveh (which is) against (the will of) the gods, and butted each other—like kids—to take over the kingship.... But they, the usurpers, who had started the rebellion, deserted their (most) trustworthy troops, when they heard the approach of my expeditionary corps and fled to an unknown country.

Again, Isaiah was correct when he prophesied that "he will hear a rumor and return to his land, and I will make him fall by the sword in his land."

---

12 Whether this was soon after his return, or years afterward, is a question.
13 *ANET* 288-89.
14 *ANET* 289-90

It does not make any sense that Sennacherib would not have conquered Jerusalem, if he could have done so. He took Sidon, Ekron, Ashkelon, and other cities in the rebellion. Hezekiah was an important figure in the revolt against the Assyrian empire. Instead of being killed for his role, Hezekiah was allowed to continue as king and his city was unharmed. The question remains why.

Could it be that the Biblical account is backwards, that is, that the II Kings 18:13-16 should follow, and not precede II Kings 18:17-19:37? Hezekiah rebels, Sennacherib does not take Jerusalem, but Hezekiah does send him tribute at a later date. It is fascinating to see that in the Book of Isaiah 36-37, almost all of the Biblical text is duplicated, *except* 18:14-16. Isaiah 36:1-2 reads:

> In the fourteenth year of King Hezekiah, King Sennacherib of Assyria marched against all the fortified towns of Judah and seized them. From Lachish, the king of Assyria set the Rabshakeh…

Do you see the dramatic difference? In this Biblical text, the stripping of the Temple and the submission by Hezekiah is missing. Certainly, it is easy to say that the editor of Isaiah, or Isaiah himself, wanted to leave that part out. It is more interesting to think that this is the primary text and that a later editor put information about Hezekiah and Sennacherib in a confusing position in the II Kings version.

We saw above that II Kings 20:12-13 (cf. Isaiah 39:1-2; II Chron. 32:31) speaks of a visit of the ambassadors of Merodachbaladan, king of Babylon, to Jerusalem. This must have been before 701 BCE since Merodachbaladan was out of power in 701 BCE; the Assyrians had seen to that.[15] Yet this passage follows everything we've been reading in the present order of the Biblical texts.

Whether we would prefer to think like this or not, the Biblical order is out of sequence. We should be open to theories that try to find a valid historical sequence without denying the historicity of the Biblical information. Even the Talmudic rabbis were willing to accept such re-ordering. They said: "There is no such thing as early or late in the Torah."

The solution that Hezekiah sent the tribute to Assyria years after the siege of Jerusalem seems to deal with all of the evidence. The issue remains that II Kings 18:17-19:37 does follow II Kings 18:13-16.

---

15 When Sargon II, the Assyrian king, rose to power, Merodachbaladan seized the throne of Babylon. In 710 BCE, Sargon II deposed him. When Sennacherib rose to power in 705 BCE, Merodachbaladan again became king of Babylon. Sennacherib deposed him in 703 BCE. The embassy to Hezekiah would seem to be in the 705-703 BCE period when the Babylonian king sought allies against the Assyrians. It would not, however, fit after this time.

One Invasion or Two?

The need to follow the Bible's sequence of events has led to a popular theory that there were two invasions.[16] In the first one, in 701 BCE, Hezekiah sent great tribute to Sennacherib. In the second invasion, around 689 BCE, Hezekiah held out and Jerusalem was spared. The order of the Biblical passages remains intact. This theory seems to assume that if there were only one invasion, then the Biblical account about the catastrophe that befell the Assyrians at the gates of Jerusalem is false and the Bible is wrong. If, on the other hand, there were two invasions, then we can reconstruct the historical events and the Bible is accurate.

Those who have pushed the second invasion theory state that a key is the name Tirkahah, the Pharaoh of the story who leads an army north to help Hezekiah and the Israelites.

In 701 BCE, Tirkahah, this theory insists, was too young to be king. At that time, Shabaka was pharaoh from 716-702 BCE and Shebitku held the throne from 702-690 BCE. Tirkaha (Taharqa) ruled from 669-664 BCE. The name Tirkahah indicates that there was a second invasion, when Tirkahah was in his prime, c.688 BCE. This case became stronger when we find the name Tirkahah in the Assyrian evidence as well. Another reason why there must be two invasions is that before the first invasion, Isaiah gave prophecies that the Israelites were going to be severely punished by foreign invaders. It doesn't make sense for Isaiah to say that the Israelites were going to be punished and then, when the enemy is at the gates, to say that they were not going to be punished so that they needn't worry. If there were two invasions, the second invasion in 688 BCE would be the one involving the miraculous deliverance of Jerusalem. This fits with the timing that Sennacherib returns home and is killed shortly thereafter, in 687/86 BCE. Those who believe that there is only one invasion must explain why twenty years separate the invasion and retreat and the assassination and death of Sennacherib.

The scholars in the two-invasion camp add Greek evidence to their arsenal. Herodotus of Halicarnassus, born about 500 BCE, was a friend of Pericles and Sophocles. He became one of the famous travelers in world history, journeying throughout the ancient East, asking questions and creating one of the most important histories of ancient times. One of his famous visits was to Egypt, where a temple priest told him a strange story. It was about an invasion by Sennacherib of Egypt. His warriors with whom he had bad relations deserted the priest-king of Egypt. All looked lost for the Egyptian king, who prayed at the temple and was told that he would be helped by the god.

An army of field mice swarmed over their opponents in the night...gnawed through their quivers and their bows, and the handles of their shields, so that on the following day they fled minus their arms and a great number of them fell. Hence the

---

16 S. H. Horn "Did Sennacherib Campaign Once or Twice Against Hezekiah?" *AUSS* IV (1966) 1-28; B. Mazar "The Campaign of Sennacherib in Judaea" *EI* II (1953) 170-5.

king still stands in Hephaestus' temple with a mouse in his hand, and with the following inscription: 'Look on me and live in safety.' (2.141)

This passage is the origin of the theory that a plague in the Assyrian camp forced Sennacherib go back to Nineveh.[17] It is true that what Herodotus describes happens in Pelusium, at the gates of Egypt. The passage in Herodotus is somewhat garbled and it could, perhaps, be an account of what actually happened at Jerusalem.

As interesting as this theory is, it has at least two major problems:

- The Bible only has one invasion;
- While it is true that Tirkahah only became pharaoh in 690 BCE, he may have led a force up from Ethiopia when he was twenty. The Bible calls him the king of Kush. He comes from the south to help. He is not in Egypt; he is not pharaoh yet. So building a theory on the Tirkahah's dates as pharaoh is dangerous.[18]

The Theory of Two Stages In One Invasion

There are scholars who think that the two parts of the Biblical passage describe two stages of the campaign in 701.[19] Since the Bible does not indicate anything about two different invasions separated by over ten years, two stages of one invasion would fit the Biblical passage better. The problem remains: Why would Sennacherib try to conquer Jerusalem after Hezekiah had already given him so much silver and gold?

Nevertheless, this is the way the Bible describes the sequence of events. Instead of assuming that we understand the logic of ancient historical events better than the Bible does, let us assume that events happened just as the Bible says they did. I will follow the Biblical sequence with citations from Josephus, who is very helpful in putting the Biblical text together with the passage from Herodotus as follows:

1. Hezekiah and his allies rebel against Assyria;
2. The Assyrians invade the area;
3. Sennacherib demands three hundred talents of silver and thirty of gold;
4. Hezekiah tries to assuage the Assyrians by giving them the silver and gold;
5. Sennacherib is not mollified; while he goes on to fight in Egypt, he sends his ministers to Jerusalem.

---

17 One of the intriguing aspects of this passage is that rats = plague. See, for instance, I Samuel 6:4, where the mouse is the symbol of plague.

18 Kenneth A. Kitchen *The Third Intermediate Period in Egypt* (Warminster, 1973).

19 B. Mazar "The Campaign of Sennacherib in Judaea" *EI* II (1953) 170-5 (Hebrew); H. H. Rowley "Hezekiah's Reform and Rebellion" *BJRL* XLIV (1962) 395-431.

Here is Josephus:

So Hezekiah submitted, and emptied his treasures, and sent the money, as supposing he should be freed from his enemy, and from any further distress about his kingdom. Accordingly, the Assyrian king took it, and yet had no regard to what he had promised; but while he himself went to war against the Egyptians and Ethiopians, he left his general Rabshakeh, and two of the other principal commanders, with great forces, to destroy Jerusalem.

Antiquities 10.1.1

While Jerusalem is besieged, Sennacherib is besieging Pelusium at the gates of Egypt. He hears that Tirkahah, the king of the Ethiopians, is on his way to fight him. Sennacherib breaks the siege because, Josephus says quoting and correcting Herodotus, a multitude of mice attacked the Assyrians. Josephus also cites Berossus, who states that Sennacherib finds Rabshakeh and his forces at Jerusalem in danger from a plague and in great fear decides to go home where he was later assassinated.

We have a theory with one invasion, which takes the Biblical, archaeological and Assyrian evidence into account. It also leaves open the possibility of a miracle.

Reviewing the Evidence

In case you're confused by this whole discussion, I assure you that the question of one or two invasions is even more complicated than I am outlining here. Scholars such as Childs[20] conclude that we simply can't straighten out the confusion. The very existence of different theories, all of which are intelligent and all of which take evidence into account, simply means that we have to keep working at the problem.

Still, there is a great deal that we can conclude. Let us review the evidence:

1. We know that Sennacherib invaded Judaea (Biblical and Assyrian evidence).
2. We know that he didn't conquer the city (Assyrian and Biblical evidence).
3. We know how the Judaeans survived a siege (Biblical and archaeological evidence).
4. We do not know why the Assyrians left, but something dramatic seems to have happened (Biblical and perhaps Greek evidence).
5. We know that Sennacherib went home and was assassinated there (Biblical and Assyrian evidence).

Dual Causality and the Deliverance of Jerusalem

The evidence does not tell us why the Assyrians left but leave they did. If you have made a commitment of that magnitude to take a city, why leave without completing your mission?

---

20 Brevard S. Childs "Isaiah and the Assyrian Crisis" *SBT* II/3, 1967 118.

- Perhaps dual causality was at work. Perhaps there was a reason, a political reason that Sennacherib wanted to go home so urgently that he picked up camp and left all of a sudden.
- Perhaps he realized that he was not going to take Jerusalem any time soon and that he was not in a position to meet the Egyptians in battle.
- Perhaps disease did fall on the camp and Sennacherib was anxious to clear out before the plague took all of his men.
- And perhaps God was involved.
- Certainly that is the way the Bible speaks of this event.
- Was it a miracle of God? Was it the timing of a plague hitting at just the right moment? Miracles can be natural events that happen at just the right moment.
- Perhaps it was dual causality, some political or natural cause, and a Divine Cause.
- Perhaps there were human acts in Jerusalem and Assyria as well as an act of God. Perhaps the humans in Jerusalem held out, drinking water from the tunnel, and then something miraculous happened.

As for me, I keep thinking about that angel of the LORD and I wonder what exactly it was that he did on that night that saved Jerusalem. I wake up in the morning and run to the walls and say, "Oh my God, Isaiah was right."

Postscript on the Theme of "Enemies at the Gates": The Miraculous Deliverance of Sacred Cities

The Huns, under Attila the Hun led his mighty forces from Asia across Europe to Rome. Attila, known fondly as "The Scourge of God," attacked but didn't take Rome. Somehow, according to history, the Pope, Leo I, convinced Attila not to take Rome.

The visual in my mind comes from a movie I saw countless times as a kid, "The Sign of the Pagan," starring Jack Palance as Attila. Attila has dreams about a man in white coming to see him. When Pope Leo comes dressed in white across the mist to see him, Attila realizes that he is participating in the fulfillment of his dream. He listens to Leo's entreaties and does not conquer Rome.

I was always fascinated by this scene because it merged in my mind with another visual, that of Alexander the Great and the High Priest of the Jewish people. I knew a story about the historical figure known as Alexander the Great (I now know too much about him to call him "Great"). In the story, Alexander is on his way to Jerusalem on his epoch-making conquest of the known world. He was going to take Jerusalem, but a High Priest comes out dressed in white. Alexander had had a dream that fit with the scene, so he decided to leave Jerusalem alone.

The two scenes converge in my mind: The priests in white, coming out of the city to meet the conquering, world-famous invader.

When I became immersed in the world of scholarship as an adult, I pursued my interest in the story of Alexander and the High Priest. By the time I finished my research, I came to the conclusion that the story was apocryphal, that is, legendary and non-historical. Alexander, as far as historians can tell, never went near Jerusalem. I now understand the story of the High Priest and Alexander as symbolic. The Jewish people, led by their ranking political and religious person, the High Priest, showed respect and submission to Alexander who in return did not destroy them or sack their beloved Jerusalem. However, the actual scene of Alexander approaching Jerusalem and being moved by the man in white who matched his dream never happened.

Once I had come to terms with the non-historical nature of the Alexander story, my mind shifted back to the Attila parallel. If the original story is legendary, what did that tell me about its later imitation? That is, I began to think that perhaps the Attila and Leo story is also legendary. Indeed, it is.

In the summer of 452 CE, a delegation of three men was sent to Attila from Rome. The meeting took place on the banks of the Mincio River. Two leading senators and Pope Leo I were sent. One senator, Trigetius, the Prefect of Rome, was an experienced negotiator who had reached an agreement with a Vandal king. The other, Gennadius Avienus, was a rich and successful politician who was in charge of Rome's water supplies. Pope Leo seems to have been the third man in the delegation. Since they were begging Attila to go away, he received the delegates while lying at ease in his tent.

Attila decided not to conquer Rome. Historians are not sure why. There had been a terrible famine in the land. There might have been malaria due to a shortage of food and water. Reinforcements were on their way. It might have been time to go home to Hungary before winter came.

A famous painting by Raphael has captured the imaginations of people across the centuries. The painting represents Pope Leo the Great who, with the assistance of God, prevented the Huns from attacking Rome. Here is a description of the painting:

> In 452 CE Pope Leo I managed to halt Attila the Hun, on his way to invade Rome, at the river Mincio near Mantua. The Eternal City was thus saved from destruction. In the fresco, Leo X, in the figure of his namesake, is riding with great dignity in the company of his retinue towards the Huns, who are galloping into the picture from the right. A mere wave of Leo's hand is enough to repel them. At left, the Pope and his attendants, poised and solemn, offer a gesture of peace to the Huns. Above them, Saints Peter and Paul wield a sword. At right, Attila and his attendants, on horseback, are scared to death of the two saints.[21]

21 The figure of the Pope on horseback is a portrait of Leo X. It was originally intended to

This painting is clearly a legendary and religious interpretation of what happened. Listen, however to how it is taken as historical:

Attila descended on Italy, sacking and pillaging cities as he moved toward Rome. It was at this point that he was confronted by Pope Leo I at the head of a delegation of Roman senators. According to the best account, Pope Leo, "an old man of harmless simplicity, venerable in his gray hair and majestic clothing," was suddenly and miraculously joined by Saints Peter and Paul, swords in their hands and clad in bishops' robes. Their appearance at this critical moment was especially noteworthy because both saints had been dead for nearly four hundred years. Whether because of this marvel or because his army was dying from heat and plague, Attila withdrew once again from the Western Europe.[22]

I am struck by the fact that there seems to be a greater acceptance of a Christian miracle than of the Biblical one.

Isaiah doesn't go out of the gates of Jerusalem to meet Sennacherib, so the stories of Alexander and Attila are not complete parallels to the Assyrian story. Yet there is a suggestive parallel in that we have three sudden withdrawals of mighty forces because of the peaceful intercession or entreaty of high religious figures and/or the miracles of God. God is involved in the Assyrian story, in the dream sent to Alexander, in the miraculous manifestations of the saints.

I am not saying that all three are made up. In fact, I take the Assyrian withdrawal as a historical fact corroborated by Assyrian documents.

Something happens to us as we learn more about history and how history is written. As we learn that much of history is legend, we tend to think that all history is legend. We get to a point when we think that a fictional story is as important and historical as a real-life event.

I am saying that the miraculous deliverance of Jerusalem led to a type of story, which we can call the "Miraculous Deliverance of Sacred Cities." First, there was an event. Then there were legends that imitated the event. Those later imitations should not prejudice us against the first event that really happened.

---

represent Julius II, but the Della Rovere Pope died before the completion of the cycle, and his portrait was substituted for that of his successor.

22 C.Warren Hollister *Medieval Europe: A Short History* (Boston, 1998) 36-7.

Chapter XI

A Time For Treason
Or
The Comfort In Destruction

I was living in Jerusalem in a dangerous time, after the invasion of the Chaldean Babylonians. Those mighty conquerors came to Jerusalem[1] and took off many of the leading citizens of my land. They even took the sacred vessels of the Temple.

Then things calmed down for a while. King Zedekiah, a descendant of King David and all of the other Judean kings, was thinking about revolting against the Babylonians. We had been living too long under their yoke. We were Judeans, the chosen ones of God. We needed to be free.

It was a dangerous time, but to tell the truth, my blood was racing with excitement. I went to the Temple to see what was going on and who was saying what.

There was Jeremiah. I despised Jeremiah. He was one of those prophets who never had anything good to say. He weakened our hands. He was always making terrible predictions. He was always saying that the people were sinful and were going to be punished. He was a lot like that other prophet, Uriah. Uriah gave a terribly rebellious speech against the last king, saying all sorts of treasonous things. The king wanted to kill him. So Uriah fled to Egypt. The king's men went all the way to Egypt and brought him back to the king. They killed him and threw his body into a mass grave. Good riddance; but somehow, somebody was protecting Jeremiah, somebody high up in the government, so Jeremiah got to live. There had been a lot of debates about whether to kill him or not, but he was there, screaming away. He made me cringe.

How obnoxious could anyone be? He wore a yoke, like he was an ox. The symbolism was that the Judeans should live under the yoke of the Babylonians. However, we didn't want to live under those foreigners. Freedom or death.

Now another prophet, one who I could respect, got up. His name was Hananiah son of Azzur. He came from the ancient and sacred town of Gibeon, a great birthplace for a prophet, if you asked me. Hananiah gave a great speech:

---

1 In what we would call 597 BCE; I will present extra-Biblical evidence below.

Thus said the LORD of Hosts, the God of Israel: I hereby break the yoke of the king of Babylon. In two years, I will restore to this place all the vessels of the House of the LORD which King Nebuchadnezzar of Babylon took from this place and brought to Babylon. And I will bring back to this place King Jeconiah son of Jehoiakim of Judah, and all the Judean exiles who went to Babylon—declares the LORD. Yes, I will break the yoke of the king of Babylon.

Jeremiah 28:2-4

Everybody understood what he was saying. He was quoting the great prophet Isaiah, the one who correctly prophesied the deliverance of Jerusalem a hundred years ago. Isaiah said that God would break the yoke of the Assyrians from the neck of our people:

And in that day
His burden shall drop from your back,
And his yoke from your neck,
The yoke shall be destroyed because of fatness.

Isaiah 10:27

Hananiah's prophecy was the new, updated version of what Isaiah said. When Hananiah spoke those words in the Temple, in front of the priests and the people, we were all thrilled. This was the best possible news possible under the circumstances. All the people who had been taken away, the sacred vessels of the Temple with all their symbolic and real monetary value, would all be brought back to their rightful place.

Jeremiah couldn't let it be. He sarcastically said "Amen! May the LORD do so!" He said that prophets usually bring bad news and that the people should be wary of what Hananiah said. If a prophet prophesied good things, it was only when those things actually happened that you knew that they had the Word of God:

So if a prophet prophesies good fortune, then only when the word of the prophet comes true can it be known that the LORD really sent him.

Jeremiah 28:9—the dramatic confrontation between Jeremiah and Hananiah got so tense that Hananiah removed the bar from Jeremiah's neck and broke it. In an incredible, symbolic gesture, and with courage worthy of a great prophet, Hananiah said that in the same way, God would break the yoke of the Babylonians.

Jeremiah did not say anything. Hananiah had clearly won. Then Jeremiah came back another day. He said that he had now heard the Word of God himself. He begged us to serve the king of Babylon. He answered Hananiah about the bars he had broken:

You broke bars of wood, but you shall make bars of iron instead.

What he meant was that even though Hananiah had broken the bars of wood, God would make bars of iron that could not be broken. The Judeans would serve the Babylonians, no matter what they said or did. Jeremiah warned us that if we didn't listen to this message, the city would be destroyed. He went further and said that Hananiah wouldn't live out the year. Jeremiah knew that Hananiah's speech was a false prophecy. How could he know this? He had already heard a very different message from God. He didn't need anyone to take his word for it. The proof would be in the poisonous pudding.

Unfortunately, Jeremiah was right. I wish Hananiah had been right. I wish the Temple had not been destroyed and Jerusalem ruined. I wish that there were a Book of Hananiah, as there is a Book of Isaiah, which recorded the prophecies about the salvation of Jerusalem that had come true.

I stood there in the Temple, watching those astonishing scenes. I believed Hananiah. I wanted him to be right. My hope and optimism, my patriotism, even my faith in God, compelled me to believe him—and the people followed him.

We revolted and the Temple and Jerusalem were destroyed.

I was wrong, dead wrong. Like Hananiah, who was dead within the year; just as Jeremiah had predicted.[2]

You Wouldn't Want to Be a Prophet

The simplistic fantasy I presented in the last section is a quick attempt to make a point: The best way to study history is to understand the challenges and choices faced by the people of a particular time and place. Hananiah vs. Jeremiah is a debate about what would happen at that time, but it is also a revealing scene for our understanding of prophecy.

Why are there no prophets today? Certainly, there are people who have the oratorical abilities of a prophet. There are those who speak for the covenant of God and rush to defend it and promote it.

Seeing into the future might seem like a great gift. Imagine if you could predict the stock market or the outcome of sports events. You would be a very wealthy person very quickly. The prophets couldn't have played the financial markets for profits if they'd wanted to. Prophecy didn't work like that. These are not the kinds of things a prophet would know. You have never heard of prophets making profits from financial markets. Jeremiah did, however, use his knowledge to make a symbolic statement by buying a field from a kinsman (Jeremiah 32:7-14); his point was that after the destruction would come, Judah would be restored and normal commercial transactions would take place again.

Think about what it would mean to see the future, to know how long you and your loved ones are going to live, to know the manner of your death. Believe me,

---

2 While the text does not come to the explicit theological conclusion that Hananiah was a false prophet, the *LXX* in 35:1 = *MT* 28:1 says exactly that.

you do not want to know these things. No one wants to hear about the consequences of our actions. We'd rather live in blissful ignorance. The personal losses of the prophets were profound. Think about being Elijah, Amos or Jeremiah. What tragic, lonely, isolated lives! Jeremiah was asked to carry out one of the most difficult tasks ever assigned to any prophet of God. During the last years of the kingdom of Judah, Jeremiah was to prophesy that because of their sin they must accept the yoke of Babylon and not resist. He was imprisoned, opposed by false prophets, threatened with death, and viewed as a traitor. Yet through him God prophesied the exile and return of the Judeans to their land.

Prophets are given what they're given. The prophets get glimpses of the wave of God, the streaming cause of God, at certain points in history. They turn their radios on and hear the news reports of what is to come and why.

However, there is dual causality. So when Jeremiah tells the people what will happen if they rebel, he does it beforehand, so that they can change their minds before it is too late. The fall of Jerusalem will not necessarily happen. They do not have to rebel against the Babylonians. They can remain loyal subjects and avert a disaster.

Unfortunately, they do not. Of their own free will, they rebel against the Babylonians and get clobbered in one of the worst catastrophes in Jewish history, so terrible that it is still remembered in an annual fast day called *Tish`ah b'Av*, the "Ninth of Av," the day when the Temple was destroyed in 587/86 BCE. More than two thousand five hundred years later, we still mourn the day these events happened.

Yet it was a day that did not have to be. Sometimes, we are our worst enemies.

How De We Know That All This Happened?

The Book of Jeremiah takes us back into the time before the destruction of Jerusalem in 587/586 BCE. Archaeology has provided a number of discoveries dating from the time of Jeremiah that give us virtually first hand evidence of the situation prior to the Babylonian invasion and siege of Jerusalem and the fall of the city. First, I will review some of the key dates:

• 605 BCE. Nebuchadnezzar becomes king of Babylon & defeats the Pharaoh Necho.

• 598 BCE. Jerusalem is captured by Babylon. Nebuchadnezzar takes the king of Judah, Jehoiakim to Babylon. Jehoiachin reigns three months and is then also taken to Babylon. Zedekiah (Mattaniah) is made king.

• 589 BCE. Zedekiah rebels against Babylon and Jerusalem is besieged.

- 587 BCE. Jerusalem falls to Babylon and the Temple is burned. Zedekiah's sons are killed in front of him and then he is blinded, and imprisoned. Captives are taken to Babylon. Gedaliah is made governor.
- 586 BCE. Gedaliah is murdered.

Do we have any record from the Babylonian side of the conquest of Judah and Jerusalem? Yes. Babylonian records verify parts of the Biblical account such as the deposing of Jehoiachin (II Kings 24:10-17) and the provisions supplied to him according to II Kings 25:27-30.[3] See also this important citation:[4]

> Year 7, month Kislimu: The king of Akkad moved his army into Hatti land, laid siege to the city of Judah and the king took the city on the second day of the month Adarru. He appointed in it a (new) king of his liking, took heavy booty from it and brought it into Babylon.

It is strange to see this notice in the annals of King Nebuchadnezzar. It is just one more entry in a log, one more annual campaign of conquest. To the Biblical psyche, it was one of the great traumas and cataclysms of all time. It was to its age what the Shoah (the Holocaust) is to ours.

In studying Biblical archaeology and in searching for extra-Biblical evidence, it is always important to remember that significant events for the Biblical record may not have been significant at all to anyone else. This does not make the events fictional. Indeed, this simple principle can be used as an argument for the possibility of the factuality of Biblical data when no other data exists.

"We Cannot See Azekah"

In the case of the Babylonian conquest of Jerusalem, as luck would have it, there is still more extra-Biblical data.

The discovery of the Lachish ostraca (inscribed potsherds) in the 1930's[5] was of great importance for the historical record. The city of Lachish, which we mentioned in the chapter on Isaiah, was one of the few remaining cities prior to the complete collapse of the kingdom of Judea (Jeremiah 34:7). Lachish was a fortress at the western approaches to the Judean hills, the southwester frontier. It was huge, encompassing some eighteen acres. The city was surrounded by a double wall and was strengthened by towers and buttresses. It had an inner and an outer gateway.

Details of the invasion of Judah by Nebuchadnezzar mentioned by Jeremiah in Jeremiah 34:7 have been dramatically verified by these letters, written to the

---

3 *ANET* 308.

4 *ANET* 564

5 The ostraca were found in the ruins of the latest occupation level at Tell ed-Duweir in southern Israel. The first eighteen were discovered by J. L. Starkey in 1935 and three more were found three years later. See Harry Torczyner *The Lachish Letters* (London, 1938) and *Te'udot Lakhish* (Jerusalem, 1940).

commander of Lachish from another outpost in the fight. According to the Book of Jeremiah, Lachish and Azekah were the last strongholds to fall:

The prophet Jeremiah spoke all these words to King Zedekiah of Judah in Jerusalem, when the army of the king of Babylon was waging war against Jerusalem and against the remaining towns of Judah—against Lachish and Azekah, for they were the only fortified towns of Judah that were left.

A letter that has been discovered powerfully presents us with a scene from inside the situation of the embattled Judeans:

And let (my lord) know that we are watching for the signals of Lachish, according to all the indications which my lord hath given, for we cannot see Azekah.

The writer of the letter, Hawshi`yahu, is telling his superior officer, Ya'ush, the governor or commanding officer of Lachish, that while his men are dutifully carrying out their responsibilities as ordered through fire-signals (a method of communication referred to, incidentally, in Jeremiah 6:1), they have lost contact with the fortress of Azekah (Tell Zakariya). It seems that Azekah had already fallen, or at least had been cut off by the enemy's forces. One cannot help but feel the fear in the heart of the writer of this letter. He and his men carry on, but they know that there is little time left. They are living on the eve of destruction.

In the letters, Hawshi`yahu seems to be defending himself against charges, perhaps of being a part of some pro-Babylonian intrigue (*Ostraca* II, V, VI). One of the letters also refers to a "prophet" who was seen to be demoralizing the people and instigating a policy of non-resistance to the Babylonians—this suggests the events surrounding Uriah the prophet in Jeremiah 26:20-21 to whom I referred above in my little fantasy (or to Jeremiah himself in Jeremiah 38:1-4). King Jehoiakim executed the prophet Uriah from Kiryath-Yearim "who prophesied against this city and against this land words like those of Jeremiah" (Jeremiah 26:20). He had fled to Egypt and was forcibly brought back to Judah to be killed for treason. Since this Uriah was already dead by the time of the letter, it could not refer to him. The story is told to emphasize the danger prophets exposed themselves to in taking on the king and his policies. In *Ostracon* VI, the writer says that the king and his official were angered against a prophet most of whose name is illegible, but who had the final suffices *yahu*. This prophet is accused of "weakening the hands" of the people, to make them slacken in their loyalty to the king and their resistance to the Babylonians. *Ostracon* III may be related in telling us that men have gone down to bring the prophet back for judgment. Unlike others, I do not think that it could refer to Uriah or Jeremiah; Uriah was already dead and Jeremiah would flee to Egypt later. These *ostraca* do show, however, exactly the king of prophetic activity that Uriah and Jeremiah were engaged in during these tumultuous and dangerous years.

A prophet such as Hananiah would be considered loyal to the kingdom; Uriah, Jeremiah, Baruch and the unnamed prophet of the Lachish letter would be considered traitors. It is fascinating to compare the Biblical text with an archaeological artifact:

> Then the officials said to the king, "Let this man be put to death, for he weakens the hands of the soldiers, and all the people who are left in the city, by speaking such things to them. That man is not seeking the welfare of this people, but their harm!"
>
> Jeremiah 38:4

> And behold the words of the prophet are not good, but to weaken our hands and slacken the hands of the men
>
> *Lachish Ostracon* VI

In both cases, one from the Bible and the other from an archaeological find, we see the same accusation leveled against those who object to the will of the state.

Treason means acting or speaking against the state; there is, however, a time for treason. When God tells you that the will of the state will destroy the kingdom and its people, it is a time for treason. God, just for the record, was only too right.

The reality of the situation as described in the Bible, and the opposition to the forces that caused it, is thus confirmed for us.

We may have proved that the Bible's account of the destruction of Jerusalem was correct. We have not, however, corroborated the story of Jeremiah. Is there any evidence concerning the prophet?

Baruch the Scribe

For all of their loneliness, at least some of the prophets had disciples and helpers who contributed to their work and perhaps shared some of their hardships. Jeremiah had a scribe named Baruch, the son of Neriah.

The Book of Jeremiah tells us that in King Jehoiachim's fourth year (c.605 BCE), God speaks to Jeremiah about the future of Judah. God wants Jeremiah to write His words on a scroll in the hope that words of warning will convince the king and his people to change their ways. Such repentance would save the people from impending disaster (Jeremiah 36:3). Jeremiah dictates his words to his scribe and friend Baruch (36:4). Since Jeremiah is in hiding for his personal safety, he sends Baruch to read the scroll in the temple.

> It was then that Baruch—in the chamber of Gemariah son of Shaphan the scribe, in the upper court, near the new gateway of the House of the Lord— read the words of Jeremiah from the scroll to all the people in the House of the Lord.
>
> Jeremiah 36:10

The scroll urges the people to accept the inevitability of Babylon's control and repent. When Micaiah son of Gemariah son of Shaphan and some noblemen hear the words, they take Baruch aside and urge him to go into hiding with Jeremiah while they appeal to the king (Jeremiah 36:11-19). As the scroll (which seems to have been taken by the officials) is read to Jehoiakim, he has the columns burned. The king then commands his son Jerahmeel and others to seize Baruch and Jeremiah 36:20-26. The king may have burned the scroll but God's words are more resilient than that; Jeremiah dictates God's words all over again to Baruch (36:32). Biblical texts and God's words are, no matter what anyone does, indestructible.

In a personally poignant passage,[6] God tells Jeremiah to dictate a prophecy to Baruch concerning Baruch himself:

> Thus said the LORD, the God of Israel, concerning you, Baruch: You say, "Woe is me! The LORD has added grief to my pain. I am worn out with groaning, and I have found no rest." Thus shall you speak to him: "Thus said the LORD: I am going to overthrow what I have built, and uproot what I have planted— this applies to the whole land. And do you expect great things for yourself? Do not expect them. For I am going to bring disaster upon all flesh—declares the LORD— but I will at least grant your life in all the places where you may go."
>
> Jeremiah 45:2-5

Baruch is not to seek "great things" for himself but is promised that his life will be spared when Jerusalem falls.[7]

When Jerusalem falls and captives are taken away, Gedaliah is made the governor of Judah (587/6 BCE). When Gedaliah is assassinated, some want to flee to Egypt to escape the control of Babylon. When Jeremiah declares God's opposition to this plan, some charge:

> You are lying! The LORD our God did not send you to say, "Do not go to Egypt and sojourn there!" It is Baruch son of Neriah who is inciting you against us, so that we will be delivered into the hands of the Chaldeans to be killed or to be exiled to Babylon!"
>
> Jeremiah 43:3

---

6 In the fourth year of Jehoiakim's reign (605 BCE).

7 Seventeen years later (588 BCE), when Jeremiah was imprisoned by Zedekiah during the Babylonian siege, Baruch was entrusted with the purchase deeds of a field Jeremiah bought as a sign of the Jews return (Jeremiah 32:1-16). Baruch was to put the deeds in an earthen vessel, "that they may last many days." This demonstrated that, "houses and fields and vineyards shall be possessed again in this land" (Jeremiah 32:14, 15).

Baruch seems to have been viewed as an ally of Babylon because he declared God's punishment by their hand.[8]

One could not reasonable expect that archaeology would provide any evidence relating to Baruch, a minor figure in the Biblical corpus. And yet the luck of the archaeological draw has netted us impressive evidence of Baruch's life and work.

Baruch's Fingerprint

In 1975, the first few pieces of 200 clay *bullae* were discovered in the shop of an antiquities dealer in East Jerusalem. The bullae, made of fingernail-sized lumps of soft clay shaped as flat disks, were affixed to a string binding a papyrus document and then impressed with the seal mark of the owner. To open and read the document, the *bulla* sealing had to be broken in order to separate it from the string. From the shape of its Hebrew characters (which changed over the centuries), scholars date the collection to the 6th century BCE, the time of Jeremiah.

Within this collection are two *bullae* believed to have belonged to Baruch and Jerahmeel, the king's son. The three lines on the Baruch *bulla* read: "(belonging) to Berechyahu son of Neriyahu the scribe." [9] Berechyahu is the longer spelling of the name of Baruch. Berechyahu means "YHWH has blessed"; "Yahu" is a shortened form of the Divine Name. The find in a royal archive that includes his patronym (father's name) suggests that he came from a prominent scribal family.

In another find, we see the clear impression of a fingerprint on the upper left of the *bulla*. It is not so far-fetched to suggest that this is Baruch's fingerprint. At the very least, such discoveries remind us that the people of the Bible were real people.

Baruch came from a prominent family. His brother Seriah was a trusted courtier in the time of King Zedekiah who was sent on a vital mission to Babylon (Jeremiah 59:64). The collection of *bulla* includes the names of many royal officials. It is more than possible that a royal archive has been discovered and that Baruch served, at one point or another, as a scribe or official in the court. Perhaps, Avigad has suggested, Baruch left his official position to aid Jeremiah. Baruch seems to have held pro-Babylonian views, a minority position at the court. It is nothing short of tragic that Baruch and Jeremiah did not convince the king and court of God's judgment and of the better political course. Jerusalem was destroyed as a result.

Still another seal-*bulla* found in excavations in Jerusalem reads, "belonging to Gemariah son of Shaphan." Gemariah son of Shaphan was a high official at the court of King Jehoiakim. We saw his name above; he was among the first audience

---

8 Both Baruch and Jeremiah were taken by force to Egypt with others who had been spared captivity (Jeremiah 43:1-7). They probably died there.

9 Shanks "Jeremiah's Scribe and Confidant Speaks from a Hoard of Clay Bullae" *BAR* Vol. XIII:5 (September/October 1987) 58-65; idem "Fingerprint of Jeremiah's Scribe" *BAR* March/April 1996. N. Avigad "Baruch the Scribe and Jerahmeel the King's Son" *IEJ* 28 (1978) 52-56; idem *Hebrew Bullae from the Time of Jeremiah* (Jerusalem, 1986).

ever to hear the prophecy (Jeremiah 36:12-13) and he tried to dissuade the king from burning the scroll (Jeremiah 36:25). The Micaiah who tried to help Jeremiah and Baruch was Gemariah's son.

This evidence should be enough to convince an objective person of the reality of the Book of Jeremiah.

Concluding Unscientific Postscript: The Hope Of Prophecy

If the prophecies are real, then there is hope. There is an incredible rabbinic story about Rabbi Aqiba. He is walking with three other famous rabbis toward Rome. They hear the sound of the traffic of Rome. The other rabbis start crying but Rabbi Aqiba starts laughing. They cry because Jerusalem is in ruins but its conquerors are riding high. Rabbi Aqiba laughs because if God has allowed the evil people to be so successful, he will certainly help good people to be successful.

Another time, when the rabbis go up to Jerusalem to the mountain of the house of the Temple, they cry to see the Temple in ruins but Rabbi Aqiba laughs. He tells them that just as God has spoken through his prophets who had predicted that Jerusalem would fall again, there were prophets who had predicted the rise of Jerusalem again.

> He said to them, "That is the very reason I have laughed. For lo, it is written, 'And I will take for me faithful witnesses to record, Uriah the priest and Zechariah the son of Jeberechiah' (Is. 8:2).
> And what has Uriah got to do with Zechariah? What is it that Uriah said? 'Zion shall be plowed as a field and Jerusalem shall become heaps and the mountain of the Lord's house as the high places of a forest' (Jer. 26:18).
> "What is it that Zechariah said? 'Thus says the Lord of hosts, "Old men and women shall yet sit in the broad places of Jerusalem"' (Zech. 8:4).
> "Said the Omnipresent, 'Lo, I have these two witnesses. If the words of Uriah have been carried out, then the words of Zechariah will be carried out. If the words of Uriah are nullified, then the words of Zechariah will be nullified.
> "'Therefore I was happy that the words of Uriah have been carried out, so that in the end the words of Zechariah will come about.'"
> In this language they replied to him: "Aqiba, you have given us comfort."
> *Sifré Devarim* 43:3:7-8[10]

I discuss and cite this story at length because it summarizes the comfort and hope that the study of prophecy and history can bring us. The rabbis, in their unhistorical way, take two witnesses in the time of Isaiah (late 700s BCE), Uriah and Zechariah, and mix them up with the later prophets Uriah (early 500s BCE) and

---

10 See Jacob Neusner *Sifré Devarim* 45.

Zechariah (late 500s BCE). The later Uriah is the prophet I have mentioned several times in this chapter; he prophesied the ruin of Jerusalem. Zechariah, living during the rebuilding of Jerusalem, is a prophet who looks forward to a glorious future for the city and its people. Rabbi Aqiba says that both prophets are witnesses to the power of God. The story points out that it is not only in the prophecy of salvation in Isaiah that we can find sustenance. Even reviewing the stories and prophecies of those prophets who predicted doom, such as Elijah, Amos and Jeremiah, can be reassuring because we verify predictions and thereby demonstrate the Will of God in history. For a God who will act in history is exactly what this world needs.

Chapter XII

Love Is Stronger Than Death
Or
What Did the Israelites of the Biblical Period Really Believe About Death and the Afterlife?

Let me be a seal upon your heart,
As the seal upon your hand.
For love is as strong as death,
Passion as mighty as Sheol.

Song of Songs 8:6

Reading these moving, poetic words, one of the most beautiful similes in the Bible, we think about the power of love. It is a touching, romantic sentiment and we are now in a position to understand this verse in all of its dimensions. Archaeology has provided us with a great deal of information about the use of seals in the ancient world.[1] Seals were often funerary offerings that were contributed to the burial for various reasons.

Commenting on the verse from the Song of Songs cited above, William W. Hallo states that " ... the beloved wishes to be as intimate with her lover as the two seals worn by him, the stamp seal carried on his wrist and the cylinder seal worn around his neck which rests on his heart."

How does the seal overcome death? In the ancient Near Eastern world, a person was buried with tools, weapons, and other private possessions including seals. A seal reflected the owner's status or occupation. So the beloved wants the status-symbol function of the seal in burial; the seal perpetuates the owner's standing in death. In the same way, the beloved declares that her lover's role in her life will outlive him; his status as her lover will persevere even in the grave. Love is as strong as death.

---

1 William W. Hallo, "As The Seal Upon Thine Arm": Glyptic Metaphors in the Biblical World," in *Ancient Seals and the Bible* eds. Leonard Gorelick and Elizabeth Williams-Forte (Malibu, Cal.: Undena, 1983) 7-17.

Hallo has helped us, in this example, to find our way back into the full meaning of the verse. I am even more moved by the power of the love expressed here now that I know what the expression meant to the poet and his/her world.

I bring Hallo's discovery as more than an example of the uses of archaeology. There is a lesson here concerning what we do not understand about a basic belief of the Biblical world. We are so unaware of the real feeling about the afterlife in ancient Israel that we cannot understand dimensions of many Biblical texts. It is instructive, therefore, to think about why a person would take tools, weapons, and seals into the grave; we are not only dealing with symbolic gestures but with the concept of a life after death which requires tools, weapons and seals.

Hold on. Haven't we always heard and read that the Bible doesn't believe in an afterlife? Do not we constantly, triumphantly proclaim the rational anticipation of modern resistance to such beliefs? Many of us admire the Bible's precocious resistance to things that we consider to be nonsense.

We have seen, however, what we have wished to see. Evidence from both Biblical texts and archaeology is accumulating that should make us revise our ironclad notion that the Bible as a whole is against a belief in the afterlife. A number of scholars, including Elizabeth Bloch-Smith and Mark S. Smith (working in tandem and individually),[2] have taken a new look at a basic assumption concerning the beliefs of the ancient Israelites.

Some background about the study of religion is necessary here. During any period of history, the official laws and beliefs of a religion do not necessarily tell us very much about what most people in that culture actually practiced or thought. The religion of ideologues and cultic functionaries will almost always be quite different from that of the common person. The religious leaders will often attempt to promote changes that they deem necessary, but the adherents of their faith will not always readily accept those changes. The average person is more likely to accept observances and ideas from other religions than will leaders whose lives are totally immersed in their particular cultic world.

In the case of Israelite religion, these simple propositions hold true for the differing attitudes toward beliefs and practices about the dead. While at a certain point in time, the official state religion in Judah attempted to rid the society of a number of aspects of the cult of the dead; the Judeans for the most part ignored the prescribed changes and went on about their business as usual. This meant that they continued to feed, consult with, and mourn the dead as they always had.

---

2 Mark S. Smith *The Early History of God: Yahweh and the Other Deities in Ancient Israel* (San Francisco: Harper and Row, 1990); E. M. Bloch-Smith *Judahite Burial Practices and Beliefs about the Dead* (*JSOT* Sup 123; Sheffield: *JSOT*, 1992).

Just because the official religion wants to rid the culture of a belief or observance does not mean that the culture is now rid of it. The people, whether because of outside influences or their own longstanding tendencies, liked their afterlife just as it had always been. A king, a prophet, or a priest might object, but that objection did not necessarily change a thing. The Bible is the product of prophets, kings and priests and does not always tell us what we would like to know about the actual religious practice of the common people. Often, we can learn what the people believed and observed by reading what the Bible denounced about their lives.

"Like The Beasts That Perish"

I will use the example of Psalm 49 to demonstrate that what certain Biblical texts say about the afterlife, and what ancient Judeans actually believed, are two very different things. I will also show that the Bible may not be as anti-afterlife as we have been led to believe.

Psalm 49 is found in the *siddur*, the Prayer Book, as a prayer placed between two recitations of the Mourner's Kaddish. As a congregational rabbi, I often lead the service at the *shiva minyan*, the service at the house of mourning. I am there to try to console the family. I have had enormous difficult reciting Psalm 49; is it consolation to read that human beings die like animals?

"Human beings do not live on in honor, They are like the beasts that perish."

I have taken up the practice of reciting Psalm 23, "The Lord Is My Shepherd," instead; God leads us safely through the valley of the shadow of death. This poem of consolation certainly seems much more appropriate for the house of mourning.

What about Psalm 49 and its stark, seemingly modern appraisal of the darkness of death? What does Psalm 49 tell us about the cult of the dead in ancient Israel? Psalm 49 contains a number of allusions to Israelite practices and beliefs about death. Verse 10 refers to the grave; verses 15 and 16 both refer explicitly to Sheol, the netherworld. Verse 15 pictures death as a shepherd. The deceased will join "the company of his ancestors" according to verse 20. Verse 12 is even more interesting:

Their graves are their homes forever
their dwelling place to all generations
they invoke their (ancestors') names over their (family) lands.

Invoking the names of ancestors means to summon the dead in order to affirm the family ownership of the land, to ensure that the land will remain in their possession forever.

The point of Psalm 49 is about wealthy people who "want to take it with them." They live and die for their wealth and property. These rich people first maintain their ancestral cult with their burials, their "eternal homes," and then wrongly comfort themselves by indulging in the custom of summoning their deceased ancestors.

The psalmist tells us that we cannot take it with us:

> For when he dies he can take none of it along
> his goods cannot follow him down.

So far, we can learn that there were practices in ancient Israel that were rejected by the official spokesmen such as the psalmist. The whole reason for the psalm is to denounce such practices as expensive burials and summoning the dead. One denounces that which is going on.

There is another aspect of Psalm 49 that needs to be emphasized:

> Sheeplike they head for Sheol
> with Death as their shepherd
> The upright shall rule over them at daybreak
> and their form shall waste away in Sheol
> till its nobility be gone.

The bad news is that you do not take it with you to the afterlife. The good news is that, first of all, there is an afterlife, and more importantly, that God can save you from a bad afterlife and take you to Himself.

> But God will redeem my life from the clutches of
> Sheol for He will take me.
>
>   v.16

Expensive Burials

What is it that the psalmist is attacking? Does he really care if some people are silly enough to believe that they *can* take it with them? Or is he responding to seriously-held, widespread practices in his religious culture?

The latter is clearly the case, as we know from the evidence of a large number of excavated mortuary remains from cave and bench tombs in ancient Judah. These tombs were the final resting-places for people who believed that they would continue in some form of existence and were thus provided with the basic necessities of life and some amenities; vessels with food and liquid, lamps for light, jewelry and amulets for protection, models to invoke sympathetic magic, personal items and tools. The body itself was dressed and adorned with jewelry including rings, earrings, necklaces, and bangles.

Remember: I am not describing what was found inside the pyramids of Egypt but in the tombs of Israelites in Judah. Food is to be eaten, jewelry to be worn. You take it with you if you're planning on using it.

In other words, Israelites during Biblical times believed not only in the vague netherworld of Sheol that we hear in the usual descriptions but in a very physical continued existence.

Family Religion

What of the reference in Psalm 49:12 to the invocation of the names of the ancestors? We are given a hint here of the religion of the people which was very strongly family-oriented. Family tombs on inherited lands were well established by the times of the Judges: Gideon, Samson, and Asahel are buried in their ancestral tombs on family lands. David retrieved the desecrated remains of Saul and his sons and buried them in their family tomb in Benjamin.

Dead ancestors were thought to have the ability to bestow and revive life or to exact vengeance. Since the dead were still alive, the living wanted to appease them, beginning with providing them with nourishment.

If one recognizes that the term *'elohim*, usually a name for God or gods, can also mean "the dead" (see I Samuel 28:13, Isaiah 8:19), then many references about "the gods of the ancestors" can be understood as "divine ancestors." Jacob and Laban call on their now-divine ancestors to safeguard the territorial non-aggression pact between them (Gen. 31:52-54).

Why the Psalmist Protested

When Psalm 49:12 rebukes the people for summoning the dead ancestors in order to preserve the family inheritance, it is striking at the very core of what Brichto has called a "Biblical complex"; Kin, cult, land, and afterlife.[3] Since the dead ancestors are endowed with the attributes of sanctity and divinity, the living are not only obligated but wise to bury them properly and attend to their needs, so that they in turn will protect their living progeny and make sure that the property remains in the family.

Why would the psalmist attack this cluster of popular beliefs? Probably in order to de-emphasize family/clan ties and focus more attention on a different cluster: King-Temple in Jerusalem-centralized worship-devotion to the state.

Take the case of Naboth in I Kings 21. King Ahab wants Naboth's vineyard and offers him a more than generous payment. Naboth replies: "The LORD forbid that I should give up to you what I have inherited from my fathers" (v.3). Naboth is not just being sentimental; it is unthinkable to give away property that he is obligated to maintain both for his ancestors and his descendants.

---

3 H.C. Brichto "Kin, Cult, Land and Afterlife: A Biblical Complex" *HUCA* 44 (1979) 1-54.

In a sense, the later kings, prophets, and writers who attacked family religion were duplicating Ahab's attempt to seize a fertile vineyard of ancestral loyalty and belief in the powers of the dead. Clan solidarity was promoted through ancestor worship and family cults of the dead. Israelite social structure was based on the family. A king wishing to change this structure and promote devotion to the monarchy, however, would want to loosen these family ties. A strong family had local power; a strong national government wanted to increase its hold over all regions of the country.

Was the monarchy successful in its attempt to change the people's attitudes toward the cult of the dead? The archaeological evidence indicates that it was unsuccessful and that the beliefs and practices associated with this cult lasted as long as the monarchy itself.

How can we read Psalm 49? Psalm 49 is a debate between two beliefs in Israelite religion. It is a painful reminder of the stark realities of death. This psalm is also a hope, nonetheless, about the afterlife of the spirit or soul.

The Sadducees and Us

While we do not know very much about the Sadducees, a party in Judea in the Second Temple period, this much is clear: they were the religious establishment, the priestly aristocracy, and they did not believe in an afterlife. Thus I am tempted to see a parallel between the periods of the First and Second Temples: in both cases, the establishment, represented by the psalmist of Psalm 49 and Sadducees, denounced the belief in the afterlife, while the common people, represented by the evidence from the Judean burials and the Pharisees, continued to hold this belief.

In modern times, modern Sadducees state emphatically, "Jews do not believe in Heaven and Hell." They seem to be threatened on two levels: since they want to be un-dogmatic, rational, and scientific, the belief in the afterlife is not part of their world-view. Also, the religious establishment may fear the uncontrollability of otherworldly thoughts; it may take people into speculation that seems "un-Jewish."

Judaism will not be able to connect to many of its people, however, until it begins to emphasize salvation, until it recognizes their true spiritual needs. Perhaps, to some extent, we must return to the conceptual framework of kin, cult, and afterlife as the basis of our religion. The normal fear of mortality, and even worse, our dread of losing our loved ones forever, is a strong motivation to believe in an afterlife. Many of us feel that, in one way or another, experience the presence, the ongoing presence, of those special people. Somehow, despite modernity and science and rationalism, we feel that love is stronger than death, and whether we wear necklaces and bracelets to the grave or not, our most heartfelt prayer is that our love will last forever.

Chapter XIII

What I Believe:
A Theology of Biblical Archaeology

Archaeology relating to the Bible seems to cause more problems for a religious person than it solves. If one knows the historical facts presented by the Bible, but does not know much about archaeology, there's no problem: The Biblical facts are simply true. The more one knows about Biblical scholarship and archaeology, however, the more one knows that many of the central facts of the Bible have been called into question.

A Minimalist says: "Very little of the Bible is true. If there is no proof that the Israelites lived in Egypt, they weren't there, or if they were, they were just a few nomads who had been detained temporarily. The Biblical story of Jericho never happened because there was no city of Jericho during the century when the Exodus supposedly took place. If there is no proof, it did not happen. If we have evidence pointing in the opposite direction, then the Bible is simply wrong."

A Maximalist, on the other hand, insists, no matter what the evidence or lack of it indicates, that all of the Biblical facts are true. We may not know why the evidence does not reflect the fact that the Israelites conquered Jericho in the 1200s BCE, but the Israelites did conquer it just as the Book of Joshua tells us. Perhaps archaeologists have been excavating the wrong site. Perhaps our methods of dating are inadequate. Whatever the case, the Bible is factual.

People such as I, who believe that we are simply looking for the truth, find ourselves walking slowly on constantly shifting middle ground. At a certain point, we need to decide what it is that we truly believe. I will tell you where I am.

I believe that the Garden of Eden is a memory of a special place and time in Anatolia in the early history of human beings, a place to which we can trace the origins of language and agriculture.

I believe that there was a Flood that left humans memories about the catastrophe and the people who survived it.

I believe that a Hebrew man rose to great power in Egypt.

I believe that the Israelites were slaves in Egypt.

I believe that the Israelites escaped from Egypt and were saved from the Egyptians who pursued them.

I believe that the Israelites went to Canaan and lived there, fighting at least some battles in order to achieve their place in that land.

I believe that there were prophets who correctly predicted many of the major events in Israelite history.

I believe that God gave Elijah a political program by which to create major changes and that his successor Elisha was involved in making those changes happen.

I believe that Amos correctly predicted a traumatic earthquake.

I believe that Isaiah correctly predicted the end of Sennacherib's siege and the salvation of Jerusalem.

I believe that Jeremiah warned his people against rebellion and correctly predicted the fall of Jerusalem.

I believe in God and I believe that the Bible is the Word of God. As I weigh the evidence from one archaeological site after another, however, I cannot help but wonder about how little archaeology has provided in sustaining the veracity of the Biblical facts. I look for the tiniest shreds of evidence. That which indicates that the Biblical background is realistic does not give me what I really desire, namely, hard proof that the Biblical facts are facts.

A sophisticated religious person can say, "I do not really care." A Jewish person could say, "The truth of the Bible does not reside in the facts. If you could prove that the Israelites were never enslaved in Egypt and that there never was an Exodus, I would still celebrate Passover. The values of freedom and caring about the oppressed are worthy of celebration, no matter what the facts are." A Christian person could say, "Even if you could prove to me that Jesus never lived, I would still celebrate Christmas. The value of redemption from sin is worthy of celebration, no matter what the facts are."

In this way, a person can be a religious believer without believing in the Biblical facts. One can be a believing Minimalist. This, to me, is too easy.

Instead, I believe in what I call a theology of Biblical archaeology. I would like to explain an uncanny fact about the identification of Biblical sites and give a theory about the reason for the current state of Biblical archaeology. As opposed to being a believer who moans over what archaeology has not provided me in my quest for truth, I will attempt to understand why God has put us in this position.

Take the example of Pithom that I have discussed at great length above. The prominent archaeologist Manfred Bietak, who is quite willing to doubt Biblical facts, feels compelled to say that Tell er-Retabeh was occupied in the Ramesside period and was contemporary with Ramesses/Piramesse, just as the Bible states. Bietak puts it this way, "So we have a Pithom in the right place at the right time in a parallel situation [to Ramesses], each blocking one of the two important entrances of the Eastern Delta." [1] Yet, there is no conclusive proof, no "smoking gun," that

---

1 Manfred Bietak "Comments on the "Exodus" in *Egypt, Israel, Sinai* 169.

places a definitive stamp on the identification Tell er-Retabeh = Pithom. So even the Maximalist scholar Hoffmeier is careful to refrain from asserting this equation.

Is Tell er-Retabeh Pithom? I think it is, but my scientific mind prevents me from being sure. In a certain way, I am relieved.

It is a basic truth that archaeology gives us "the luck of the draw," what the spade happens to find. However, it has become "curiouser and curiouser" to me that we never seem to find the bit of proof that will render our conclusions conclusive.

If you believe in God, if you really believe in the will of God to influence events in this world, you have another choice. You begin to think about the uncanniness of the missing pieces. It is as if, one begins to think, God wants it this way, that to provide conclusive proof would make belief obsolete.

Imagine if you will, that we could find evidence of Moses and the Israelites at Mt. Sinai, using pottery datable to the 1200s BCE. It would be great for the owners of the kiosks and motels near the traditional, or that would be constructed near, the newly discovered, Mt. Sinai. Then, what would happen to the mystery of the unknown Mt. Sinai? We would climb a mountain, but it would only be a mountain, hardly as grand or majestic as a lot of other mountains in this world. Without the temporary supernatural phenomena of God descending on a mountain in a cloud, the fire and the shaking, Mt. Sinai would just be a height in the desert.

Site identifications are, after all, only the sites where things happened. Finding them does not lead to the discovery of the inner resources to survive this life. Only belief can provide this strength. Only leaps of faith can bring us to the other side of the chasm.

Belief without the mystery, without the temptation to doubt, without the spiritual jump across the gap, is just going with the facts. That, spiritually speaking, is no big deal.

A Minimalist can say, "You do not find the proof because it is not there. The Israelites weren't in Egypt, or at Mt. Sinai, and they didn't conquer the land of Canaan."

For someone in the circle of belief, however, there is another possibility. I suggest that God wants belief to be just that, belief, and not mere acceptance of the facts. To believe means, by definition, the conceptualization of something that is not apparently there.

I do not write this for the non-believers and the Minimalists. They have their own problems. I write this for those who are pining for the evidence that would prove the facts of the Bible. I predict that we will never find conclusive evidence because God wouldn't want us to find it.

As I've discussed above, I am a member of an ongoing archaeological dig in the Northwest Sinai, attempting to determine if our site is the Biblical Migdol. The geography is right, the parallel hieroglyphic inscriptions are right; we have inscriptional and material evidence of a fort, a temple, and tombs. However, we have not found the bit of evidence, the special "something" that would proclaim that the site is Migdol, which we need to make the definitive identification.

The other members of my team would be unhappy with me for saying this, but I do not think we're going to find it.

My colleagues may get frustrated. I just smile; God has an incredibly deep sense of humor. We just do not understand how wise and funny He is.

BIBLIOGRAPHY

Abd el-Maksoud, Mohamed. "Fouilles récentes au Nord Sinai, sur le site de Tell el-Herr: Première saison, 1984-85" *Cahiers de Recherches de l'Institut de Papyrologie et d'Égyptologie de Lille* 8 (1986) 15-16.

――――. "Une nouvelle fortresse sur la route d'Horus: Tel Heboua 1986 (Nord Sinai)" *Cahiers de Recherches de l'Institut de Papyrologie et d'Égyptologie de Lille* 9 (1987) 13-16.

Aharoni, Yohanan. *The Land of the Bible: A Historical Geography* (Philadelphia, 1979).

Ahlstrom, Gustav. "Merneptah's Israel" *JNES* 44 (1985) 59-61.

Albright, William Foxwell. "Further Light on the History of Israel from Lachish and Megiddo" *BASOR* 68 (1937) 22-26.

Amit, Yairah. "The Dual Causality Principle and its Effects on Biblical Literature" *VT* 385-400.

Avigad, Nahman. "Baruch the Scribe and Jerahmeel the King's Son" *IEJ* 28 (1978) 52-56;

――――. *Hebrew Bullae from the Time of Jeremiah* (Jerusalem, 1986).

――――. *Discovering Jerusalem* (Nashville, 1980).

Ballard, Robert D. with Malcolm McConnell *Adventures in Ocean Exploration: From the Discovery of the Titanic to the Search for Noah's Flood* (Washington, D.C., 2001).

Ben Zvi, Ehud. "On the Reading 'bytdwd' in the Aramaic Stele from Tel Dan." *Journal for the Study of the Old Testament* 64 (1994) 25-32.

Bietak Manfred. *Avaris and Piramesse: Archaeological Exploration in the Eastern Nile Delta* (London, 1981) 253.

――――"Canaanites in the Eastern Delta" in Rainey *Egypt, Israel, Sinai* 43.

――――. "Comments on the "Exodus"" in Anson F. Rainey Egypt, Israel, Sinai; Archaeological and Historical Relationships in the Biblical Period (Tel Aviv, 1987) 169.

――――. *Tell El-Dab'a* Vol. 2 (Vienna: Verlag Der Osterreichschen Akademie der Wissenschaften, 1975) 217-220, fig. 45.

Biran, Avraham and Joseph Naveh. "An Aramaic Stele Fragment from Tel Dan." *Israel Exploration Journal* 43 nos. 2-3 (1993) 81-98.

――――. "The Tel Dan Inscription: A New Fragment." *Israel Exploration Journal* 45 (1995) 1-18.

Bloch-Smith, E. M. *Judahite Burial Practices and Beliefs about the Dead* (*JSOT* Sup 123; Sheffield: JSOT, 1992).

Brand, P. *The Monuments of Seti I and their Historical Significance: Epigraphic, Art Historical and Historical Analyses* (Ph.D. Dissertation, Toronto, 1998).

Brichto, Herbert Chanan. "Kin, Cult, Land and Afterlife: A Biblical Complex" *HUCA* XLIV (1979) 1-54.

Bryce, J. *Transcaucasia and Ararat* (London, 1877).

Buber, Martin. "The "Tree of Knowledge"" in *On the Bible* (New York, 1968).

Caminos, R. A. *Late-Egyptian Miscellanies* (London, 1954).

Cassuto, Umberto. *A Commentary on the Book of Genesis: Part Two From Noah to Abraham* translated by Israel Abrahams (Jerusalem, 1974).

Childs Brevard S. *Isaiah and the Assyrian Crisis* (SBT II/3, 1967)118.

――――. "A Traditio-Historical Study of the Reed Sea Tradition" *VT* 20 (1970) 412-14.

Clements, R. E. *Isaiah and the Deliverance of Jerusalem* JSOT Supplement Series 13 (Sheffield, 1980).

Crawfoot, J. W. and G. Crawfoot. *Early Ivories from Samaria* (London, 1938).

Cross, Frank Moore. *Canaanite Myth and Hebrew Epic* (Cambridge, Mass.: Harvard University Press, 1973) 112-44.

Cryer, Frederick H. "Of Epistemology, Northwest-Semitic Epigraphy and Irony: The 'BYTDWD/House of David' Inscription Revisited." *Journal for the Study of the Old Testament* 69 (1996) 3-17.

Davies, G. I. *The Way of the Wilderness* (Cambridge 1979).

Davies, Philip. "House of David' Built on Sand: The Sins of the Biblical Maximizers" *BAR* 20 no. 4 (1994) 54.

Delitzsch, Franz J. *A New Commentary on Genesis II* tr. from German (Edinburgh, 1888).

Dever, William G. "A Case-Study in Biblical Archaeology: The Earthquake of Ca.760 BCE" *Eretz-Israel* 23 (1992) 27-35.

Duncan, J. E. *Milton's Earthly Paradise: A Historical Study of Eden* (University of Minnesota, 1972).

Eakin Jr., Frank E. "The Reed Sea and Ba'alism" *JBL* 86 (1967)378-84;

Eissfeldt, Otto. *Ba'al zaphon, Zeus Kasios und der Durchzug der Israeliten durchs Meer* Beitrage zur Religiongeschichte des Altertums, Heft 1 (Halle, Niemeyer, 1932).

Facaros, Dana and Michael Pauls. *Turkey* (Chester, Connecticut, 1988).

Freedman, David Noel and Andrew Welch. "Amos's Earthquake and Israelite Prophecy" in *Scripture and Other Artifacts: Essays on the Bible and Archaeology in Honor of Philip J. King* ed. by Michael D. Coogan, J. Cheryl Exum, and Lawrence E. Stager (Louisville, Kentucky, 1994) 188-98.

Gardiner, Alan. H. "The Geography of the Exodus: An Answer" *JEA* X (1924) 87-96;

———. *Late-Egyptian Miscellanies (Brussels, 1937).*

———. "The Delta Residence of the Ramessides" *JEA* 5 (1918) 127-71.

———. "Tanis and Pi-Ra'messe: A Retraction" *JEA* 19 (1933) 122-28.

Gevaryahu, H. "Baruch ben Neriah the Scribe" in *Zev Ligevurot* (1973) 191-243 (in Hebrew).

Giamatti, B. *The Earthly Paradise and the Renaissance Epic* (Princeton, 1966).

Ginsberg, H. L. *The Israelian Heritage of Judaism* (New York, 1982).

Giveon, Raphael. *Les Bedouins de Shosu de documents Egyptiens* (Leiden, 1971).

Graves, R. and R. Patai. *Hebrew Myths: The Book of Genesis* (London, 1964).

Hallo, William W. "As The Seal Upon Thine Arm": Glyptic Metaphors in the Biblical World," in *Ancient Seals and the Bible* ed. by Leonard Gorelick and Elizabeth Williams-Forte (Malibu, Cal.: Undena, 1983) 7-17.

Halpern, Baruch. "The Stela from Dan: Epigraphic and Historical Considerations" *BASOR* 296 (1994) 63-80;

Hamza, Mahmud. "Excavations of the Department of Antiquities at Qantir (Faqûs District) (season, May 21st - July 7th, 1928)" *ASAE* 30 (1930) 31-68.

Haran, M. "The Exodus Routes in the Pentateuchal Sources" *Tarbiz* XL (1971) 113-43 (Hebrew).

Hayes, William C. *A Papyrus of the Late Middle Kingdom in the Brooklyn Museum* (Papyrus Brooklyn 35. 1446 (New York, 1955).

———. *Glazed Tile from a Palace of Ramesses II at Kantir* (New York: Metropolitan Museum of Art, 1937).   195

Heidel, Alexander. *The Gilgamesh Epic and Old Testament Parallels* (Chicago, 1949).

Helck, W. "Ikw und die Ramses-stadt" *VT* 15 (1965) 35-48.

Hoffmeier, James K. *Israel in Egypt: The Evidence for the Authenticity of the Exodus* (New York: Oxford, 1997).

———. "Of Minimalists and Maximalists" *BAR* 21 No. 2 (1995) 20-22.

———. "The Recently Discovered Tell Dan Inscription: Controversy and Confirmation." *Archaeology and the Biblical World* 3 no.1 (1995) 12-15.

Hollister, C.Warren. *Medieval Europe: A Short History* (Boston, 1998).

Horn S. H. "Did Sennacherib Campaign Once or Twice Against Hezekiah?" *AUSS* IV (1966) 1-28.

Hort, G. "The Plagues of Egypt I" *ZAW* 69 (1957) 84ff. and "The Plagues of Egypt II" *ZAW* 70 (1958) 48ff.

Jakobson, R. and M. Halle. *Fundamentals of Language* (The Hague, 1956).

Kaufmann, Yehezkel. *The Book of Joshua* (Jerusalem, 1959) 128 (in Hebrew).

King, L. W. *Babylonian Religion and Mythology* (London, 1889).

King, Philip J. *Amos, Hosea, Micah—An Archaeological Commentary* (Philadelphia, 1988).

Kitchen, Kenneth A. "Egypt, the Levant and Assyria in 701 B.C." *Fontes Atque Pontes: Eine Festgabe für Helmut Brunner* ÄAT vol. 5 (1983) 243-53.

———. "Egyptians and Hebrews, from Ra'amses to Jericho" in *The Origin of Early Israel - Current Debate* ed. Shmuel Ahituv and Eliezer D. Oren (London, 1998) 78.

———. "Genesis 12-50 in the Near Eastern World" in *He Swore an Oath: Biblical Themes from Genesis 12-50* ed. by R. S. Hess et al (Cambridge, 1993) 77-92.

———. "Joseph" in *International Standard Encyclopedia* vol. 2, 1125-30.

———. "Joseph" in *New Bible Dictionary* 617-20.

———. "Joseph" *ISBE* vol. 2 1127.

———. *Pharaoh Triumphant: The Life and Times of Ramesses II* (Cairo, 1990).

———. "Review of Redford's A Study of the Biblical Story of Joseph" *Oriens Antiquus* 12 (1973) 223-242.

———. "Tell el-Borg: Preliminary Epigraphic Report 2: Further Ramesside Blocks" (August 2000) 8.

———. *The Third Intermediate Period in Egypt* (Warminster, 1973).

Kramer, Samuel Noah. "Blood-Plague Motif in Sumerian Mythology" *Archiv Orientalni* 17 (1949) 399ff.

Leach, E. R. "Levi-Strauss in the Garden of Eden" *Transactions of the New York Academy of Sciences* (New York, 1961) 386-96.

———. "Genesis as Myth" in *Genesis as Myth and Other Essays* (London, 1969).

Lemche, Niels Peter and Thomas L. Thompson. "Did Biran Kill David? The Bible in the Light Of Archaeology." *Journal for the Study of the Old Testament* 64 (1994) 3-22;

Levi-Strauss, C."The Structural Study of Myth" *Myth: A Symposium* ed. T. A. Sebeok (Bloomington, 1955).

Marcolongo, Bruno. "Evolution du paleo-environnement dans la partie orientale du Delta du Nile depuis la transgression flandrienne (8,000 B.P.) par rapport aux modeles de peuplement anciens" *CRIPEL* 14 (1992) 23-31 and fig. 1.

Mazar, B. "The Campaign of Sennacherib in Judaea" *EI* II (1953) 170-5 (Hebrew).

Mellaart, J. "Excavations of Catal Hyük, 1963, Anatolian Studies" *Journal of the British Institute at Ankara* vol. XIX, 1964.

———. *The Archaeology of Ancient Turkey* (London, 1978).

Millard, A. R. "Sennacherib's Attack on Hezekiah" *Tyndale Bulletin* 36 (1985) 61-77.

Morier, James. *A Second Journey through Persia, Armenia, and Asia Minor, to Constantinople, Between the Years 1810 and 1816 (London, 1818).*

Mysliwiec, K. *Eighteenth Dynasty before the Amarna Period* Iconography of Religions, 16: Egypt, 5 (Leiden, 1985).

Naville, Edouard. "The Geography of the Exodus" *JEA* X (1924) 18-39.

———. *The Store-City of Pithom and the Route of the Exodus* 3 (London, Egypt Exploration Society, 1883).

Neev, D. and G.M. Friedman. "Late Holocene Tectonic Activity along the Margins of Sinai Subplate" *Science* 202 (1978) 427-9.

Nims, Charles F. "Bricks without Straw" *BA* 13 no. 2 (1950) 22-28.

Oppenheim, A. L. "Mesopotamia" in C.C.Gillispie ed. *Dictionary of Scientific Biography* vol. 15 (New York, 1978) 637.

Oren, Eliezer D. "An Egyptian Fortress on the Military Road between Egypt and Canaan" *Qadmoniot* 6 (1973) 101-103 (Heb.).

———. "How Not to Create a History of the Exodus: A Critique of Professor Goedicke's theories" *BAR* 7:6 (1981) 46-53.

———. "Migdol: A New Fortress on the Edge of the Eastern Nile Delta" *BASOR* 256 (1984) 7-44.

———. "Military Architecture along the 'Ways of Horus': Egyptian Reliefs and Archaeological Evidence" *Eretz-Israel* 20 (1989) 8-22; 21 (1990) 6-22.

———. "Sinai, Northern" in *The New Encyclopedia of Archaeological Excavations in the Holy Land* vol. 4 (Jerusalem and New York, 1993) 1386-1396.

———. "The Overland Route between Egypt and Canaan in the Early Bronze Age" *IEJ* 23 (1973) 198-205.

———. "The 'Ways of Horus' in North Sinai" in *Egypt, Israel, Sinai: Archaeological and Historical Relationships in the Biblical Period* ed. by Anson F. Rainey (Tel Aviv, 1987) 69-119.

Parrot, Johann Jacob von. *Journey to Ararat* trans. by W. D. Cooley (London, 1845).

Petrie, W. M. F. *Hyksos and Israelite Cities* (London, 1906) 30 pls. 32A, 34, 35C).

Porada, Edith. "The Cylinder Seal from Tell el-Dab'a" *AJA* 88 (1984) 485-88.

Prest, J. *The Garden of Eden: The Botanic Garden and the Re-Creation of Paradise* (New Haven, 1981).

Rainey, Anson. "The 'House of David' and House of the Deconstructionists" *BAR* 20 no. 6 (1994) 47.

Redford, Donald B. *A Study of the Biblical Story of Joseph* VTS vol. 20 (Leiden, 1970).

———. *Egypt, Canaan and Israel in Ancient Times* (Princeton, 1992) 98-129.

———. "Exodus 1,11 *VT* 13 (1963) 401-18.

———. "Perspective on the Exodus" in *Egypt, Israel, Sinai* 140-42.

———. "Pithom" *Ld'ef* IV: 1054-58.

———. "Pi-Hahiroth" in *ABD* V371.   197

———. "The Ashkelon Relief at Karnak and the Israel Stela" *IEJ* 36 (1986) 197.

———. "The Egyptological Perspective on the Exodus Narrative" in Anson F. Rainey *Egypt, Israel, Canaan: Archaeological and Historical Relationships in the Biblical Period* (Tel Aviv, 1987) 137-62.

Rendsburg, Gary A. "On the Writing of *bytdwd* in the Aramaic Inscription from Tel Dan" *Israel Exploration Journal* 45 (1995) 22-25.

Ricke, H., G. R. Hughes, and E. F. Wente. *The Beit el-Wali temple of Ramesses II* (Chicago, 1967).

Robinson, Arthur H. and Barbara Bartz Petchenik. *The Nature of Maps: Essays Toward Understanding Maps and Mapping* (Chicago, 1976).

Rowley, H. H. "Hezekiah's Reform and Rebellion" *BJRL* XLIV (1962) 395-431.

Ryan, William and Walter Pitman. *Noah's Flood: The New Scientific Discoveries About the Event That Changed History* (New York, 1998).

Sarna, Nahum. "Israel in Egypt: The Egyptian Sojourn and the Exodus" in Hershel Shanks ed. *Ancient Israel* (Washington, 2000).

Sasson, V. "The Old Aramaic Inscription from Tell Dan: Philological, Literary and Historical Aspects." *Journal of Semitic Studies* 40 (1995) 11-30.

Sauer, James A., "The River Runs Dry," *Biblical Archaeology Review* July/August, 1996.

Schneider, Tsvi. "Six Biblical Signatures: Seals and Seal Impressions of Six Biblical Personages Recovered" *BAR* (July/August 1991).

Schniedewind, William M. "Tel Dan Stela: New Light on Aramaic and Jehu's Revolt." *Bulletin of the American Schools of Oriental Research* 302 (May 1996) 75-90.

Schulman, Alan R. "On the Egyptian Name of Joseph: A New Approach" *SAK* 2 (1975) 236.

Scolnic, Benjamin Edidin. "The Flexible Word of God: Thoughts on the Other Pole of Biblical Authority" *Judaism* 36:3 (Summer, 1987) 331-38.

Seeligmann, L. "Menschliches Heldentum und göttliche Hilfe: Die doppelte Kausalitat im alttestamentlichen Gesschichsdenken" *ThZ* 19 (1963) 385-411.

Seters, John Van. *The Hyksos: A New Investigation* (New Haven, 1966).

———. *Prologue to History: The Yahwist as Historian in Genesis* (Louisville, 1992).

Shafei, A. B. "Historical Notes on the Pelusiac Branch, the Red Sea Canal and the Route of the Exodus" *Bulletin de la Societe Royale de Georgraphie d'Egypte* 21 (1946) 231-87.

Shalem, N. *Seismicity in Palestine and in the Neighboring Areas* (unpublished manuscript cited in Jacob Milgrom "Did Isaiah Prophesy During the Reign of Uzziah" *Vetus Testamentum* 14 (1964) 179.

———. "The Earthquakes in Jerusalem" *Jerusalem* 2 (1949) 22-60 (in Hebrew).

Shanks, Hershel. "Jeremiah's Scribe and Confidant Speaks from a Hoard of Clay Bullae" *BAR* Vol. XIII:5 (September/October 1987) 58-65.

———. "Fingerprint of Jeremiah's Scribe" *BAR* March/April 1996.

Shannon, C.and W. Weaver. *The Mathematical Theory of Communication* (Urbana, 1949).

Shea, William. "A Date for the Recently Discovered Eastern Canal of Egypt" *BASOR* 226 (1977) 37.

Smith, Mark S. *The Early History of God: Yahweh and the Other Deities in Ancient Israel* (San Francisco: Harper and Row, 1990).

Snaith, Norman. "Yam Suf: The Sea of Reeds: The Red Sea" *VT* 15(1965) 395-98.

Sneh, Amihai, Tuvia Weissbrod and Itamar Perath. "Evidence for an Ancient Egyptian Frontier Canal" *American Scientist* 63 (1975) 542-48.

Soggin, J. A. *The Prophet Amos* (London, 1987).

Speiser, Ephraim Avigdor. "The Rivers of Paradise" in *Oriental and Biblical Studies* ed. by J. J. Finkelstein and M. Greenberg (Philadelphia, 1967) 23-34.

Stadelmann, Luis I. J. *The Hebrew Conception of the World: A Philological and Literary Study* (Rome, 1970).

Strabo. *Geography* V Books 10-12 trans. by Howard Leonard Jones (Cambridge, 2000).

Thompson, Thomas L. "Dissonance and Disconnections: Notes on the *bytdwd* and *hmlk.hdd* Fragments from Tel Dan" *Scandinavian Journal of the Old Testament* 9.2 (1995) 236-40.

Tomimura, D. "A propos de l'origine du mot égyptien "Neuf-Arcs"" *Oriento, Bulletin of the Society for Near Eastern Studies in Japan* 24 (1981) 114-24.

Torczyner, Harry. *The Lachish Letters* (London, 1938).

———. *Te'udot Lakhish (Jerusalem, 1940).*

Tyldesley, Joyce. *Daughters of Isis: Women of Ancient Egypt* (London, 1994).

Uphill, E. *The Temples of Per Ramesses* (Warminster, 1984).

Ussishkin, David. *The Conquest of Lachish by Sennacherib* Publications of the Institute of Archaeology 6 (Tel Aviv, 1982).

Valbelle, Dominique. "La (Les) Route(s)-D'Horus" *in Hommages Jean Leclant* vol. 4 Bibliothèque de l'École des Hautes Études 106 (Cairo: IFAO, 1994) 379-86.

Von Parrot, Johann Jacob. *Journey to Ararat* trans. by W. D. Cooley (London, 1845).

Von Rad, Gerhard. *Genesis* (Philadelphia, 1961).

———. *Old Testament Theology* I (Edinburgh and London, 1962).

Ward, William. *Egypt and the Mediterranean World 2200-1900 B. C.: Studies in Egyptian Frontier Relations in the First Intermediate Period (Beirut: American University Press, 1971).*

———. "The Egyptian Office of Joseph" *JSS* 5 (1960) 144-50.

Wright, G. Ernest. *Biblical Archaeology* (Philadelphia, 1957).

Yadin, Y. *Hazor: The Rediscovery of a Great Citadel of the Bible* (New York, 1975).

Yadin, Y., Y. Aharoni, T. Dothan, I. Dunayevsky and J. Perrot. *Hazor II: An Account of the Second Season of Excavations, 1956* (Jerusalem, 1960).

Jacob Neusner

The Aggadic Role in Halakhic Discourses. Lanham. February 2001. University Press of America. Academic Studies in Ancient Judaism series. Volume I

The Aggadic Role in Halakhic Discourses. Lanham. February 2001. University Press of America. Academic Studies in Ancient Judaism series. Volume II

The Aggadic Role in Halakhic Discourses. Lanham. February 2001. University Press of America. Academic Studies in Ancient Judaism series. Volume III

A Theological Commentary to the Midrash. Lanham. April 2001. University Press of America. Academic Studies in Ancient Judaism series. Volume I. *Pesiqta deRab Kahana*.

A Theological Commentary to the Midrash. Lanham. March 2001. University Press of America. Academic Studies in Ancient Judaism series. - Volume II. *Genesis Raba*.

A Theological Commentary to the Midrash. Lanham. April 2001. University Press of America. Academic Studies in Ancient Judaism series. Volume III. *Song of Songs Rabbah*

A Theological Commentary to the Midrash. Lanham. April 2001. University Press of America. Academic Studies in Ancient Judaism series. Volume IV. *Leviticus Rabbah*

A Theological Commentary to the Midrash. Lanham. June 2001. University Press of America. Academic Studies in Ancient Judaism series. Volume V *Lamentations Rabbati*

A Theological Commentary to the Midrash. June 2001. University Press of America. Academic Studies in Ancient Judaism series. Volume VI. *Ruth Rabbah and Esther Rabbah I*

A Theological Commentary to the Midrash. June 2001. University Press of America. Academic Studies in Ancient Judaism series. Volume VII. *Sifra*

A Theological Commentary to the Midrash. July 2001. University Press of America. Academic Studies in Ancient Judaism series. Volume VIII. *Sifré to Numbers and Sifré to Deuteronomy*

A Theological Commentary to the Midrash. August 2001. University Press of America. Academic Studies in Ancient Judaism series. Volume IX. *Mekhilta Attributed to Rabbi Ishmael*

The Unity of Rabbinic Discourse. January 2001. University Press of America. Academic Studies in Ancient Judaism series. Volume I: *Aggadah in the Halakhah*

The Unity of Rabbinic Discourse. February 2001. University Press of America. Academic Studies in Ancient Judaism series. Volume II: *Halakhah in the Aggadah*

The Unity of Rabbinic Discourse. February 2001. University Press of America. Academic Studies in Ancient Judaism series. Volume III: *Halakhah and Aggadah in Concert*

TITLES

Texts without Boundaries. Protocols of Non-Documentary Writing in the Rabbinic Canon, Lanham, 2002: University Press of America. Academic Studies in Ancient Judaism series. Volume Two. *Sifra*

Texts without Boundaries. Protocols of Non-Documentary Writing in the Rabbinic Canon, Lanham, 2003: University Press of America. Academic Studies in Ancient Judaism series. Volume Three. *Sifré to Numbers.*

Texts without Boundaries. Protocols of Non-Documentary Writing in the Rabbinic Canon, Lanham, 2003: University Press of America. Academic Studies in Ancient Judaism series. Volume Four. *Sifré to Deuteronomy.*

Texts without Boundaries. Protocols of Non-Documentary Writing in the Rabbinic Canon, Lanham, 2004: University Press of America. Academic Studies in Ancient Judaism series. Volume Five. *Genesis Rabbah.*

Texts without Boundaries. Protocols of Non-Documentary Writing in the Rabbinic Canon, Lanham, 2004: University Press of America. Academic Studies in Ancient Judaism series. Volume Six. *Leviticus Rabbah.*

Texts without Boundaries. Protocols of Non-Documentary Writing in the Rabbinic Canon, Lanham, 2004: University Press of America. Academic Studies in Ancient Judaism series. Volume Seven. *Pesiqta deRab Kahana.*

Texts without Boundaries. Protocols of Non-Documentary Writing in the Rabbinic Canon, Lanham, 2004: University Press of America. Academic Studies in Ancient Judaism series. Volume Eight. *Esther Rabbah and Ruth Rabbah.*

Texts without Boundaries. Protocols of Non-Documentary Writing in the Rabbinic Canon, Lanham, 2004: University Press of America. Academic Studies in Ancient Judaism series. Volume Nine. *Song of Songs Rabbah.*

Texts without Boundaries. Protocols of Non-Documentary Writing in the Rabbinic Canon, Lanham, 2004: University Press of America. Academic Studies in Ancient Judaism series. Volume Ten. *Lamentations Rabbah.*

Texts without Boundaries. Protocols of Non-Documentary Writing in the Rabbinic Canon, Lanham, 2004: University Press of America. Academic Studies in Ancient Judaism series. Volume Eleven. *Mekhilta Attributed to Rabbi Ishmael.*

Texts without Boundaries. Protocols of Non-Documentary Writing in the Rabbinic Canon, Lanham, 2004: University Press of America. Academic Studies in Ancient Judaism series. Volume Twelve. *Abot deRabbi Natan.*